The Kundalini Book of Living and Dying

By the Same Author

Secrets of Numerology
Destiny, Science and Spiritual Awakening
Kundalini : The Journey Back to Our True Home
Kundalini for Beginners
Secrets of Kundalini Awakening
All you wanted to know about Hatha Yoga
All you wanted to know about Nadis and Chakras
All you wanted to know about Kriya Yoga
All you wanted to know about Kundalini
All you wanted to know about Dreams
All you wanted to know about Aura
All you wanted to know about Psychic Development
All you wanted to know about Mantras
All you wanted to know about Bhakti Yoga
All you wanted to know about Karma Yoga
All you wanted to know about Jnana Yoga
All you wanted to know about Tantra Yoga
Secrets of Shaktipat

The Kundalini Book of Living and Dying

Gateways to Higher Consciousness

RAVINDRA KUMAR, Ph.D.
JYTTE KUMAR LARSEN

MOTILAL BANARSIDASS PUBLISHERS
PRIVATE LIMITED • DELHI

First Indian Edition: Delhi, 2007
(First Published in 2004 by Red Wheel/Weiser, LLC, York Beach, ME with offices at : 368 Congress Street Boston, MA 02210)

ISBN: 81-208-3215-9

MOTILAL BANARSIDASS
41 U.A. Bungalow Road, Jawahar Nagar, Delhi 110 007
8 Mahalaxmi Chamber, 22 Bhulabhai Desai Road, Mumbai 400 026
236, 9th Main III Block, Jayanagar, Bangalore 560 011
203 Royapettah High Road, Mylapore, Chennai 600 004
Sanas Plaza, 1302 Baji Rao Road, Pune 411 002
8 Camac Street, Kolkata 700 017
Ashok Rajpath, Patna 800 004
Chowk, Varanasi 221 001

For Sale in Asia only

Printed in India
BY JAINENDRA PRAKASH JAIN AT SHRI JAINENDRA PRESS,
A-45 NARAINA, PHASE-I, NEW DELHI 110 028
AND PUBLISHED BY NARENDRA PRAKASH JAIN FOR
MOTILAL BANARSIDASS PUBLISHERS PRIVATE LIMITED,
BUNGALOW ROAD, DELHI 110 007

CONTENTS

PART FOUR

Gateways to Higher Consciousness, 129

PART FIVE

Exploring Reality through Kundalini, 205

This book is dedicated
to my grandmother, the late Bhagwati Devi,
and my father, the late Ganga Singh,
who guided me when they were on earth
and who are still guiding me from the higher realms.

FOREWORD

IN THE COURSE OF MY SPIRITUAL study, I have had marked episodes of activated kundalini energy. When they first occurred, there was little in the way of literature to place these experiences into a meaningful context in my life. Even today, despite more research, this important part of our consciousness is not fully appreciated. That's why Dr. Ravindra Kumar's *The Kundalini Book of Living and Dying* is such a significant work; it explains the nature of kundalini, why it is important, and how any person can bring its benefits into his or her life. In the process of enlightening ourselves, we contribute mightily to the enlightenment of the soul of global humanity. Our ability to evolve as human beings and as souls, our ability to unite with God, our ability to leave behind forever hate, war, and terrorism will be facilitated—even determined—by kundalini.

This energy of enlightenment resides within each and every one of us, often dormant until we make the choice to seek unity with God. In our ensuing spiritual study and practice, we awaken the sleeping power within, and we are profoundly changed—physically, mentally, and spiritually. The hallmarks of kundalini are phenomena such as surges of electricity in the body, detachment from the body, intense heat and fire, buzzing sounds, a feeling of being in the presence of God, and awareness of spiritual presences such as angels. More important, however, are the benefits that lie beyond the phenomena: creativity, genius, enhanced well-being, longevity, and, most significant of all, enlightenment.

Experiences of kundalini have been recorded around the world since ancient times. Kundalini is the divine fire of God and the gods, the *samadhi* of adepts, the raptures of saints, the healing power that floods through the hands of healers, the inspiration of invention, the intense happiness of a peak experience. The average person may think that kundalini belongs only to those whose spiritual practice elevates them into a rarified atmosphere of consciousness, but this is not so. Kundalini is universal, available to all. Anyone who prays or meditates regularly is likely at some point to feel the power of kundalini.

My own experiences resulted from spiritual study, meditation, and intuitive/psychic development. Not knowing much about kundalini in the beginning, I initially viewed these experiences as isolated episodes. As

I learned more about kundalini, I realized the importance of understanding its role in the development of consciousness, and of encouraging it to become more active in a gradual and productive manner.

Some years ago, I was privileged to meet Dr. Ravindra Kumar and become familiar with his work. Dr. Kumar is a man of great spiritual depth, knowledge, and wisdom. Through his years of study and spiritual practice, he has come into an understanding of truth that he shares in the jewels of many works. This book, *The Kundalini Book of Living and Dying*, is the crown jewel of that work. Dr. Kumar weaves together Western and Eastern philosophy, religion, esotericism, mysticism, science, and psychology to explain from different viewpoints the nature of the soul and the nature of reality. From his own experience, he has developed the Integral Path, a practical way for the spiritual seeker to open kundalini and develop spiritual consciousness. Specific instructions and exercises are given throughout.

The more we know about kundalini and how to bring it into flower within us, the more we will benefit from it, both as individuals and as part of the collective soul of humanity. Kundalini furthers our wordless understanding of the nature of creation, our part in the whole of all things, and our ultimate unity with God.

The essence of kundalini is eloquently captured in Psalm 19, which reads in part:

The heavens are telling the glory of God;
and the firmament proclaims his handiwork.
Day to day pours forth speech,
and night to night declares knowledge.
There is no speech, nor are there words;
their voice is not heard;
yet their voice goes through all the earth,
and their words to the end of the world.

In them he has set a tent for the sun,
which comes forth like a bridegroom leaving his chamber,
and like a strong man runs its course with joy.
Its rising is from the end of the heavens,
and its circuit to the end of them;
and there is nothing hid from its heat.

When kundalini is awakened through attunement to the higher planes, we are quickened in the heat of divine fire. The splendor of divine love flows through us. It is vital that we recognize the kundalini power within and learn how to cultivate it in the name of truth and love. The more we do so, the less we will descend into fear and hate. In fact, ultimately, we will not even be able to do so, for our collective soul consciousness will be firmly anchored in the light and unconditional love of the godhead. We will truly reside in the kingdom of God. This future will not happen, however, unless we choose it. This book provides an excellent guide to help us realize that choice.

—ROSEMARY ELLEN GUILEY, PH.D.,
author of *The Encyclopedia of Saints and Breakthrough Intuition*

PREFACE

THE EMINENT SWISS PSYCHIATRIST Carl Jung said that it is psychologically beneficial to have death as a goal toward which to strive. Mozart called death the key to unlocking the door to true happiness. Shakespeare wrote that when we are prepared for death, life is sweeter. The French philosopher Michel de Montaigne said "to practice death is to practice freedom."

Although Dr. Ravindra Kumar does not come right out and say it, this book is about "practicing death." Strange words, but like Jung, Mozart, Shakespeare, and Montaigne, Dr. Kumar has discovered the fountain of wisdom. When we drink from this fountain, we learn how to lead a much more enjoyable and meaningful life in the present lifetime. It is one big paradox: practice death, embrace death, and learn how to live now.

"Death is indeed a fearful piece of brutality," Jung offered. "There is no sense in pretending otherwise. It is brutal not only as a physical event, but also far more so psychically. [However] from another point of view, death appears a joyful event. In the light of eternity, it is a wedding, a *mysterium conjunctionis*. The soul attains, as it were, its missing half. It achieves wholeness."[1]

It's extremely difficult for the average Western materialist, whether or not he or she subscribes to a religion, to comprehend such sage reasoning. "The idea of death, the fear of it, haunts the human mind like nothing else," wrote anthropologist Edwin Becker in his 1974 Pulitzer prize-winning book, *The Denial of Death*. Becker explained that to free oneself of death anxiety, nearly everyone chooses the path of repression. We bury the anxiety deep in the subconscious while we busy ourselves with our jobs, escape into fictitious stories, hit little white balls into holes, show off our shiny cars, and pursue material wealth as we seek a mundane security we expect to continue indefinitely. We give meaning to Kierkegaard's "Philistine"—man fully concerned with the trivial, man striving to become one with his toys.

Of course, along the way, some take time out for love and service, the things that count, but sooner or later those repressed anxieties concerning death begin welling to the surface, causing stress, anxiety, fears, and depression.

Becker called repression the enemy of mankind. Psychiatrist Robert Jay Lifton, author of *The Broken Connection*, said much the same thing, stating, "In real psychological ways, one must know death in order to live with free imagination."[2]

The key to living the unrepressed life, according to both Becker and Lifton, is having a sense of immortality, a firm belief that this life is part of a much larger and eternal life. Jung, Mozart, Shakespeare, and Montaigne all had that sense. Without it and without the defense mechanism of repression, man races toward extinction, or, as Jung put it, "marches toward nothingness."

Developing that sense of immortality is not usually achieved simply by attending church or synagogue once a week. We must practice death daily. As Socrates put it, "practicing death" is merely pursuing philosophy "in the right way," and learning how "to face death easily." It means searching for higher truths, cultivating an awareness of the larger life, being able to visualize other realms of existence, discerning our motives, contemplating our actions, pondering our deeds. It calls for meditation and study, including reading all the great books of religion as well as the works of various seekers, scholars, sages, seers, saints, and swamis—people like Jung, William James, Emanuel Swedenborg, Alice Bailey, Rudolf Steiner, Swami Ramakrishna, Mary Baker Eddy, Teresa of Avila, John of the Cross, Grace Cooke, Edgar Cayce, Allen Kardec, Hildegard of Bingen, and others.

Many people think nothing of devoting an hour a day to exercise in pursuit of physical well-being. Practicing death for an hour a day can do the same for spiritual well-being. It releases us from the fetters of repression. It helps us on the road of evolution from darkness to light, from unconsciousness to consciousness, from spiritual depravity to spiritual enlightenment, from ignorance to knowledge, from imperfection to perfection.

This book can help the seeker understand what it means to practice death and then to actually practice it. It shows the seeker how to better understand life, to savor it, to harmonize with it, to find inner peace, tranquillity, and repose, to move closer to being one with the creator, and to make a graceful transition to the world of higher vibration when the time is right.

—MICHAEL E. TYMN, Book Review Editor,
Academy of Religion and Psychical Research

ACKNOWLEDGMENTS

I HAVE BEEN FORTUNATE TO HAVE spiritual initiations from gurus of outstanding reputation. I bow down my head to the lotus feet of these gurus.

Through my visualization of previous births I discovered Master Pythagoras, who was my guru in 600 B.C. and who has helped me in other lifetimes, too. In this lifetime, I received simple initiation from Siddheshwar Baba at his ashram outside of Delhi in 1986. He was formerly Dr. B. S. Goel, author of *Third Eye and Kundalini.* In 1987, Eckankar Guru Sri Herald Klemp of Minnesota initiated me. Since then I have been meeting some unknown saints in dreams and getting initiated by them. I was given a mantra that stays with me to this day.

Recently, I was lucky to receive simple initiation from the popular lady saint Guruma at her ashram near Sonepat. Then I got in touch with Guru Deepak Yogi, who gave me Shaktipat initiation with a touch and mantra. Later I was authorized to give intitiation in Shaktipat and kriya yoga by Dr. Swami Krishnananda Saraswati of Kali Mandir, Uttarkashi, who is the disciple of H. H. Swami Narain Tirth of Shankarmath, Uttarkashi, and Siddha Yogashram, Varanasi (Kashi).

Eventually, I came to know about the Tirth lineage of gurus and was initiated by Swami Parmananda Tirth of Indore, who is the disciple of the powerful Shaktipat guru Swami Shivom Tirth, who himself is the disciple of a well-known guru, the late Swami Vishnu Tirth Maharaj.

I am also grateful to my mother, Mrs. Lakshmi Devi, and to Jytte's mother, Mrs. Ellen Marie Anderson for their love and blessings.

Sincere thanks are due to Michael E. Tymn and Jonathan Barber for their regular and complete editing of the manuscript, without which it would not have been in this nice shape. Thanks are also due to Margaret Dempsey and Brigitte Arora for some useful suggestions.

Many thanks to Wm. Henry Belk II, Rev. Richard Luis Batzler, Dr. Claire G. Walker, Dr. John F. Miller, Gopi and Neela Chari, Dr. Rosemary Ellen Guiley, Dr. Bonny Greenwell, Barbara Harris Whitfield, Boyce Batey, and Dr. Rabia Lynn Clark for the lively and useful discussions I had with them.

I'd like to record my gratitude to my brother, Jitendra Singh, my son, Atul Singh, and my daughter, Seema Singh, for their encouragement and for carrying out my duties whenever I am out of India.

I'd like to record my thanks to my disciple, Advocate Anjani Kumar Pradhan for looking after the Academy's activities efficiently as its Executive Secretary, especially when I am out of the country. Thanks are also due to my disciple Munish Kumar Shukla for that matter.

Last but not least I wish to thank my cousin Ramola Singh for spiritual association and interests, for promoting a vegetarian restaurant in support of the Yoga Centre, and for introducing me to advocate Ravindra Kumar, who worked successfully toward the formation of a spiritual group of people and for the establishment of the ashram in Etah, India.

INTRODUCTION

EACH OF US HAS A SPIRITUAL ENERGY dormant below the base of the spine. In the East, it is referred to as the *kundalini*. But by whatever name it is called, it is the common denominator in all major religions.

If this energy is awakened and converted into inner power, we become transformed. We develop an understanding of higher truths and view death not as an enemy but as a minor transition in the larger scheme of affairs. We are able to see the life of the soul—the eternal part of us.

A person with an awakened kundalini sees the universe regularly through visions and "out-of-body" spiritual experiences. (Interestingly, temporary spiritual experiences are also possible through occurrences such as dreams, drugs, anesthesia, and near-death experience. But these are like getting a "visitor's visa" to the other side, while the kundalini makes provision for permanent residence.) One experiences life after death even before dying. A wider view of the eternal life of the soul enables one to gauge the significance of his present physical existence in true perspective.

This wider understanding reduces much of one's anxiety in different spheres of life, besides eliminating the fear of death as an end to everything or a leap into the unknown. It builds an inner peace and inspires us to lead a fuller and righteous life. At the same time, it allows a smooth and peaceful transition to the realms of higher vibration when we discard our earthly shells and move on to the other side.

The "other side" in the scriptures of major religions of the world—Buddhist, Hindu, Christian, Tibetan, Mohammedan, and Egyptian, as well as the Theosophical Society—is divided into six "upper" realms (described in different ways by different religions) existing beyond our physical plane: the ethereal, the astral, the psychic, the spiritual, the cosmic, and the nirvanic. Thus, there are seven divisions of the universe altogether, beginning with the physical. The "Seventh Heaven" of Western mythology has its origin in this concept. Modern authorities like Sri Aurobindo, Osho Rajneesh, Carl Jung, Geraldine Cummins, Gladys Osborne Leonard, and Martinus also corroborate these.

Our evolving soul is destined to ascend these six realms to attain its ultimate goal—a merging with the Divine Soul. This merging also implies a close proximity to God, while retaining one's individuality. The seven realms are believed to correspond to seven chakras or centers of consciousness and energy within the human body, with the kundalini as the starting point at the base. Awakening one's kundalini (or attaining one's full potential) consists of activating these chakras successively.

The awakening of kundalini is the true meaning of being "born again" or "twice-born." As Christ said, only the twice born can enter the kingdom of heaven. I was fortunate to have experienced such an awakening in 1987. It changed my entire outlook on life, and after teaching mathematics for more than thirty years in eight countries, I shifted my focus to religion and psychology. I resigned from mathematics, so to speak, in 1994 and dedicated myself fully to spiritual growth and to helping others grow spiritually.

I have discussed spiritual matters, including the awakening of the kundalini, in three earlier books—*Secrets of Numerology* (1992), *Destiny, Science and Spiritual Awakening* (1997), and *Kundalini for Beginners* (2000). In this book, I have attempted to harmonize the key points from those three books, while elaborating on them in order to present the reader with a shortcut Integral Path toward kundalini activation and enlightenment.

From my own experience as well as that of others I've encountered, it is my firm conviction that an activated kundalini is the prime factor responsible for an individual's outstanding performance in any walk of life, be it in arts or sports, science or war. This book shows you a succinct, shortcut Integral Path devised from a combination of scientific and classical methods to attain your infinite potential in this world and hereafter.

Here's wishing you luck on your progressive journey to greater peace of mind and thence to eternal bliss.

DR. RAVINDRA KUMAR
(Swami Ravindranand)
Founder/Director
Academy of Kundalini Yoga
61, Vashisht Park, Pankha Road,
New Delhi-110046
Email (India): kumarravi@mail.com
Ph.: 65956688; Mobile: 9891467723
Email (Denmark): jytteravi.kumar@mail.tele.dk
Phone: (45) 36169250
Website: www.quantumsoulaware.com

PART ONE

The Other World

Chapter One

THE AWAKENING OF THE TWICE-BORN

I experienced death and, paradoxically, in death, I awakened to a new life. I was living in Zimbabwe in 1987. At 5 A.M. on a balmy October morning, while praying to God, I asked him to help me on my path toward enlightenment. Feeling despair at my inability to access him, I felt tears flow from my eyes. My rosary beads had fallen from my hands and I no longer sensed the world outside. Suddenly, I saw my dead body being carried on the shoulders of four people as they repeated the words, "Ravindra Kumar is dead." Emerging from this all-engrossing and miserable situation, I felt relieved, peaceful, and happy; a new horizon had opened before me. I felt that something had shifted in me. I did not know it then, but this was my spiritual rebirth. My state of bliss and cheerfulness was overwhelming as I got up from my chair and left the room. The Zimbabwe sunrise was beginning to blossom as I went out for my usual long walk, bringing newfound happiness with me. Going to the mathematics department later that morning, my heart was no longer in my work. Telling others about my experience, I found they could not comprehend it. From that day on, I began losing interest in mathematics, my profession for more than twenty-seven years.

Continuing to chant mantras and meditate as I had in the past, I was about to take tea in the evening about two weeks later, when suddenly my body began to twist like a snake. My tongue felt as if it were coming out of my mouth, and there was immense heat coming from the crown of my head. Running out of the house, I took a brisk walk for half an hour, and then cycled on an indoor machine at home for another 20 minutes. I then had a cold drink and rested. The next day, the university doctor examined me and listened to every detail of my experience. He said clearly, if I had not been so healthy and physically fit I would be paralyzed today. In his experience, physically weak practitioners can undergo paralysis as a result of too much meditation. Because I had been regularly practicing hatha yoga exercises, chanting mantras, and reading tantric literature for several years, the awakening of the kundalini did not cause paralysis in me. However, the doctor advised me to discontinue all meditative practices and not to lecture at the university for two weeks.

On that day in October 1987, after discontinuing all types of chanting and meditation, a wonderful series of experiences began to unfold for me. I continued to pray each morning and, on three occasions in the period of two months, I witnessed the Mother Goddess clad in a red silk sari with shining silver bangles. She sat smiling at me. Oh, what a beautiful face and shining eyes! I saw myself dressed in white, bowing down to her as she blessed me with her right hand touching my head. Following these visions, I was very cheerful and content. My focus shifted from mathematics to religion and parapsychology. I started writing articles based on my experiences. They were published in *The Journal of Religion and Psychical Research.*

All faiths and traditions have talked about the primordial or unstruck sound one hears internally in successful states of meditation. It is this sound that takes the soul toward God. My experiences with the sound began in the middle of the night when I got up to answer the call of nature. At around 2 A.M., I heard a persistent sound, like the blowing of a conch shell or an airplane flying over the house. I asked everyone in the house if they heard anything unusual. The household denied hearing anything. In the morning, I went to the university hospital where the doctor examined me. He said there was nothing wrong with my ears. He had heard of cases where people hear internal sounds that either subside or continue, but that, in my case, there was nothing to worry about. I still live with that sound today. It has become more clear and pronounced over the years.

My experiences with outer light started in 1984 while practicing meditation. I was teaching at the University of Port Harcourt, Nigeria, at that time. Suddenly, on hearing a lightning sound, as if electricity had jumped between two poles, my eyes opened and I saw a six-inch-high and four-inch-wide column of white light standing four feet from my head. Amazed at seeing it, I looked around to find the source, but could find none. Shortly, the light began to flicker and move left as it diminished in size, vanishing completely after traversing about three feet. This light was cool and bright and did not hurt my eyes; rather it felt soothing. After that event, my faith in the divine increased. I became happier, less concerned with the external activities around me, and more interested in my thoughts and feelings about God.

An experience with inner light came two months after my awakening in 1987. In the early morning, as I was about to leave my bed, I saw blue light through my inner eyes. Unusually attracted to it, I kept my eyes closed and continued to concentrate on the light. After a while, I opened my eyes and found the light still there. Whether my eyes were open or closed, the blue light stood there, remained 10 to 15 minutes, and then disappeared. Now when I close my eyes, the first thing I see is the blue light.

I had experienced what, in the East, is known as kundalini, a spiritual awakening from within. Kundalini is the spiritual energy that lies dormant at the base of the spine. It is in the form of a snake, coiled three and a half times, with its mouth closing the opening of the central nerve along the spine, called *sushumna*. Most of us have only 15 to 20 percent of our brain active at any given time. When kundalini awakens, sleeping parts of the brain begin to open and the person begins to acquire unusual powers. This makes a person a genius in his or her field of work. Outstanding achievements in any worldly field, as well as spiritual awakening or enlightenment, are the natural consequences of the arousal of kundalini.

Life before Awakening

Looking back on my life before that eventful day in 1987, I see my spiritual path had been predestined. My mother once told me that, as a child, I had no interest in material things, that I didn't care for balloons, whistles, or other toys as other children did. Remaining quiet, undemanding, content, and happy, I would simply hold my mother's finger and walk quietly with her and my father. I wondered if this was a carryover from a previous life or a new behavior. While in college, I was honored by being named captain of the gymnastics team. Maybe I should have experienced some special pride at wearing the jacket proclaiming me captain, but I did not. Always an excellent student as well as a good athlete, I enjoyed extracurricular activities. Yet I never took the pleasure in my accomplishments that it seemed I should have. In any gathering, I found myself alone, even though my skills as humorist and singer should have given me recognition and companionship. Always preferring solitude, sitting alone, and thinking, I would coax and cajole myself into treading the unfrequented ways. Not that I did not like the company of people; I simply needed regular time for introspection and the search for meaning in my life. I used to feel a sort of constructive dissatisfaction with regard to material objects and worldly relations.

Nature favored me from early childhood, providing the perfect environment for my inner development. I was ten months old when my mother left me with my grandmother so she could study in a teachers' training school. My elementary school and college education occurred away from my parents. Living in dormitories, I cried because I missed my parents and felt so lonely. In my professional life, I taught in five places in India and eight countries around the world. Every two years, I transferred to a new country, each time to a new setting, new house, new people, new circumstances, or new car. Thus I was forced to forget old comforts and friends and to develop new relationships. This helped remove the fear of the unknown from my heart, and I became accustomed to accepting new adventures. This constant change developed an attitude of detachment that became habitual.

Teaching at various universities, I devoted my free time to exercise and yoga in the morning and long walks in the evening. In 1982, with no planning, I picked up a book on mantras from Delhi. It was as if something had taken me to the place where the book was on display. Bringing the book to Nigeria where I was teaching, I selected some mantras and began chanting for two to three hours every day. I was used to going to bed early, between 9:30 and 10 P.M., and waking between 2:30 and 2:45 A.M. I would wash myself and sit meditating and chanting mantras from 3 to 6 in the morning. I would also read various scriptures and case histories of God or Self-realized people from around the world for nearly three hours every day. My sex life was regular and I drank alcohol in moderation, living a life that combined hatha yoga (yogic postures), bhakti yoga (devotion through chanting and meditation), jnana yoga (reading scriptures and searching for my Self), and tantra yoga (recognition of sex drive) for several years.

A candle under a container of water cannot provide enough heat to boil the water. However, when a stronger heat is placed under the water, it will bring the water to a boil and convert it into steam. In the same way, if sufficient spiritual forces are applied, they will precipitate the sleeping energy within. And just as water converts into steam, man, who is God in the making, converts into God. Then, an energetic blast is experienced within and we have the kind of experiences I have described. The chemistry and physiology of the body begin to change. One specific phenomenon I noticed was a heightened activity taking place within my testicles and a fluid flowing upward toward my brain. Sometimes, I would feel nerves breaking in my brain. My interest in sexual activity changed dramatically while I lived as a near recluse. Prior to this period, I would have regular and prolonged sex; now I was more casual about it and at times would even withdraw in the middle of the act and go to sleep. I experienced inner happiness, cheerfulness, and contentment. I also stopped thinking about the past and speculating about the future, and became indifferent to the present.

Freedom from Fear of Death

Everyone has some experience of fear and anxiety in their life. Fear is a normal response that includes feelings of disquiet or alarm elicited by the realistic expectation of pain, danger, or disaster.[1] For example, if a thief enters your house and asks at gunpoint that you give away all your valuables, your heart begins to beat faster, your body begins to shake and tremble, sweat appears on your forehead, you are embarrassed and scared to death. Anxiety is an irrational or overwhelming fear. It is one's subjective distorted view of the circumstance. It is often based on an irrational belief. Death anxiety is defined as an overwhelming fear of death and/or dying and usually involves an all-encompassing fear about whether one will continue to exist in some form or fashion after physical death. It includes unrelenting fear of dying and anxiety about the unknown. It is man's biggest fear and we deal with it daily, although most people repress it. In repressing it, they give rise to many other physical and psychological ailments. The message of this book is that we can overcome the constant fear of death through a spiritual awakening and live an unrepressed life.

Freedom from death anxiety, therefore, requires proof of three components of life after death: a surviving soul, a positive afterlife, and God. The uniqueness of this book is that it provides this proof through personal experiences and corroborates it through various faiths and traditions. It is likely that your death anxiety will be overcome by the time you have finished reading this book. The last chapter presents a proven practical method for awakening one's own spiritual energy within and finding freedom from death anxiety.

A large number of researchers in the field of past-life regression have convincingly shown the continuity of existence before birth and after death.[2] This confirms the words Lord Krishna spoke in the Bhagavad-

Gita some five thousand years ago. Other great ones, such as Gautam Buddha, Jesus Christ, Pythagoras, Confucius, and Zoroaster, have further confirmed the continuity of existence. The reason for death anxiety is that people are so attached to the physical pleasures that they have no time to go into meditation themselves to find the proof. Those who have gone into meditation have found the proof and realized their own existence-knowledge-bliss. Meditation ultimately gives the experience of death while still living and liberates one from the fear of death once and for all. Modern people take temporary measures through drugs or distractions, which give only short-lived relief; the dragon of fear shows up again later in life. A permanent solution comes only through the awakening of one's dormant spiritual energy.

Not only is my fear of death gone, but I find dying to be a sweet game one can play anytime. Quoting St. Paul, "I die daily." The fear of the unknown is gone for me, since I now know the other side so well. For the past fifteen years, I have been going out of my body and exploring various realms. The kind of life to be found on the other side depends on your personal evolution on earth. Although God is indefinable, you can experience him, depending on the intensity of your desire. People have experienced him as a touch, as a vision, as sound and light, and as a physical manifestation of their most cherished formulation of him. My own experiences are briefly elaborated in the next section.

The Reality beyond, Seen Personally

Soon after experiencing my awakening of kundalini in 1987, I received firsthand knowledge of various astral subplanes. I traveled to these places of light and saw living conditions similar to those on earth. One difference was that the laws of physics did not apply there. People lived in their astral bodies, similar in appearance to their earthly physical bodies. At times, I found myself on planes higher than the astral without a physical body. My existence was either as a ball of light or simply without any dimension. There was no sun or moon, no duality of any kind. For example, there was only pleasant light and no shadow of any kind. Such planes are spiritual regions that constitute three-quarters of creation, while only one fourth of creation has life within a solar system like ours.[3] I experienced myself as a formless point of awareness. During this process, you may see dreams that come in the four stages described by Jung and others.[4] In the final stage, you may see the manifestation of an infinite God in a finite form of your liking.

With these experiences, I received the proof of myself as a permanent soul living a useful and happy afterlife and having a loving association with God. Needless to say, I have no place for death anxiety in my life, and I look forward to the day when I will translate to the other side. We can choose our own method to achieve higher consciousness. However, the recommended method is the Integral Path laid down in the last chapter of this book—a path that may eventually lead to spiritual enlightenment.

Kundalini rises through the seven central chakras (vortices of energy) on awakening. Out-of-body travel to higher realms while asleep occurs as a natural phenomenon when the third chakra, also known as the *manipura* chakra or solar plexus, awakens. Knowing unconditional love is a result of awakening the fourth, *anahata*, chakra or heart center. One requirement of the first commandment of Moses is, "Thou shalt love thy neighbor," which is not what we normally do in life. The moment we think we can, we remember the day our neighbor did something we judged as wrong, and we will or choose not to feel love for him. When the heart chakra opens, we transcend negative thoughts; understanding and compassion replace judgmental thoughts. You love your neighbor regardless of what he may have done. Inner happiness and cheerfulness are your emotions, and a pleasant smile is naturally on your face. You become indifferent to the temporary phenomenal happenings surrounding you.

The opening of the *vishuddhi* chakra, or throat center, gives the power of clear speech and freedom from dis-ease. This is one reason yogis look younger than their actual age. The opening of the sixth center, called the *ajna* chakra or eyebrow center, accompanies the (ego) death experience. Your ego fragments into a thousand pieces, and there is a spiritual resurrection. Devoid of ego, childlike, you qualify to enter the kingdom of God. Remember the words of Master Jesus, who said that only a childlike person may enter the kingdom of God. This kingdom is within you. Here you are unconditionally happy and unconcerned by the events of the material world because you have found the nonmaterial and permanent source of happiness. Gone is any dependence on temporary sources of pleasure or distraction, such as alcohol, smoking, sex, winning a lottery, seeing friends, watching television, shopping, or traveling. You become independent of material things and live as a contented and cheerful person, with no requirements. That is how a liberated person or a yogi lives.

A person at this stage is known as "twice-born" in the words of Master Jesus. The second birth takes place when one's dormant spiritual energy awakens. The physical body received at the first birth is spiritualized in the second birth. With the second birth, we automatically enter the kingdom of heaven, or higher realms. Seven-ness is an underlying principle of the universe, and a common denominator in various faiths and traditions around the world. Human awareness has seven levels; the universe divides into seven realms or planes. We are a permanent soul, or Atman, transcending layers of ignorance as we rise through our levels of awareness. The soul has paranormal powers. Scientists compare these personal case histories to quantum objects. We can choose from various methods for raising our consciousness to higher levels. One time-tested method is to awaken our kundalini, the dormant spiritual energy we all possess.

Chapter Two

EVIDENCE AND MOTIVATION OF THE DIVINE PLAN

During the past two decades, I have experienced out-of-body, or soul, travel on a different level of awareness. I have traveled to various higher realms and communicated with other souls. I had always been intrigued by the idea of consciously speaking to someone living in a higher realm. The opportunity to do so came after my father passed over. In September 1995, three years after my father's death, a clairvoyant friend in North Carolina assisted me in making contact. A spirit spoke through him, saying that Ganga Singh (my father) was not strong enough to talk to me directly. However, as caretaker of the place where my father was recovering, he offered to converse with me and relay whatever my father said, while my father would hear me directly.

Through this helpful spirit, my father described a hospital setting where large numbers of people were recovering. After a long rest, his broken leg was mending and soon he would be transferred to a region of brighter light. He was feeling very relaxed. He wanted me to remove his possessions from the house where he had lived so his attention would not be distracted, and requested that he be emotionally released by all of his relatives. I asked if he had met my grandmother (his mother) yet, and he replied that she was in a higher region where he could see her but that he could not go there directly. He wanted me to tell his wife (my mother) that he was very well and that no one should worry about him.

We then spoke about other family matters. I expressed my sorrow at not being at his side when he left this world. He was also sorry, missed being with me, and wanted to embrace me. He suggested we could meet in a dream thirty days later, if I agreed. Naturally, I said yes. Exactly thirty days later, we were walking and talking together in my dream.

The next opportunity to visit my father came in June 2000, at the home of my friend in North Carolina. In this vision, having recovered his strength, my father spoke to me directly, greeting me with folded hands. I experienced much joy, since now my father was talking to me directly, rather than through another. Immediately, I lowered myself in prostration to touch his feet—a traditional Indian gesture of respect and reverence. Saying we were no longer father and son, but now two fellow souls, he expressed his pride at my progress and offered to guide me in my quest for spiritual knowledge. When asked if he remembered his wife, he replied, "Which one?" Other souls had partnered him in other lifetimes. He confided in me, revealing his new type of existence. In this existence, he sometimes felt like a cloud. He could take form if he wished; however, he felt no need. In this place, neither eating or drinking was necessary. It was a realm of unearthly colors, such as he had never seen. The entire atmosphere was so lovely that it was beyond the capacity of earthly language to express. Going to meet friends or relatives required only a thought, but usually they would come to see him in groups. Several radiant and serene teachers came from time to time to offer lessons.

Curious, I inquired about his next incarnation. He said that the choice had not come up yet. The concept of time did not exist and he was happy learning and enjoying his new life. Needing to go, he assured me that I could visit him whenever I wished. When I asked him if my visit had caused him any trouble, he reassuringly said, "No, not at all."

My medium friend suggested that I could talk to his spirit guide, Guru Kirpal, who had translated from earth a few years ago. Guru Kirpal was the same spirit who had helped me communicate with my father when he was still indisposed. On another occasion, I had an hour's conversation with Guru Kirpal. He told me that he resided only on the mental plane. He explained that souls on the mental plane, and on a still higher level, have very subtle bodies, sometimes visualized only as a flash of light. They engage in spiritual pursuits and are teachers who visit whenever assistance is required.

After witnessing myself as a soul conversing with my father on the astral plane and with Guru Kirpal on the mental plane, my natural next step was to seek other planes of existence and levels of consciousness, or what I call levels of awareness.

The Properties of the Soul

The term *soul* is well defined in the Oxford dictionary as the nonmaterial part of a person, believed to exist forever. In the Webster lexicon, it is defined as an entity without material reality, often regarded as the spiritual part of a person. Combining these definitions with my personal experiences, I personally define *soul* as a nonmaterial and spiritual part of a person, which exists forever.

The Bhagavad Gita[1] relates the teachings of Lord Krishna, spoken several millennia ago. It characterizes the soul as an entity that is neither born nor dies. The soul has not come into being, does not come into being, and will not come into being. It is unborn, eternal, ever-existing, and primeval. It is not slain when the body is slain. As the embodied soul, it passes, along with our earthly body, from boyhood to youth to old age. Likewise, it passes into another body at death. An aware person is not bewildered by such a change. Those who are seers of the truth have concluded that the temporal or material body does not endure, but that for the soul, there is no change. They have concluded this by studying the nature of both. No one is able to destroy the imperishable soul. Just as a person putting on a new garment gives up the old one, the soul accepts a new material body, giving up the dead one. The soul can never be cut by weapons, nor burned by fire, nor wet by water, nor withered by wind. It is everlasting, omnipresent, and eternally unchanged. Understanding this, we need not grieve for the body. All beings are unmanifest in their beginning, manifest in their interim state, and unmanifest again when transformed. So, is there need for lamentation?

When Lord Krishna spoke of the truths of the Bhagavad Gita on the battlefield of Mahabharata some five thousand years ago, it was not the first time those truths had been voiced. Tens of thousands of years ago, on the planet Sun, the sage Manu taught the principles of the Bhagavad Gita. The same principles will be taught once again at some future date. Aldous Huxley called it perennial philosophy.[2] As more details about the physics of the soul surface, it is a pleasant surprise to see psychics, clairvoyants, and past-life-regression therapists independently discovering the same principles. Whatever the form, the soul is a consciously aware energy, a feeling being with memories, unresolved issues, and a sense of humor.[3] It is mightier than space, stronger than time, deeper than the sea, and higher than the stars.[4]

Traveling is an important aspect of the soul. It is connected to the body by a silver cord that stretches to unlimited lengths when it explores.

This cord is released only at the time of physical death. The conscious mind governs the journey of the soul out of the body or back into the body. Although soul-travel experiences take place mainly during sleep, the soul also goes out for small trips during waking hours, although we may not consciously be aware of it. These are some of the signs, indicating out-of-body experiences:

1. Dreams of flying that feel real;
2. Dreams of visiting deceased loved ones;
3. Dreams of being close to a loved one living in a far-away place, with a sad feeling of a forced separation on waking;
4. Dreams from which you awaken in the middle of the night, but cannot open your eyes, move your body, or speak;
5. Dreams from which you are shaken awake in the middle of the night, although you go to sleep again after waking.

There are brief moments when the soul goes out of the body while awake. This happens during intense emotional states, such as worry for a sick loved one, desire to be with a loved one who is far away, homesickness, the wish to check up on the children, or concern about responsibilities in progress somewhere else. You may feel as if you are daydreaming or going blank. During such an experience, you may kiss or hug someone; the person will not know it consciously, but will have a feeling of being loved. Many times, you may feel someone is calling you by name; in fact, a soul is actually around and calling you, but you cannot see anyone. There is a barrier in the conscious mind not allowing it to know everything the soul knows. That is why, when the soul goes out, the mind goes blank. The soul has visited the loved one, but the conscious mind does not know about it. The soul uses the body and mind for the experiences of the current incarnation. The body and mind are limited within the five senses, but the soul is not. Gary Zukav discusses how, as we evolve spiritually, our intuitive perceptions also evolve and we become multisensory beings.[5]

Although soul-travel dreams may occur spontaneously, some people have learned to induce them. The sleep state is one way to have an out-of-body experience, but not the only way. Terrill Wilson described his method of working consciously.[6] His first success came after one year of practice in concentration. By visualizing the environment and history of an area, he could arrive at his desired destination. Over the years, he soul-traveled to many realms and interacted with other beings. Over time, he improved his formulas for travel and included them in his books. In the end, however, he pointed out that spiritual awakening, and not soul travel, will bring us where we are destined to be.

There are other situations where soul travel takes place. If you go to bed with an unsolved problem in mind, the soul may go out of the body and meet other souls to find the solution—and you wake up with an answer. You do not consciously know the homework done by the soul, but you are happy for the information. The soul regularly talks to spirit guides. When you are physically unable to take a vacation, the soul may travel out of the body and visit some beautiful place, such as a favorite garden or mountain meadow. You wake up with a smile, refreshed, but unconscious of the gift delivered by the soul.

Robert A. Monroe established an institute for soul travel in the United States after writing several books on the subject. In these books, he describes three techniques. The first is the mind-awake/body-asleep method, in which one remains conscious when the body goes to sleep. While one slowly enters the twilight zone between waking and sleeping, the soul becomes lighter and lighter and finally moves out through the top of the head, becoming a subtle body that looks back on the physical body. The second is the rotation method, in which one visualizes turning over without using the physical arms and legs while in the state between waking and sleeping, and then thinks of floating away from the body. The third method uses sexual energy to arouse passionate energy and then sublimates that energy instead of releasing it physically. One imagines the energy as a white globe rising from the root chakra to the eyebrow or crown chakra, then moving from the body. During soul travel, there may be many sensations, like buzzing or vibrating. Everyone will experience their own style.

The Creation of Souls

Although the birth time of a soul cannot be traced, some believe it was fifteen billion years ago. Many writers also refer to old and new souls, claiming that old souls have lived many lives, gaining wisdom in the process, while young ones are just stepping onto wisdom's path. Old souls leave their bodies quickly as the body dies. Average souls do not leave so rapidly, and younger souls may remain linked to the earthly environment for a time after death.[7] Highly advanced souls are often found in humble circumstances. A rich diversity of beliefs and contentment in solitude are measures of the emotional and spiritual maturity of old souls. New souls, on the other hand, are believed to be going through a process of continual creation.

In the Eastern spiritual tradition of enlightened Indian gurus and Tibetan lamas, the soul has never been born and can never die. Its energy is in the same infinite state as cosmic consciousness, or God. All that exists or ever will exist arose in the same universal moment. Whenever enlightened men and women in the West have written on this topic, their views seem to be in agreement with their Eastern counterparts.

These are only two ways of seeing the experience of the soul. As there are infinite possibilities, both of these may be correct within the framework of those having the experience. Our beliefs or understandings will condition our experiences. To cope with the concept of infinity, we may need to create the experience of birth to give us a reference point that is closer to our understanding of what it is to exist in time and physical space.

Past-life therapist Michael Newton has regressed a number of people using hypnosis to collect information about the creation of souls. Two categories of his patients report remembering a "soul nursery," complete with incubator mothers who help hatch the eggs and care for newly born souls. The nursery is a vast space of vaporous, swirling energy currents infused with intense light. Soul production originates in a molten mass of high-intensity vitality, energized by an amazing love force. The pulsating, undulating pink mass swells in the middle, increasing in size; it pushes outward and separates as a new soul, alive with energy and uniqueness, is born. New souls are distinct masses of white energy, sheathed in golden light, gliding majestically in orchestrated lines of progression. Incubator mothers in their delivery suits receive them and nurture them in their incubator cells until they are ready. This is a realm of love and beauty cradled in a beatific glow of orange-yellow light, with infinite violet darkness beyond. Each soul has unique characteristics instilled by a perfection that cannot be described. No two souls are alike.

The Divine Plan

Creation offers to the soul an opportunity to develop the world and the soul to the highest possible potential. Unlimited lifetimes are allowed each soul to attend earth school. Perfection already exists, but each soul has to reach that realization of perfection individually. This requires going through a variety of "down-to-earth experiences," until Self-realization is achieved.

A soul may be born as a male or female in a series of lives, such as the present Dalai Lama in his thirteenth incarnation, or the present Guruma in Sonepat (India), in her sixth consecutive incarnation as a female saint. The past-life researcher Joan Grant remembered her seven previous lives, four as a male and three as a female.[8] The soul alternates between male and female incarnations to experience both sides of the coin, until a balance between the masculine and feminine nature is acquired. This is the goal of the evolutionary process on earth, taught by different faiths and traditions. Ardhanareeshwara, the half-male, half-female figure of Lord Shiva in India, the hermaphrodite in Judaism and Gnosticism, and the androgynous god/goddess in Greek mythology all point toward this reality. King David of the Old Testament is a good example. His rebellious son challenged him for the throne. David fought and killed his son, giving proof of his masculine energy. But then he wept for many days grieving for his lost son, giving proof of his female energy. If his faithful minister had not stopped David's excessive mourning, the king's balance—and the battle—would have been lost. We should all endeavor to become equally intellectual and intuitive to achieve this balance.

Likewise, a soul is sometimes born as a poor person, sometimes as a rich person, in order to experience both situations and, ultimately, to strike a balance. Sometimes one is born as an oppressor, sometimes as a pawn. Sometimes one is born in the East, sometimes in the West. Buddha gave the example of a stringed musical instrument. If the strings are too tight or too loose, the instrument will not produce melodious sounds. When a balanced tension develops in the strings, a harmonious situation is created. This principle applies to human life as well. Under the divine plan, the soul is offered all possible opportunities to achieve to this balance. Whenever such a balance is attained, the soul graduates from earth school. In the remaining years of that life, a person lives without desires or attachment, happy and cheerful, unchained to the past, with an absence of speculation about the future and a lack of concern regarding the present.

Levels of Awareness

Taking an analogy from an apparent cosmic design of seven-ness, other writers propose that there are seven major levels, believing the universe to be a *torus*, its seven colors corresponding to the seven stages. These seven stages are related to seven kingdoms that cumulatively increase in power, starting with light and ending with people. Seven-ness appears in sound waves in the seven fundamental tones of Western music. Indian music also has seven basic tones. There are seven colors in the rainbow. The atomic elements are arranged in the seven rows of the periodic table. In the Kaballah, seven *sefiroth* correspond to seven levels of substance. In metaphysics, there are seven major chakras. Modern researchers of the brain/mind and levels of consciousness use a seven-level symbolic interpretation. One scientist has said: "If sevenness is a cosmic property, then it could represent a constraint imposed by the creation pattern in the generation of space-time." Quantum physics also has something new to say about creation patterns and individuals who explore other realms that may give us clues.

I personally agree with the proposition that seven-ness is a cosmic property and that a creation pattern imposes a constraint on the generation of space-time. I have given details elsewhere about seven levels of transformation through the opening of all seven chakras after the passage of kundalini.[9] Sri Aurobindo stated that *purusha* exists on all levels of existence. Purusha means masculine energy and intelligence. It is balanced by *prakriti*, the feminine or emotional energy. All beings contain both purusha and prakiti, as well as the potential to bring them into harmony. By meditating, one can travel to various levels of existence in the astral body with angels or guides (see, for example, the recent case of Echo Bodine[10]).

The properties of the soul at the seven levels can be described as follows:

Level 1: The time of unconsciousness and karma is the beginning, when we are concerned with survival. Living in fear, we are unaware of the connection that exists between all living beings. People at this level ignore their inner voice, misunderstand the law of karma, fear a power outside themselves, and act in a selfish way, worrying about their own gratification. Love, in the greater sense, has not awakened within them.

Level 2: The awareness here is similar to level 1, but the people have begun to love others, are less self-concerned and less fearful. Others are separate to them. Although they occasionally revert to their old ways, their hearts are opening to others.

Level 3: At this level, faith in spirituality develops; one believes more in unity than separation. Understanding cause and effect (what we send out is what we get back), they accept their responsibility and the law of karma. Some follow a religious path with spiritual understanding, and all take steps in a positive direction toward a broader belief system. They risk being emotionally open and understand the similarities between themselves and others.

Level 4: At this level, some still have karma to balance and lessons to learn through further incarnation. Having spent various lives enduring difficult times on levels 1 to 3, they open to a greater understanding of reality. They are inquisitive, join organizations of a metaphysical or spiritual nature, and begin to search for truth. The battle between physical addictions and spiritual values is a mark of level 4. Recovery from addiction takes place at this level. The impermanence of the physical world is realized and detachment arises. They enjoy the lessons they have learned and values they have accrued. They meet life with an open heart and may be independent of organized religion. Their wounds and pains are healing, negative acts are amended, responsibility is taken, and an interest in spiritual evolution develops. Many souls at this level may move to level 5 or choose to come back to earth and help their fellow beings. They are angels or avatars.

Level 5: No longer believing in a need for struggle and conflict, souls of the fifth level are not compelled to return to earth. At this level, realization of oneness with God and all creation is manifest. Level 5 is the beginning of Nirvana. The soul, when integrated on this level, does not need to incarnate further, although the option remains. Souls here no longer experience grief or resentment, or blame God for creation. Unconditional love is the hallmark of this level. Here, souls are teachers and guides. Their karma is released, as negative beliefs are healed. They are angelic.

Level 6: This is the level of bliss, and cannot be measured with earthly yardsticks. Souls at this level have transcended limited consciousness and soon enter level 7.

Level 7: This is the level of universal consciousness.

Chapter Three

DYING, DEATH, AND THE AFTERLIFE

Difficulty in the dying process is proportional to the level of attachment to the physical world. Conversely, ease in the process of dying is proportional to the spiritual evolution of the person. A team of helpers guides the soul after physical death to a place where one lives with others in soul/astral form and prepares for rebirth. An individual with awakened spiritual energy, or kundalini, bypasses this place and is automatically placed in a realm where they grow further toward God. Past-life regressionists report what their subjects or case studies have seen, while yogis report what they themselves have seen. According to past-life regressionist Newton, "It is the people represented in these cases who are the real messengers of hope for the future, not the reporter."[1] He rightly admits the limitation of working with people who are still incarnating. To gain information from realms higher than the astral, one either has to be in touch with souls who have broken the chain of reincarnation, or be a yogi him- or herself. This is where kundalini comes into the picture. A practitioner with an awakened kundalini is capable of connecting him- or herself with the higher realms.

Many people have learned about the meaninglessness of life on one hand, and acquired knowledge of the beyond on the other. With the knowledge of a meaningful existence of life after death, it is natural for the fear of death to vanish. Through metaphysics, yoga, meditation, or other means, individuals around the world have awakened their dormant spiritual energy. With this awakening, they have experienced death while still living. As a result, their fear of physical death is gone forever. As a natural consequence of this awakening, people have found knowledge of life after death, and the existence of other planes of reality.

Death of the Physical Body

On the physical plane, we possess both a physical body and an etheric body. Although the etheric body is similar to the physical body, it is not bound by the same physical constraints. The physical body (*sthool sharira*)* is composed of solid, liquid, and gaseous elements, the three densest components of the physical world. Accordingly, the body has bones, blood, and gases corresponding to these three elements. The etheric body is made of four kinds of ether (*akashic* elements), which are more subtle than the three elements of the physical body. The function of the etheric double (*pranamaya kosh* or *chhaya sharira*) is to receive light energy from the sun and pass it to the nervous system as nourishment. Humans live by this energy.

The soul is surrounded by causal, mental, astral, physical, and etheric bodies. At the time of death, the soul, or Atman, is released from two of its bodies—the physical and the etheric. The etheric body cannot normally be seen, but clairvoyants or yogis, with their divine eyes, can see it. It consists of infinite pinpoints of flashing light. The seven centers of energy called chakras can be seen glowing in its central line. There is no greater authentic proof than the etheric body with its seven chakras, which we all possess, to show the reality of kundalini, which passes through these chakras on awakening. The etheric body hovers around the physical body for about twelve days after death before moving on. This is one reason why Hindus celebrate the twelfth and seventeenth days after someone's death in a spiritual way, to help release the etheric body. Etheric bodies have been seen lingering around the grave for several days.

Death can be slow and frightening, or a quick and beautiful process. At its onset, the weaker parts of the body close down first. Life energy stored by the etheric body moves upward from the feet toward the head. Parts of the body stop functioning one by one. Poison in the blood starts showing its effect, because the life energy that kept it in check is leaving. If the soul/Atman does not want to leave the physical body due to attachment, one may suffer in strange ways. One of my close relatives com-

*For definitions of this and other terms, see the glossary.

plained of being bitten by scorpions and snakes, suffering for almost an hour. He said he wanted to die, but was not allowed. The death of an older person may be relatively simple and comfortable when they have understood the meaninglessness of life. They may have conquered the five enemies (greed, lust, anger, attachment, and ego) to some extent. Yogis who have already experienced death in meditation leave their bodies swiftly. However, for an average person, the poison starts spreading and a state of coma approaches.

In a state of coma, the twilight zone of semi-consciousness, a person may see their whole life pass before them, including events going back in time to early childhood. At this point, the soul is its own judge. Judgment has always been self-judgment. One feels happiness and bliss corresponding to good deeds, and grief and repentance corresponding to harmful deeds. One is in a clear state of awareness, regardless of mental conditions during life, and a decision may be made about future lives. Whatever is not necessary is dropped from the astral body and whatever is required according to the final thoughts or sentiments remains. Correspondingly, the person finds their home in the appropriate subdivision of the astral plane, which lies next to the physical plane. Angels or pure beings on the higher realm are known to help those arriving at the next life, in accordance with the balance of karma—a perfect and flawless law of nature or God. A yogi, or person with awakened kundalini, bypasses this stage, as he or she has already seen their future life on one of the higher realms in the state of meditation.

After watching this "film" of one's life, the astral body (*sukshma sharira*) slips from the physical body. The gateway for detachment from the astral body is through the crown center for those who have conquered the five enemies—greed, lust, anger, attachment, and ego. For others, there may be different exit sites. The astral body is linked to the physical body by a silver cord. This silver cord becomes thinner and thinner, and finally severs completely at the time of death. In dream states, when the astral body is journeying into the astral planes, it is always linked to the physical body by this silver cord, which is infinite in length.

Properties of Life outside the Physical Body

Several books have appeared on out-of-body experiences, written authentically through research and personal experiences.[2] Robert Monroe and Dr. Ian Stevenson are two well-known writers on this subject. Monroe and Stevenson conducted hundreds of experiments on themselves and others to view life outside the physical body. Their findings show that, when the individual is outside the physical body, there are feelings of freedom and unconditional happiness. In fact, one may not wish to return to the physical body. This experience may occur either as a male or as a female, according to Monroe. One particular male always enjoyed being a female whenever outside his body.

Near-Death Experience

There are individuals who appear to die or come close to death, and then return to life. In many cases, it happens in hospitals on the operating table while under general anesthesia. People report phenomenon similar to the experiences of mystics. The term *near-death experience* comes from Dr. Raymond Moody, who, in his book *Life After Life*, hinted at an "entity" that survives physical death. Likewise, Rosemary Ellen Guiley's descriptions of life beyond death, given by those who have such experiences, include:

> a sense of being dead, or feeling themselves floating above their bodies, pain free, feeling bliss or peacefulness. Traveling down a dark tunnel toward a light at the end; meeting non-physical beings who glow, many of whom are dead friends and relatives; coming in contact with a guide or Supreme Being who takes them on a life review, during which their entire life is put into perspective without rendering any negative judgments; and finally, a reluctant return to life.[3]

Although there is no scientific proof of near-death experiences at this time, there is enough anecdotal material to support them. Innumerable cases are available in which the clinically dead report details of the operations performed on their bodies and conversations they heard in other parts of the hospital while apparently out of their bodies. Most of these individuals lose their fear of death and begin believing in an afterlife. Many of them become more spiritual and begin to believe in some type of God. Some people acquire heightened intuitive or psychic abilities. Their outlook is so changed that many of them find it difficult to adjust back to a normal life. Some philosophers theorize that near-death experiences are an opening toward enlightenment or a gateway to higher consciousness. One can imagine the transformation yogis undergo as they experience death whenever they are in deep meditation or trance, or during soul travel in dreams.

Recent Communications with Close Relatives

Jasper Swain, a magistrate at Pietermaritzburg, South Africa, had regular communications with his son, who died in an accident. In the words of Mike, the deceased son of the magistrate:

> As I said, thought is all powerful here. For example, if I want to own a brand-new Jaguar, all I have to do is visualize the car in my mind, and it is created right there before my eyes, out of the energy of this world.[4]

According to Mike, if two people are far away from one another and they want to make contact, telepathy is the normal way. Think of the fellow you want to speak to, and bingo! He is right there. They contact each other as easily as we use the telephone—except that they do not need a telephone. If someone wants to talk to you, you hear him in your mind. If you want to go to him, you merely exert your will and you are right there! Everything seems to be perfect. Bodies never get tired. Illness and sickness do not exist. It is a world of perfection, according to Mike. The soul that inhabits our bodies operates like a system of electrical impulses. The New Testament agrees that the human personality does survive the barrier of death. Master Jesus himself revealed his etheric body to his disciples. He even showed them the nail holes in his hands. In other words, he re-created his earthly body out of etheric matter, out of the electric impulses that activated the flesh-and-blood body. Being a master, he was empowered to do so, for an enlightened master has full control of all energy levels on earth and can use them at will.

Continuing the description of the body he now possessed, Mike said:

> There is quite a difference between the "me" that lives in this world, and the "me" that lived in your world! My body does not need food or drink to keep it going; nor does it need sleep to restore it. There are no excretory organs in our bodies. For example, when I drink a glass of water, it just diffuses itself, throughout my system, and that is that! In other words, it is converted into energy.

Mike described different levels of existence in the region. A person from the lower level finds it very difficult, if not impossible, to enter the higher level. This is because of his coarser vibrations, compared to the finer vibrations of the higher plane. Similarly, a person from the higher level can enter a lower level, but he will not stay there for long, since his finer vibrations will soon start feeling uncomfortable.

Thus telepathy, telekinesis, levitation, precognition, clairvoyance, materialization of objects, and other ESP (extra-sensory perception) powers are natural tools of life on the astral plane. Sometimes they infiltrate the physical plane and are exhibited through certain people. Duke University in North Carolina has been conducting research on these subjects since 1920 under the direction of Professor J. B. Rhine, who died a few years ago. Although these phenomena have been reproduced in the laboratory, it has not been possible to fit any physical or mathematical model to any of them. Indeed, this may never be possible, since, to do so, you must find a way to contain the infinite in a finite frame. However, these researches do give you a glimpse or taste of the astral plane while you are still on the physical plane. And, of course, they motivate us to explore further.

Those who live the life of a yogi can say good-bye to this physical plane once and for all, and become an inhabitant of the astral plane or a higher plane of the spiritual realms. Here, there is happiness, a sense of freedom, and no desire to return to the physical body. However, some intelligence watches over them and directs them to re-enter their body. This is especially true for those who have had near-death experiences.

In the astral realm, people live in groups in their astral bodies and they continue talking about their earthly lives with each other. They have the freedom to live as a male or female. Whenever a person is about to die on earth, all the group-souls on the astral realm come to know about it through direct channeling, and the intimate relatives and friends gather around and may talk to the person on their deathbed. Before arriving at one's own soul group—we may call it one's "true home"—the soul may have to pass through a kind of hospital, where it recovers from illness or injury. However, if one hasn't had any illness at death, one arrives directly at the "true home." Here, souls continue learning lessons from various teachers until they are ripe for their next incarnation.

No linear time concept exists here. Judgment is based on observation only. Soul groups continue incarnating on earth in different bodies and have a variety of relationships with each other. Traveling from one group to another is similar to immigration from one country to another on earth, and is not always easy or straightforward. This view is supported by the views of Sri Herald Klemp of Eckankar when he says,

> There is a minor channel (gateway) that links corresponding regions of the Astral and Physical planes. In fact, each country in the world today exists because of a spiritual gateway between it and a corresponding place upon the astral plane. Europe, Asia,

India, Asia Minor, Africa, North and South America, and every other area of earth have a corresponding gateway.[5]

Heaven and Hell

The lower divisions of the astral plane are for people creating their own hell. With repeated efforts and great difficulty, teachers pull some of them out of their self-created prisons. For example, a woman who had killed her own daughter-in-law was so full of self-pity and self-judgment that she could not imagine the reality of happiness. O'Brien, a researcher who works in large-group sessions to encourage people to contact relatives who have passed over, convinced her, brought her out of her own web, and helped her into a higher division.[6] This is part of our natural evolution, and capable souls are always eager to help those who need it. This is in contradiction to orthodox religion, which says that there are hells of punishment where sinful people suffer after death. Once I visited Tiger Garden in Singapore, which has a large section displaying varying conditions one can suffer in hell. In reality, we all allow our negative beliefs to create our own hell. Like-minded people may gather together and live in a condition of self-created and shared hell. Martinus, the Danish philosopher, claims:

> This sphere is known on the physical plane as "purgatory" and has furthermore through superstition been called "hell." There will thus be a certain unpleasant zone for all beings with imperfections to pass through after physical death. But the "eternal fire" or "everlasting damnation" with which the primitive imagination has equipped it certainly does not exist.[7]

According to Martinus, the individual arrives here with a mission of learning not to make more mistakes, or commit suicide or murder again. It can be unpleasant, but it is the path to perfect life and a direction toward God. He goes on to say, this area is only a small part of the whole spiritual zone, which otherwise constitutes an ocean of light and bliss—in its most profound analysis, a place of divine blessing. With this in mind, there can be no justifiable basis to mourn the early death or departure to another world of friends and relatives excessively.

People with noble and serene thoughts are found in higher subdivisions that have heavenlike conditions but are not actual heavens. Here, too, like-minded people may group together and live in a heavenlike state.

Heaven and hell have an entirely different reality from what is projected by some religions. This is also confirmed by the soul-travel experiences of yogis such as Yogananda, Muktananda, Sivananda, and many others.[8]

Accidental Death and Suicide

These cases need special attention because of their increasing frequency in the world. Sudden death is much different from natural death. People who die from old age or long illness may have weakened desires and less attachment to the world, taking them to a higher subdivision on the astral plane. In cases of sudden death, the person may not be prepared and worldly desires of a basic nature may remain. This may lead them to the lower divisions of the astral plane.

There are two kinds of people in this category: those living a pure and generous life, and those living a selfish life full of anger and self-satisfaction. Those of the first category remain forgetfully and peacefully asleep until, one fine day, they are awakened by some good soul and led upward. Those of the second category remain fully alert in this dark and dense subdivision and become a source of trouble. For the satisfaction of their unsatisfied animal desires, they enter the body of another angry, merciless person, or a person who is ready to do anything for the satisfaction of their low physical desires. They fuel that person's sentiments and encourage him or her to do the worst possible. They assume a ghastly form. They may lure people with negative thoughts to do harmful things. However, they cannot affect people of good moral character. Only when someone is driven toward a lowly act can they prove harmful. Such spirits can be seen clairvoyantly around areas of prostitution, butcher shops, and bars.

Researcher and author A. P. Senate observed that those who commit suicide—particularly those who have planned it for some time and have the scheme well set in their minds—may then repeat this act in several years. The spirit of a girl who committed suicide by jumping into the Thames was seen repeating this tragedy for twenty years. The time and method were the same as those of the original suicide.

Suicide is one act that has been unanimously discouraged by everyone. According to Sri Herald Klemp of Eckankar, "if you commit suicide, it will haunt you in your next life. You will have more misery than ever."[9] Shri Shirdi Sai Baba said:

> You must enjoy the fruit, good or bad, of your past actions; if the enjoyment be incomplete, suicide will not help you. You have to take another birth and suffer again. So instead of killing yourself,

> why not suffer now and finish up your store of the fruit of past deeds and be (done) with it once and for all?[10]

In the words of Leadbeater:

> The position of the suicide is further complicated by the fact that his rash act has diminished the power of the ego to withdraw its lower portion into itself, and therefore has exposed him to various additional dangers; but it must be remembered that the guilt of suicide differs considerably according to its circumstances, from the morally blameless act of Seneca and Socrates through all degrees down to the heinous crime of the wretch who takes his own life in order to escape from the entanglements into which his villainy has brought him; and the position after death varies accordingly.[11]

The opinion of Martinus is:

> For the individual who commits suicide the unpleasantness is further increased by the dreadful disappointment that death is not, as he had believed, a deliverance from his difficulties but that he, on the contrary, in addition to being still fully conscious of them, has now also inflicted upon himself the suffering that he will, to a certain extent, have to endure an abnormal spiritual existence with the prospect of a repetition of these difficulties in his next physical life on earth. He thus witnesses the fact that he cannot run away from his fate. Had he put up with those difficulties until death had occurred of its own accord, his spiritual existence would at least have been more normal and strengthening for his next terrestrial life.[12]

Discouragement of suicide agrees with the teachings of almost all religions. The central advice of the saints is that one should live life to its natural end and undergo the associated sufferings in this life. One cannot set aside the suffering, which is experienced as a lesson, by committing suicide. One has to reincarnate again under similar circumstances until the lessons are learned. Therefore, less suffering is created with the decision to accept and balance negative karma now.

The permanent element, soul, incarnates on earth in a physical body to learn by experiencing the results of its negative actions and judgments. However, the temporary element, ego, which deals with the phenomenal existence of the physical body, has forgotten the soul's mission to undergo learning and rebels under the adverse circumstances by committing suicide. On returning to the higher realms, the soul realizes the mistake of the ego and plans to return to earth in another incarnation to complete the necessary learning. It is nature's design that amnesia puts the soul with its memories in the unconscious, and the individual lives a life governed by the ego. The role of metaphysical or yogic practices is to bring the memory of the soul to the conscious level. There are indications that some individuals may retain a partial memory of their mission on earth. This memory will help them cooperate with their soul's mission.

Chapter Four

THE ASTRAL PLANE

The physical plane, earth, is the densest of all the realms of the universe. The first of the higher realms is the astral plane. The astral region, the immediate neighbor of our physical plane is, according to Leadbeater, the second of these planes. Objects and inhabitants of the astral plane are real in exactly the same way as our own bodies, our furniture, our houses, or our world are real—as real as Taj Mahal. "In our solar system," he claims, "there exist perfectly definite planes, each with its matter of different degrees of density. Some of these planes can be visited and observed by persons who have qualified themselves for the work, exactly as a foreign country might be visited and observed."[1]

In his book, Leadbeater describes the life and characteristics of the astral plane. According to him, an astral plane has seven subdivisions, each with a corresponding degree of materiality or density. When we speak of a soul rising from one plane or subplane to another, we do not think of it as moving in space, but rather as consciousness transferring from one level to another. One world with its scenery and inhabitants seems to fade slowly from view, while another of a more elevated character dawns in its stead. Yet, there is a physical dimension for each plane or a subplane.

> Matter of all sub-planes is to be found here on the surface of the earth, but the astral plane is much larger than the physical, and extends some thousands of miles above its surface. The law of

> gravitation operates on astral matter, and if it were possible for it to be left entirely undisturbed it would probably settle into concentric shells.[2]

At the time of the separation of the astral body, the person normally falls asleep. This sleep may extend from a few days to a few months, depending on the physical condition of the person before death. One who has been sick may sleep longer. The souls of dead friends and relatives know in advance the time of death of the dying person and are normally found around the person at the time of death. This is confirmed in the instance of my father, who died in September 1992. He saw childhood friends and relatives in their astral bodies during the last few days before his death. Volunteers escort those who do not have a friend or a relative from a higher realm. There are many souls up there always ready and able to help a departing soul—or from their point of view, an arriving soul.

The gross elements of desire are precipitated at this stage and the person automatically moves to one of the seven divisions of the astral plane to which they belong according to their attachments or evolution. Just as there are seven divisions of the astral plane (*bhuvarlok*), from gross to subtle, so the judgments and desires of the person are separated from the most gross (outside) to the subtlest (inside). Artificial control of beliefs during life is broken now and individuals appear in their real form. When sleep is broken, they find themselves on a division of the astral plane vibrating with the same frequency as their precipitated emotions and desires. Selfishness and narrow-mindedness are grosser than the subtle sentiments of helping others. Thus social workers or politicians, who outwardly served others but were inwardly living a narrow-minded selfish life, would find themselves on the second plane. One stays there until finding freedom from selfish and narrow views, then moving automatically to the third or fourth subplane. In physical life, people may be living in a big comfortable house, but their narrow views bring them to the lower plane of narrowness. Comparatively, people who lived in an ordinary house in the physical world but unselfishly served humanity will find themselves directly on the third subdivision. This is not to say that wealth, in and of itself, shows selfishness or narrowness of values. Philanthropy has helped and harmed the world, depending on the beliefs and intentions generating the action.

The lowest, or first, subdivision may correspond to the most selfish and brutal people who have committed heinous crimes. Since like attracts like, this is the plane for such people who live in their narrow and selfish mentality. So a morose atmosphere prevails and it may be an approximation of hell. Hell, pictured in various religions as a place where people are tortured in many ways, is a fiction created by the leaders of those religions. Perhaps the early teachers wanted to give a physical shape to the lowest subdivision for the understanding of people without abstract imaginations.

Initially, people on the astral plane may not understand they are dead. Or they may wish to visit their friends and relatives on earth, due to their attachment to them. For either reason, they may come to earth as astral bodies and try to assume physical form to talk to their loved ones. They call the name of the person, but there is no response. Sometimes you may have a faint feeling of someone calling you, although you do not see the person. After repeated failures in getting a response from the living person, the astral being may understand that he or she is dead and return to the astral plane. Normally a guide accompanies them to the astral plane. Martin and Romanowski have described a large number of cases of this kind in detail in their book, *We Are Not Forgotten* (1991).

The astral plane may have the appearance of heaven, since everything appears attainable. Yet, there is no single or absolute heaven as described by some religions. The heaven of the scriptures is, again, a fantasy of religious teachers. However, you still have the constraints of the astral body that suffers from the effects of its desires. It is only on the next plane above the astral plane that you cease to have an astral body and, thus, no suffering. This happens after the second death, which we are going to discuss a little later. A person with an awakened kundalini and living in the earthly world has regular visits to various subdivisions of the astral plane. Aspirants receive foreknowledge of the higher realms as part of their learning of the nature of God-consciousness.[3]

A good example of the powers of the astral plane being expressed on the physical plane is the creation of thoughtforms. Alexandra David-Neel lived in India and Tibet for twenty years and participated fully in tantric rituals along with a regular practice of yoga and meditation.[4] Through the power of thought, she created a monkey (*tulpa*) who could be her companion. For some years, it provided her with help and companionship. However, after some time, it developed its own individuality and refused to obey her fully. He became a nuisance and, with great difficulty, she was able to remove him. This is reminiscent of the creation of the goddess Durga by the other gods. Through their collective power of thought, they brought her into being so she could fight the demons and save the gods. The psychic being of Sri Aurobindo or the Higher Self of Carl Jung, created by the soul over a series of earthly incarnations, can now be understood. This psychic being has an individuality of its own and is the benevolent factor bridging the gap between the soul and God.

In old age, the organs of a person become weak, youthful physical form is lost, and the senses are unclear. However, on arrival on the astral plane all these defects are healed. The person lives in a youthful body and never feels tired, hungry, or thirsty. Sometimes a defective part in the body lingers on in the memory. These souls are placed in a mansion, which may be called a hospital, somewhere on the fifth division of the astral plane, where they are given rest and the defective part is gradually cured. It is a purgatory, a station on the way. A person's way of thinking, emotions, and knowledge attained in the physical world may remain exactly the same.

Power, position, and money all come to an end on the astral plane. Only purity of heart, love, and goodwill matter and, on the basis of these things alone, one is respected. Simple and neglected people on earth, who were in fact pure and spiritual, rise to higher subdivisions on the astral plane and are highly respected. The soul body (causal body) of a person who leads a life of purity and spirituality is very beautiful and lustrous. Such a person normally goes to the third subdivision, often called the "Summerland," after death. This realm is studded with mountains, beautiful gardens, rivers, and lakes. Houses are surrounded with beautiful, eternally blooming flowers of unearthly colors. No rain, thunderstorms, or things of that nature disturb the atmosphere. Some call it a paradise earth without fear, hatred, jealousy, competition, or selfishness. According to Ivor James, it cannot be the replica of earth, which is degenerate. Poets and writers have seen glimpses of such places in their trances when they write. Who says we are dead? Worldly people are in fact dead (or asleep) because they live in a state of confusion, very far from reality. A person, who has no desire on the astral plane, receives everything over there. That is the paradox.

Contact with saints or higher souls furthers the evolution of inhabitants of Summerland. Having spiritual feelings, these souls are ready to enter new experiences. After going through a condition of temporary coma, they awaken in the fourth or fifth subdivision or a still-higher one. Nature is more and more beautiful in these higher divisions, as the vibrations become more refined and subtle.

New feelings and experiences develop on the astral plane, according to the virtues of the person. Feelings of the heart are no longer hidden from others, because they immediately convert into colors around the astral body. Thus, one naturally lives a pure life; all relationships are open, unlike those on the earth. Those who think only about themselves (as on the earth plane) would not be happy here on the astral plane. On the lower subdivisions, people continue with worldly habits, such as eating and drinking, until they understand these are no longer needed to survive. On higher subdivisions, people are free from such needs and live a productive life leading toward spiritual perfection.

The astral plane has vast libraries containing innumerable books on all possible subjects, and extraordinary research facilities. Researchers can continue their work either on earthly or astral matters with great satisfaction. In the absence of our usual concept of time, time here is measured in the form of experience. The period one spends on the astral plane may vary from five years to five hundred years to five thousand years, depending on the experiences of the person that are necessary, either for the next worldly incarnation, or for moving upward to the mental plane. There are no limitations.

A word about the "gray world," a state suspended between the physical and astral planes. Life here can be very troublesome and uncertain, since the person belongs nowhere. A tense and saddened atmosphere, together with innumerable people of the same kind, surrounds people who have a narrow view or have lived a selfish and dry life that has been full of criminal and heinous acts on earth. At this stage, if they do not repent their low deeds, they slip into this gray world. The gray world is a state suspended between the physical and astral planes, an abode of criminals and doers of heinous acts who are not ready to repent their activities. The atmosphere here is dim and dark. However, one is not condemned to stay here forever. As soon as awakening strikes, there is always an evolved soul to help and the person is lifted to a higher subdivision. No call for help is unheard.

The first, or lowest, subplane is dark, dense, and difficult, comparable to the condition of a person required to live in the center of a mountain. It is an abode of hardened criminals and dreadful creatures. These are conditions described by all religions as orthodox hell (with the difference that they are created by the person's own beliefs). This is the *pret-lok* of Hinduism, where the bad souls seek to enter the bodies of others for the satisfaction of base desires. Here one finds thoughtforms of hundreds of millions of people charged with *prana* (life energy), created by subhuman minds due to anger and hatred. These affect people with similar thinking on earth by providing stimulation to them.

The second subplane is less dark, less dense, and more refined than the first. It is the abode of highly materialistic people. Souls who awaken here after sudden death do not realize they are dead. Souls caught here are in in-between states. An example would be soldiers of World War I still looking for someone to kill. Here, great waves of loving souls come to help confused souls come out of their psychic shock. They are taken to "nursing homes" situated on the fifth subplane of the second plane.

One should remember that each plane has a further seven subdivisions, or perhaps even more than that. Each of the first and second subplanes may have innumerable souls on different subdivisions, according to their states of consciousness and variations. Accordingly, the highest subdivision of the second subplane may have souls who are more refined and ready to move to the next subplane.

The third subplane is the first "lighted area" of the astral plane, called the Summerland by many writers. Those who have lived a harmless life, not necessarily spiritual but benevolent beings, may awaken here and think they have come to heaven. It may appear to be a copy of earth without its negative attributes. There are mountains, rivers, lakes, houses, streets, and gardens similar to earth. Some say the flowers also assume a human form. People live in an atmosphere similar to that on earth and retain the same habits of eating, drinking, dressing, traveling, and meeting friends and relatives. Everything materializes through the power of thought. As the soul grows and interacts with high souls and saints, it passes through a coma, before finding itself awake in the fourth or the fifth subplane, or even a higher one, according to one's consciousness.

The fourth subplane is a fully lighted area with finer vibrations than the third plane, grander physical surroundings, and more celestial beauty. This division has a special place for children. The fifth is brighter yet, with higher vibrations. This is perhaps the most important division from an activities point of view. Far more beautiful and luminous than all the heavens created by the minds of religion, this could be the happy hunting ground of native peoples. Religious bodies congregate here, believing themselves to be the only ones saved, happy, and rewarded. Many spiritual guides of people on earth have their homes here. However, the teachers are not really great and there is a language barrier—communication occurs through mediums. People appear to be in the prime of life here; bodies become younger and perfect. There are books, libraries, and centers of research. Thousands of souls engage in research on either astral or earthly subjects. For any particular study, the facilities available are fantastic. People are unaware of time passing. They think there is nothing better than what they have here; it is the end of everything. Learned people, poets, artists, scientists, great persons, and saints all belong to this region. Hospitals for reviving souls and providing them with new bodies are found here.

However, the ideal of even higher conditions still appeals to the intellectuals and they realize this is only a way station. From the realm of spiritual mind, they receive ideas and, after a temporary coma, they may move to the sixth or seventh division. The sixth is very well lighted, similar to the fifth plane, but with still higher vibrations. It is much more refined, more advanced, and highly developed artistically or philosophically. It has fantastic landscapes. The seventh is the heavenly world, yet still astral, since the real heaven lies on the next plane—the mental plane, called *devachan* in Sanskrit.

Table 1. Layout of the Subdivisions of the Astral Plane

SUBPLANE	SALIENT FEATURES
Physical	Living with senses, creation and dissolution of karma, real opportunity for evolution
Gray world	State suspended between astral and physical planes, unrepentant hardened criminals
First	Dark, dense, and difficult for living, bad souls looking for satisfaction through others
Second	Less dark, less dense, highly materialistic people, not believing being dead
Third	First lighted area, Summerland, benevolent people, and good living conditions
Fourth	Fully lighted area, grander physical surrounding, celestial beauty, nice for children
Fifth	Brighter, healing and spiritual development, churches, schools, and libraries
Sixth	More refined/advanced, fantastic landscapes, artistically/philosophically developed
Seventh	Heavenly worlds, yet only astral, much balanced karma, real heaven on next plane

Although an absolute layout of the subdivisions of the astral plane can never be made, Table 1 gives an approximation. One may live for thousands of years on the higher subdivisions, since the conditions are perfect and there is no passage of time. Astral worlds do not have physical dimensions and do not revolve around a physical sun as the earth does. Hence, one has to learn through spiritual evolution that this is not the real or final heaven. The "second death" takes place and the astral body dies. One awakens on the lower mental plane, called heaven, or *swarglok*.

Chapter Five

THE MENTAL AND HIGHER PLANES

For the inhabitants of the astral plane, there comes a time when the spiritual mind is restless to enter into new experiences. The astral body begins to die and the soul awakens in a spiritual body in a spiritual world, called *devachan* in Sanskrit. This is the soul's "second death," the transition from the astral to the mental plane. While on earth, the soul lives in a physical body made of physical elements (earth, water, fire, air, and ether). On the astral plane, it lives in an astral body made of astral atoms with finer vibrations. On the mental plane, it has a mental body made of atoms with still finer vibrations.

The Mental Plane

The mental plane has two divisions: the lower division is heaven (*swarglok*), the upper is the causal plane (*maharlok*). It is the astral body that responds to desires (karma), resulting in attachment or detachment, or good and bad. When this body has been shed, one is out of all duality and the soul experiences complete happiness and bliss. No words can describe the feelings there. On the lower division, or heaven, the soul has a mental body; on the upper division, it has a causal body. The causal body is the first manifested form around the soul—that is, the beginning of a body with form for all time to come, for as long as the soul lives in the lower worlds below the causal plane. Above the causal plane, the soul journeys by itself, without any form or body around it.

Sometime after his physical death, using his yogic powers, Sri Yukteshwar said the following through his materialized temporary body:

> I live in that part of the astral plane which is known as Hiranyalok. I help many developed Souls coming from earth, in getting freedom. People here are free from the problems of eating, drinking etc. One can meet here with one's mother, father, son, daughter, wife or husband etc., not only from the previous life, but also from several lives before the previous one. One is free from untimely death, decease and old age. It is only intuition, which works out every thing here. One only needs the will here to accomplish anything or everything.[1]

The *hiranyalok* talked about by Sri Yukteshwar is perhaps *swarglok* (heaven), since he talked about moving to the causal plane from there. He also spoke about staying in the hiranyalok for a long time, which is only possible in swarglok. According to many others, one can meet with relatives of the previous life on the astral plane, but relatives from their other lives can be met with only in swarglok.

I had a chance to talk to Guru Kirpal through a medium in North Carolina. He told me he is living on the mental plane and that there are many saints and highly evolved souls there as well. Sri Yukteshwar Giri also lives on the mental plane. This suggests that most Self-realized souls live on the mental plane and help people on the lower planes in their process of evolution. These high souls can talk to other souls and travel to lower planes for interaction.

To understand the interpenetration of the various planes, let us look at an example. Take a bottle and fill it with water, sand, ash, and some pieces of stone. Shake it and then put it on the table. After a while, you see that the heaviest pieces of stone have settled near the bottom and the lighter ones are on top of them. Above the stones, you see the particles of sand and then the ash. Surrounding everything, you find water. Water being the least dense of all, it is at the highest region where no other matter can remain. At the same time, water is found in every division of the bottle. Similarly, ash is the next element and, in that region, sand and stones are not found; but at the same time ash is also seen in every lower division of the bottle. So the second division has two elements—water and ash. Next, in the third division, you find sand, ash, and water, but no stones. And in the fourth division, you see all the four elements—water, ash, sand, and stones. Even so, the highest and first, or "divine," plane has only divine elements in it. The second, or "monadic," plane has divine and monadic elements in it. The third, or "atmic," plane has divine, monadic, and atmic elements in it. The fourth, or "intuitional," plane has divine, monadic, atmic, and intuitional elements in it. The fifth, or "mental," plane has divine, monadic, atmic, intuitional, and mental elements in it. The sixth, or "astral," plane has divine, monadic, atmic, intuitional, mental, and astral elements in it. And the seventh and last, or "physical," plane has all seven elements in it—divine, monadic, atmic, intuitional, mental, astral, and physical.

As a person evolves from the physical to the astral plane, they leave the physical elements behind and become composed of the upper six elements only. When they further evolve from the astral to the mental plane, astral elements are also given up forever, and the person possesses only mental, intuitional, atmic, monadic, and divine elements. On further evolution, they say good-bye to the mental elements, and are now made up of intuitional, atmic, monadic, and divine elements only. On reaching the atmic plane, they are made of atmic, monadic, and divine elements only. On the monadic plane, they possess only the monadic and divine elements. And finally, when the highest-order soul merges into the divine and becomes one with it, one does not have even the monadic elements and is made purely of the divine element, truly in the image of God himself. Monad being the first manifestation from the divine source, its extinction means the unmanifested self in the divine realm of God. However, just as water has contact with all the lower divisions in the bottle, so a divine person has contact with all the lower planes. One can visualize all the seven planes in a circular form around the physical plane, just like the skins of an onion in circular layers, one above the other. There are elements of each plane penetrating all the lower planes.

Seven planes divided into 7 subdivisions make for 49 subdivisions. Out of these 49, the last two (solid and liquid) constitute the visible world, which can be seen through the physical eyes. The rest of the 47 elements constitute the invisible world, which can be seen through clairvoyant eyes only. The last plane has all the 49 elements in it, from solid to divine. The 48th plane does not have the solid element, but it has all the other 48 elements, from liquid to divine. The 47th plane does not have the last two elements, solid and liquid, but it has all the remaining 47 elements, from air to the divine.

Spirit individualized becomes a soul. Its beginning is the original and biggest secret of all time. Thus, the soul, or Atman, is an element of God and this element, in its original form, remains established and present on the monadic plane. In its original form, it is pure and uninvolved. When the ray of this element descends into the lower plane, the attributes of that plane gather around it. When it descends to the next lower plane, attributes of the second lower plane make the second cover (of its attributes) around the soul. Descending onto the third plane, the third cover of attributes envelops the soul. Proceeding in this manner, when the soul reaches the lowest, or seventh, physical plane, it has in it the attributes of all seven planes as various layers or covers around itself. On the journey back home, these layers or covers are removed one by one and the soul shines again in its original form.

The personality of an individual is a grouping of four lower bodies—mental, astral, etheric, and physical. This group is a perishable one, and is formed around the basic body, called the causal body, which is created from the elements of the upper division of the mental plane, called the causal plane, or *maharlok*. The causal body is the personal carrier of the soul and it is imperishable. It is the center of creation and storehouse of unmanifested and abstract thoughts. Experiences of the individual from previous lifetimes remain stored in the causal body in seed form. Each time the soul reincarnates, these seeds flower into new experiences. Since the causal body is made of pure Atmic elements, it stores only the virtues collected so far, such as tolerance, forgiveness, compassion, humility, devotion, courage, capacity for and competence in work, wisdom, and intuitive knowledge. In each successive incarnation, these virtues are added and, in a particular incarnation, they appear as an integral part of the nature of the person. Negative attributes, such as weakness, vice, corruption, selfishness, exploitation, covetousness, and self-gratification, do not find a place in the causal body because of the purity of its elements. However, the personality, which is made of mental, astral, etheric, and physical bodies, stores the weaknesses and shortcomings of the soul, which do manifest in successive incarnations. For example, a person who may have broken a leg in a previous life finds insufficient strength in that leg in the present incarnation. The astral body, which is a product of the *kama-lok* (plane of desires) stores in itself the weaknesses of the person that are added to the causal body. But they fade away with the death of the personality and the causal body, and only virtues remain in the end.

There are two kinds of thought: thought manifested in form and abstract thought. An average person can contemplate thoughts with form only; abstract thinking is not easy. This means that an average person does not contemplate thoughts of tolerance, forgiveness, compassion, humility, and devotion. Accordingly, an average person can reach only to the lower division of the mental plane, or swarglok, the arena of manifested form.

Most people's ultimate ambition is to reach and enjoy the good life of heaven. Religion tells them they will be with God. This is the climax of thought in the manifested form. There is nothing beyond it, they believe, and they stop there.

The second category, abstract thinkers, includes only a very small part of humanity—artists, psychologists, doctors, professors, and researchers in various fields of study. Such people may have an experience of the causal plane, or maharlok. They may reach into this world of abstract thought.

Like all other planes, the mental plane is also divided into seven subdivisions. The upper division, called the causal plane, is divided into three parts, while the lower division, called heaven, is subdivided into four. Heaven is the plane of unconditional happiness, since the astral body, which is the cause of desires, has been dropped at the time of entry into the mental plane, after the second death. Life in heaven is contented, since you do not need anything outside yourself.

Beyond the Mental Plane

Beyond the mental plane is the realm of those who contemplate God without attributes, the *Nirguna Brahman*, or those who are abstract thinkers on a level that involves intuitive wisdom from beyond. They belong to the intuitional, or "buddhic," plane. And above the intuitional plane is the realm of those who have either contemplated Atman or soul, or who, through their regular metaphysical or yogic meditational practices, have realized the high self of Jung, the Atman of the Hindus, the *Ruha* of Sufism, the Light of the Void of Buddha, or the Father of Lord Jesus Christ. They belong to the Atmic plane, the plane of Nirvana or liberation, which provides freedom from the false and breaks the bond of reincarnation or the cycle of death and rebirth once and for all. Thoughtful people from all beliefs and walks of life have reached this stage. This region is composed of exceptionally beautiful mountains, rivers, trees, fruits, and flowers and is illuminated without an obvious source. You see yourself as a dimensionless point of awareness, moving freely with the speed of thought, having no hunger, thirst, or desires, in a state of perpetual bliss incomparable to any pleasure on earth. You have the ability to see in all directions and have an intuitive knowledge that you do not need to know anything at all. You have an intuitive belief that you have always existed and always will. This is the state of *Sat-Chit-Ananda* (Existence-Knowledge-Bliss)—the attributes of Brahman or God. Since the soul (Atman) is akin to God (*Paramatma*), you receive an intuitive understanding of God. Thus Self-realization leads to God-realization intuitively. Such a person does not have any requirement on earth; they are not interested in the past, or in speculating about the future. They are naturally unconcerned about the present. They move around the globe as self-contented and liberated persons, happy and free.

Experiencing a higher plane while sitting on a lower plane does not mean that you travel bodily to that plane. In fact, the higher plane is experienced right where you are sitting. The consciousness moves from lower planes to higher ones. Consider the experiment with the bottle containing water, ash, sand, and stones. Sitting at the bottom of the bottle, you see only the stone and sand if your consciousness is vibrating with thoughts of a solid. You see only water if your consciousness is vibrating with thoughts of a liquid, although both stone and water are present at the same place. Similarly, the physical plane has elements from all the planes, but you will live the reality of only the plane corresponding to the level at which your consciousness is vibrating. Clairvoyants live in the reality of the astral plane, although they sit on the physical plane. Saints live the reality of the mental, or Atmic, plane, according to the development of their consciousness, although they sit on the physical plane. One finds a new abode on that plane after death, for which one has qualified oneself by raising one's consciousness. After all, the vast universe has different layers or dimensions with varying densities, represented by various planes.

The Seven Divisions of the Universe

The universe appears to be divided into seven realms. This observation has been made in corroboration with the experiences of evolved individuals around the globe, scientific investigations, scriptures from various faiths and traditions, and from my own experiences. There are many yogis who awakened their kundalini and then wrote accounts of the higher realms based on their personal experiences. The books by Swami Yogananda Paramahansa, Swami Muktananda, Swami Satyananda Saraswati, Dr. Ramesh Paramahansa, Gopi Krishna, Dr. B.S. Goel, Swami Sivananda, Nisargadatta Maharaj and Swami Vishnu Tirtha are examples. I trust that knowledge of the dying process and of the higher realms or heavens will prompt individuals to find a means of awakening their own dormant kundalini.

The timeless scriptures of Hindu philosophy, the Vedas and Upanishads, are well supported, verified, and confirmed by modern research in the West. Western research is based mainly on cases of automatic writing, mediums, near-death experiences, past-life regression, and out-of-body experiences. Volumes have been written on these subjects in the past two centuries.[2] Many of these books have been produced through automatic writing, in which a physical being holds the pen while the writing is directed by a nonphysical being. Leadbeater divided the universe into seven planes:

> The names usually given to these planes, taking them in order of materiality, rising from the denser to the finer, are the physical, the astral, the mental, the buddhic, and the nirvanic. Higher than this are two others, but they are so far above our power of absorption that for the moment they may be left out of consideration.[3]

According to Hindu philosophy, summarized by Mehta and Vaze[4] and the knowledge gathered through the study of the *Egyptian Book of the Dead,* the *Tibetan Book of the Dead,* the Theosophical Society, Eckankar, hundreds of research projects carried out in the West over a period of 150 years, case studies of renowned mediums such as Edgar Cayce, Stephen O'Brien, and Michael Newton, the experiences of the saints and prophets available from time to time, and a variety of near-death experiences and cases of contacting the spirit of a dead friend or relative collected by J. D. Goyal,[5] the universe appears to be divided into seven grand divisions as shown in Table 2 on page 46. Each of the seven planes is further divided into seven subplanes.There are, therefore, 49 subplanes altogether in the universe. Table 3 on page 47 gives the distribution according to Hindu philosophy.

A natural question to ask at this juncture would be, how long does a person stay on the astral plane? It is a difficult question to answer, nevertheless, there is some information available that is based on research. The length of stay on a plane depends on the stage of evolution and state of mind one has reached. Artists, scientists, philosophers, poets, writers, and followers of a spiritual path spend the least time on the astral plane (less than 10 years) and the maximum time in heaven (several hundred years). Honest seekers, those who contemplate ideal justice, mental health workers, social reformers, humanitarians, and philanthropic and spiritual people may spend hundreds of years on the astral plane and 500 years on the lower mental plane. Those who do not think badly of others, average citizens and believers in religion, may stay for 50 to 60 years on the astral plane and 200 to 300 years in swarglok. Narrow-minded and selfish people may live for less than 100 years on the astral and up to 200 years on the

Table 2. Seven Divisions of the Universe and Their Properties

S. NO.	THE PLANE	VEDIC PLANE	ATTRIBUTES	PROPERTIES
1	Divine	Adi	Basic Nature	Unmanifested
2	Monadic	Anupama	Basic Nature	Manifested
3	Atmic	Nirvanic	Sankalpa (Will)	Spiritual
4	Intuitional	Buddhic	Love (Pure)	Inner Knowledge
5	Mental (Mahar lok) (Swarg lok or Heaven)	Causal-Karana (Upper division) Mental-Manasa (Lower division)	Thought	Analytical Intellect
5	Astral (Bhuvar lok)	Kama-Desire	Sentiments	Attachment/ Detachment
7	Physical (Bhu lok)	Sthool	Karma	Sensual Knowledge

Table 3. Seven Divisions of the Universe According to Hindu Philosophy

S. NO.	HINDU PLANE (LOK)	BRAHMAN PLANE (LOK)	ATTRIBUTES OF THE PLANE	BODY ACCORDING TO THE PLANE
1	Go lok	Adi lok	Attributeless God—Nirguna Brahman (Unmanifested)	Monad (Spark of God)
2	Vaikunth lok	Monadic lok	Basic nature—Saguna Brahman (Manifested)	Atman
3	Satya lok (Plane of truth)	Atmic lok	Atmic element	Anandamaya kosh (Intuition and bliss)
4	Tap lok (Plane of austerities) Jnana lok (Plane of wisdom)	Buddhic lok	Para/Inner Wisdom	Vigyanamaya kosh (Will, action, intellect)
5	Mahar lok (Causal plane) Swarg lok (Heaven)	Manasik lok	Abstract thoughts Thoughts with forms	Manomaya kosh—Manasik sharira (Mental body)
6	Bhuvar lok (Astral plane)	Sukshma lok	Artistic, compassionate, benevolent; properties of purity (satogun), activity (rajogun), and rigidity (tamogun)	Pranamaya kosh (Astral body, etheric double)
7	Bhoo lok (Physical plane)	Sthool lok	Memory, light, life, activity; gaseous, liquid, solid	Annamaya kosh (Physical body)

lower mental plane. Superstitious minds may spend 100 years on the astral plane and they may visit the mental plane for short periods. Barbarians are normally expected to spend 100 years on the astral plane and they reincarnate on the physical plane without getting a sense of the mental plane. Low, mean, and immoral persons—those living in pride, covetousness, lust, anger, gluttony, envy, and sloth—are expected to live for more than 100 years on the astral plane and they immediately reincarnate on earth without receiving a glimpse of heaven. These are rough estimates. There may be people who spend thousands of years on a subdivision of the astral plane before either reincarnating or proceeding to a higher plane. Similarly, there may be people who spend thousands of years in heaven before either reincarnating or proceeding to the causal plane. There may be higher souls who proceed directly to the mental, intuitional, or even the Atmic plane without spending a moment on the lower planes. People of the most heinous nature may live on the first subdivision of the astral plane for several thousand years before anything better or worse can happen for them.

Chapter Six

KUNDALINI AND THE GATES OF HEAVEN

We now know the universe is divided into seven realms of varying frequencies. We belong to the most gross and solid physical plane. Its neighbor is the astral plane, and next to that lies the mental plane, subtler yet. The subtlest realm is the plane of divine existence. Most commonly, you travel to the astral plane in your astral body in your dreams. It also happens in special circumstances—during sickness, anesthesia, or trance. You can also travel to the astral realm under hypnosis with the direction of a regressionist, but then you have to find one you trust and you may not remember your journey afterward. During near-death experiences, travelers into the subtle realms get a taste of their afterlife. But these experiences are not under your control and may only happen once. We came from our true home in the heavenly realm and that memory haunts us subconsciously. In a particular lifetime, when the meaninglessness of possessions and emotional attachments creeps into our minds and hearts, we begin the journey back to that true home.

The most authentic and permanent way of opening the gates of heaven is through the awakening of kundalini. It is the time-tested and classical method developed by the yogis over several millennia and written about in ancient scriptures such as the Vedas and Upanishads. In all faiths and traditions, the process is similar, but the technical details and names differ.

Kundalini is the spiritual energy lying dormant at the base of the spinal column. When it awakens, it passes through seven chakras, or energy centers, along the spinal column. These seven chakras are related to the seven universal divisions of the universe and, through them, you receive natural and permanent access to the heavens. Once kundalini awakens and crosses the third chakra, it never completely returns to the base. This phenomenon is irreversible and it places you irrevocably on your way to your true home. There is a feeling of happiness and peace in your heart. Your questions are replaced with knowing and you begin living a more contented life.

The passage of kundalini is calibrated and you meet with definite signs at each chakra in the form of colors and sounds. The colors are the colors of the rainbow. In descending order, they are violet, indigo, blue, green, yellow, orange, and red (VIBGYOR). Thus, when your first chakra, below the base of the spine, opens, you see the color red; when the second chakra opens, you see the color orange, and so on. Yogis at a high stage of evolution see the color violet. Similarly, you hear the sound of thunder when your first chakra opens up, the sound of the sea roaring or a lion when your second chakra opens, and so on. The names and locations of the chakras, together with the corresponding colors and sounds, are shown in Table 4.

A transformation of the personality takes place with the opening of each chakra as the kundalini passes through it. When the root chakra opens, one transcends the eternal enemies greed, lust, anger, attachment, and ego. When the sacral center opens, one transcends sex. With the opening of the navel center, one crosses the boundary between the lower and higher worlds, and the practitioner begins to visit heavenly worlds in dreams, visions, and trances. One begins to have some control over life's events. When the heart center opens, one's heart is filled with divine love and the practitioner begins to show unconditional love for everyone. This is when you love your neighbor unconditionally, as the Old Testament requires. With the opening of the throat center, one achieves freedom from falsehood and the power of speech and self-expression. The opening of the throat center activates a point in the skull called the *bindu*, from which nectar flows into the body allowing the practitioner to achieve rejuvenation and freedom from disease. Those who achieve this look younger and have an added charm to their personality. The road to the kingdom of heaven is open for them now. With the opening of the sixth center, between the eyebrows, one's ego is fragmented into a thousand pieces and one witnesses the death of ego in some definite form. In my case, it was personified as my dead body being carried by people on their shoulders in accordance with the Indian custom. I could hear people saying, "Ravindra

Table 4. The Chakras and Their Properties

S. NO.	CHAKRA	LOCATION	COLOR	SOUND
1	Root Center	Midpoint between anus and genitals	Red	Thunder
2	Sacral Center	End of the tailbone	Orange	Roaring of sea or lion
3	Navel Center	Solar plexus	Yellow	Tinkling bells or running water
4	Heart Center	Center of chest	Green	Buzzing of bees
5	Throat Center	Level of throat pit	Blue	Single note of a flute
6	Eyebrow Center	Midpoint between the eyebrows	Indigo	Humming sound or thousand violins
7	Crown Center	Top-center of head	Violet	Music of woodwinds

Kumar is dead." Dr. Elizabeth Kubler-Ross experienced the "terrific pain, which her patients were undergoing at the moment." She asked for help from God, which was not given to her in a way she understood. After the experience of death comes the experience of resurrection, accompanied by unprecedented joy and bliss. At this point, one may see a cherished and adored form of God and experience his kingdom

The opening of the crown center takes place in flashes. It is a time when one's body opens for the soul to merge with the absolute. Most practitioners decide to continue to live until their allotted time on earth is finished. They want to impart the knowledge they have gained to others. This could be for two reasons: either they love everyone unconditionally and want to help them achieve liberation, or they do not want to leave any reason for returning to earth in further incarnations. Generally, yogis at this stage keep some worldly interest alive so ties are not completely cut. As an example, Ramakrishna Paramahansa used to eat delicious food every day. When someone asked the reason for it, he said, "You asked this question too early. I wanted to remain with you people a little longer." It is said that, three or four days later, he transferred to his heavenly abode. Yogis continue to live the same kind of life, with similar interests to other people, but they are completely changed from the inside, which others may not see. Sometimes, people judge yogis from their external lifestyle and misunderstand them, since they cannot see the transformation inside. Lord Jesus constantly said, "I and my Father are one," but no one understood him.

The great sage Shankaracharya observed two important signs of a liberated person:

> He who is liberated from the body and is himself perfect, abides in enjoyment like a worldly man full of desires created by past karma [does]. But he lives quietly as a spectator, free from desires and changes, like the center of a wheel.
>
> Want of enquiry into the past, absence of speculation about the future, and indifference [as to the present], are the characteristics of a jivanmukta [liberated person].[1]

A liberated person continues to live the same style of life as before realization, but is no longer bound by karma. This can be understood with the example of cycling. To keep the bicycle rolling, one has to peddle constantly. But when the peddling is stopped, the bicycle does not stop. It keeps moving as if still being peddled. Desire in a yogi ceases to exist at the point of liberation, yet his or her appearance of living a normal life remains the same and continues. The difference is that one does not endeavor for material satisfaction any longer, and experiences life with nonattachment—as a witness, not as a participant. Others may criticize yogis for this, but the fact is that they are internally transformed, and whether or not a particular experience occurs is not important. They may be eating, drinking, making love, and playing games as before, but there is no yearning after things. Rather there is peace, tranquillity, and contentment under all circumstances. Just as the bicycle slowly comes to rest after the peddling is stopped, worldly activities gradually come to a halt in the life of yogis. Nevertheless, yogis may be keeping some interest alive to keep their physical bodies from annihilation. The state of permanent happiness or bliss is so rooted in them that they do not need to know about the past and future, or remain attached to the present.

Kundalini

The importance of kundalini was known in most ancient cultures. Elizabeth Claire Prophet has repeatedly mentioned in her writings that the high adepts of the lost Atlantean civilization had mastered kundalini and imparted knowledge of it and the seven chakras to aspirants. According to Jasper Swain, adepts on the astral plane have been advising earthlings to deal with kundalini very cautiously.[2] To show that this knowledge existed in other ancient faiths and traditions, it is sufficient to consult the writings of several experts in the field.

After researching kundalini for several years and authoring fifteen books on consciousness and enlightenment, John White writes:

> Although the word Kundalini comes from the yogic tradition, nearly all the world's major religions, spiritual paths and genuine occult traditions see something akin to the Kundalini experience. The word may not appear in the traditions, but the concept is there nevertheless, wearing a different name and symbol, yet recognizable as a key to attaining godlike nature. It has been described in the ancient records of Tibet, Egypt, Sumer, China, Greece and other cultures and traditions, including early Judaism and Christianity. The Pharaoh's headdress, the feathered serpent of Mexico and South America, the dragon of Oriental Mythology, the serpent in the Garden of Eden, all are indicative of Kundalini. So is the caduceus, the twin snakes coiled around a staff, symbolic of medical practitioners. The

> caduceus is said to be derived from the god Hermes, founder of the hermetic tradition of higher knowledge.[3]

Gene Kieffer, president of the Kundalini Research Foundation in Connecticut writes:

> If you awaken Kundalini fully, and if the transformative process proceeds in a healthy way to its ultimate conclusion, you will become a spiritual genius and a world teacher. You will be compelled to action.[4]

According to Robert Scheer:

> In the Inca and Maya worlds of Mexico and Guatemala, the most powerful god is Quetzalcoatl, the winged serpent. Farther south, in Peru, you can find images carved in ancient stone sanctuaries representing the puma, condor and serpent, symbols of the three realms: our earth, the world above and the world below. In the carvings are seven holes stacked one above the other—one for each of the seven chakras. According to early Quechua mythology, these seven hollow spaces were originally filled with gold, crystals or gemstones . . . the energy the Incas called Kori Machakway is the same transformative power that the Hindus refer to as Kundalini, the golden serpent energy that is situated at the base of the human spine . . . he lists many words that are common to both the Quechua and Sanskrit languages . . . power should be used in service to others, a lesson that could just as easily have come from a Hindu guru as from a descendant of the ancient Incas.[5]

People temporarily experience the reality of the heavens or of the realms of the universe through various types of out-of-body experiences described in this chapter. However, it becomes a permanent reality on the awakening of kundalini. Additionally, a person with awakened kundalini becomes a spiritual genius and a world teacher. Knowledge of higher realms or heavens in advance helps in triggering the awakening of kundalini when proper methods are adopted. Kundalini is a universal phenomenon known in various parts of the world under different names. The awakening of kundalini is further associated with the witnessing of the soul and the transformation of consciousness discussed in the chapters to come.

PART TWO

The Soul as Traveler

Chapter Seven

THEORY OF THE UNIVERSE AND THE SOUL

Seekers from cultures all over the world have been searching for the soul and its properties since time immemorial. Soul knowledge dawns in a person when he or she finds success in contemplative practices, in one form or another. One sure way of attaining this knowledge is through the awakening of kundalini. In this chapter, I endeavor to present further knowledge of the soul and its properties as collected by seekers up to the present time. These findings can help the practitioner in two ways: contemplation on the soul can trigger the awakening of kundalini, and confusion caused by the sudden awakening of the dormant energy can be lessened, smoothing the journey.

The sixth century B.C. is unforgettable as the birth-time of spiritual giants around the world: Buddha and Mahavira in India, Pythagoras in Greece, Confucius in China, Zoroaster in Persia, and the Druids in Europe. These figures all made history on the path of Self-realization. These were no ordinary events; either a super-human mind beyond earth initiated them or, more rationally, human evolution had reached the stage of spiritual quest. And after this blooming of awareness, a series of individuals continued to emerge on the spiritual path in all parts of the world. In the same way, the nineteenth century should be remembered for the birth of four geniuses who emphasized the existence of the soul or Atman: Madame H. P. Blavatsky (1831–1891) of Russia, Sri Aurobindo Ghosh (1872–1950) of India, Carl Gustav Jung (1875–1961) of Switzerland, and Martinus (1890–1981) of Denmark, who, on gaining independent realization, presented his own theory of soul and God.[1] At about the same time, the world saw the birth of quantum physics, which provides scientific proof of the existence of the soul or Atman and confirms the timeless perennial philosophy of religion. Quantum physics found that the attributes of the soul are similar to the properties of the electron. Hence, the soul can be known and understood through the electron. It can be inferred that the soul is the nonlocal aspect of human beings.

Given two entities, if they can know about each other or transfer information from one to the other, even if they are separated by a distance that is more than light can travel in a second, then the two entities are said to possess the nonlocal property. We know that light travels at a speed faster than that of any other entity in the universe. Since we know that electrons and souls can "know" about each other, there must be some agency that travels faster than the speed of light. This is called the nonlocal property, which is possessed by both electrons and souls. This nonlocal agency is said to be divine. Through it, all souls can be in contact with each other. Moreover, through it, the absolute consciousness can be in contact with each and every soul.

Scientist and astronomer Sir Fred Hoyle questioned the basic propositions of scientific theory and subsequently established a reputation for brilliant and radical thought.[2] He is associated with the Steady State theory of the universe and has been developing the meaning of existence in the finest scientific tradition. He concluded that Darwin's theory is mistaken; it does not explain the crucial question of variations among species. Sir Hoyle believes that the basic information we have has come from outside the earth. He believes life did not start on earth, rather somewhere else. According to him, the Big Bang theory does not lead to a connection between the early stages of life and what we see now, and hence is incorrect. In his opinion, the religionist cannot understand the origin of humanity and so thinks that people must somehow have been created, which is mistaken. Similarly, the scientific theory that matter must have been created by the Big Bang, because science cannot yet explain where matter came from, is also erroneous. The universe, many scientists feel, must have evolved from previous conditions. The Big Bang theory tries to build a large theoretical structure on quicksand, while the Steady State theory provides a firm backdrop against which events can work out. In other words, there is a guiding intelligence laying a foundation for existence. Hoyle thinks this intelligence in the universe is trying to cope with something, but does not give perfect solutions—that we are perhaps a small reflection of the intelligence that produced us. He suggests that we are the local representatives of the larger intelligence, and this agrees, to some extent, with formal religions.

Professor Hoyle thinks we may be heading toward a stage in which the objective may not be too far from being achieved. "The religious people have got it with St. Paul on the road to Damascus," he claims. "The sudden light—it's just like that in science. There is a turning point."[3] Laboratory tests leading to the conclusion that tiny particles in space have a very decisive property was the moment on the road to Damascus for him. Particles in space have the characteristics of living material, which he calls the "infra-red thumb print." It is just a feeling within you; it is light on the road to Damascus. Einstein's remark, "God may be subtle but he is not malicious," impressed Sir Hoyle as an appropriate summation of scientific philosophy. Life possesses the universal thumbprint property and we are a component in a large-scale system. When enough people have gone through the crisis of sudden understanding—the light dawning on the road to Damascus—and form a group belief, they begin to teach this to others.

Hoyle feels formal religion is a 3,000-year-old prejudice. And unless people move away from this prejudice and away from scientific thinking devoid of spirituality, another planet will have failed. Nevertheless, there are many planets; some will get through and survive. It doesn't look particularly good for this world, however. Hoyle observes:

> We have reached the stage where we can destroy ourselves a hundred times over in half an hour and that is a pretty grim possibility. Unless people sort themselves out, I do not think there is much time ahead. Although many things that I've said are not favorable to religion in detail, this business of a religious instinct, the sanctity of truth and so on, are signposts that will prevent our self-destruction.[4]

Sir Alister Hardy, commenting on the phrase "road to Damascus" used frequently by Hoyle in his book *Revelations: Glimpses of Reality*, says the phrase means a "sudden revelation," or something very important that influences the whole outlook of an individual—something to which he might give the name of God.

> I feel intellectually ashamed of the modern academic attitude to what one might call the study of the nature of LIFE. The most important feature about living things is the nature of consciousness. At present it is largely ignored, because one cannot see a

> method of investigating it; but there can be no doubt that it is there, and not just confined to man.[5]

Although Blavatsky, Aurobindo, Jung, and Martinus may not have had the afterlife in mind, their proposition of the spirit or soul fits completely with the properties of the astral plane outside earth and of the other higher realms. The blending of these concepts—the scientific electron, the spiritual soul, and the higher realms of various scriptures—tends to give a very good explanation of the creation of God. The present chapter endeavors to prove the nonlocality and general quantum nature of the soul through this blending of "psi-evidence," quantum physics, the experiences of saints, and the descriptions given in various scriptures.[6]

Spirituality, Religion, and Science

Religion existed long before science came into being. Science has been with us for only about five hundred years, coming perhaps with the invention of astronomy by pioneers such as Galileo and Copernicus. Since science deals with objectivity, it appeals easily to the human mind, as scientific results can be seen through our own eyes. On the other hand, the subjectivity of spirituality is not easy to grasp since we have to become a part of the process ourselves. The results are only experienced subjectively; they cannot be shown objectively. For some, however, they can be felt. It is at this stage that Descartes separated science from religion some four hundred years ago. But now, in the so-called New Age, especially with the arrival of quantum physics, physicists are loosening the grip of the orthodox definition of reality, although some do not want to admit it publicly at present.[7] Paul Twitchell of Eckankar said religion and science are going to merge into each other and a new theory will emerge in the twenty-first century. J. B. Rhine began to show signs of fatigue in his later years when no physical or mathematical models could possibly be fit into any of the paranormal phenomena experimented with at Duke University. In fact, physicist R. L. Morris admitted that, whatever concessions physics may give to paranormal phenomena, no explanation could ever be possible.[8] I would go a step further and hypothesize that science is eventually going to lose its identity and finally merge into spirituality. More and more scientists are now admitting that they cannot explain phenomena until they become a part of it by way of meditation. When this happens, spirituality and the paranormal will remain, and science, as a separate philosophy, will vanish. This was life in the lost civilization of Atlantis some twelve thousand years ago. This was the life that erected the many pyramids in Egypt and Mexico, something for which modern science has been unable to account.

To see how science has been following the spiritual foundation of religion by arriving at the same conclusions long held by spiritual reasoning (not religious dogma), we proceed as follows. Innumerable instances can be quoted from Hindu scriptures where the special character Narad Muni disappears at one place, instantly reappears at another, and communicates with a being instantaneously without opening his mouth. Time in *swarglok* (heaven on the lower mental plane) moves extremely slowly; for example, after spending only a year or so in swarglok, one might find, on return to earth, that two to three generations have passed. Lord Krishna used to appear with a large number of *gopis* (milkmaids) simultaneously at several places when they were involved in *rasalila* (a group dance). You could only see these beings on a higher realm such as swarglok. Nor was there any question of measuring the speed of travel, since Krishna could disappear and reappear instantly, despite the distance between the two places.

Events described above are normal characteristics of the astral and mental planes. Yogis and saints have, from time to time, also experienced these events on earth. Scientists, however, are only beginning to find hints of such possibilities through the study of quantum particles. A quantum object can appear at more than one place simultaneously; it can manifest as a particle; it can disappear in one place and reappear at another; it can influence other quantum objects regardless of the distance between them.[9]

My hypothesis is that quantum properties are the natural tools of a soul on the higher realms, gained upon surrendering the physical body at death. Of course, these properties become more refined each time the soul moves to a higher realm. The behavior of subatomic particles on the physical plane is analogous to the behavior of people on higher realms, since astral entities are subatomic in nature. The secret doctrine of Madam H. P. Blavatsky expresses the following conclusion: "Everything in the Universe, throughout all its kingdoms, is conscious: i.e., endowed with a consciousness of its own kind and on its own plane of perception."[10] Likewise, according to Satprem:

> The future belongs to those who give themselves unreservedly to the future. And we assert that there exists a future far more marvelous than all the electronic paradises of the mind: man is not the end. . . . We seem to invent ever more marvelous machines, ceaselessly expand the limits of the human, and even progress

> towards Jupiter and Venus. But that is only a seeming, increasingly deceptive and oppressive, and we do not expand anything: We merely send to the other end of the cosmos a pitiful little being who does not even know how to take care of his own kind, or whether his caves harbor a dragon or a mewling baby. We do not progress; we inordinately inflate an enormous mental balloon, which may well be exploding in our face. We have not improved man; we have merely colossal zed. . . . The truth is, the summit of man—or the summit of anything at all—does not lie in perfecting to a higher degree the type under consideration; it lies in a "something else" that is not of the same type and that he aspires to become. Such is the evolutionary law.[11]

Beversluis observed:

> The central point is the new understanding of the universe which is no longer perceived as consisting of solid bodies moving in space and time but rather, according to quantum theory, as a field of energy pervaded by consciousness. Western scientists, for the first time, have seriously faced the fact that if they want to understand the universe, they have to understand their own consciousness. A leader in this development was David Bohm, for he was one of the first scientists to take seriously the place of consciousness in scientific understanding.[12]

This emphasized only one point, that the scientific achievements, which are of a very finite nature, may be good for the physical comforts of humans, and they may continue; however, to understand the infinite universe one has to concentrate on consciousness. The universe has been defined in chapter 1. *Consciousness* is defined as the understanding of the infinite potential we already possess. An illustration of that has been demonstrated through the properties of the quantum particle. Dr. Claire Walker asks if consciousness works on the principle of nonlocality and wonders if the soul, since it is nonlocal, is also psychic.[13] My answer to both questions is "yes."

Chapter Eight

CONSCIOUSNESS, EGO, SELF, AND GOD

Sri Aurobindo and C. G. Jung, working independently and treading divergent paths, converged at the same conclusion—that behind the conscious mind of the individual lies an unlimited psychic region that is as real as the physical world. This was no ordinary event. Indeed, it is perhaps one of the most outstanding achievements of the twentieth century. Although the facts have been known to various religions in varying degrees for a long time, the modern world needs logic and proof before it can believe the mysticism found in spiritual knowledge but suppressed by religious dogma. This proof is well provided by these two giants of the modern era.

Through these two, subjectivity has been converted into objective study and direct experience. Jung arrived at his conclusions based on his own dreams and the dreams of his patients, while Sri Aurobindo's conclusions were based on his direct experiences through yoga and meditation. However, during his visions of death in 1944, Jung also had direct experiences in which he found himself floating "in a state of purest bliss thronged round with images of all creation," and the physical world appeared to him "downright ridiculous" and as a "segment of existence which is enacted in a three dimensional box-like universe especially set up for it."[1] Nevertheless, Jung's scientific way of writing, developed methodically, forced him to explain the supra-physical in terms of the physical. "He could not discriminate between different ingredients of visions and archetypes. This has resulted in a lot of confusion in his theory of archetypes."[2]

There is an obscure region below the conscious mind called the unconscious by Jung. He divided the unconcscious into two parts: the personal and the collective. The unconscious of Jung is the "subconscient" of Sri Aurobindo, who also divided it into two parts: the individual and the universal. The personal unconscious, or individual subconscient, is the storehouse of suppressed and subsided material from the present life that was once floating in the conscious mind. "This material remains in the seed form in the subconscient and comes up again when allowed."[3] Dreams in the sleeping state are the unfolding of these impressions. The universal subconscient, on the other hand, comes from the inconscient, which is also the source of the conscious mind of humans, and of the instincts and impulses for life. The universal subconscient, or the collective unconscious, is formed in the process of evolution, right from plant life and the animal kingdom, and is the heritage of humanity. Both thinkers agree that this stratum of psyche is autonomous; they attribute to it direct and immediate knowledge of objects and events. It preserves the past and perceives the future—for example, dreams predicting future events. According to both of them, it is the immeasurable sea from which the conscious mind emerges like an iceberg. It is the source of paranormal phenomena such as telepathy, telekinesis, and clairvoyance. Ordinarily, this part of the psyche is unapproachable to the conscious mind; it reveals itself only in altered states or dreams.

According to Sri Aurobindo, the universal subconscient, of evolutionary origin, is only the lower part of the subliminal. The higher subliminal is due to the direct descent of the superconscient to the principle of mind, life, and matter. According to both authors, the conscious mind receives knowledge of its future course through intuitions of the collective unconscious, and this cannot be the total history of the conscious. According to Sri Aurobindo, the higher subliminal functions are a part of the Atman; "it is that which endures and is imperishable in us from birth to birth, untouched by death, decay or corruption, an indestructible spark of the Divine."[4] It is through *sadhana* (yoga, meditation, chanting of mantras, or other metaphysical practices) that a yogi passes through the lower regions, encounters personal memories that block his inner growth, and finally expands subliminal consciousness into cosmic consciousness.[5] In view of Dr. S. P. Singh:

> Just as Freud, in his idea of the unconscious, had confused the personal unconscious and the collective unconscious which, as Jung has shown, are entirely of different origin and nature, so Jung in his idea of the collective unconscious seems to have con-

fused the lower and the higher spheres of the subliminal which, as shown by Sri Aurobindo, are still more disparate from each other in their origin and nature.[6]

Archetypes and Visions

The archetypes of Jung are the visionary beings of Sri Aurobindo. They are the same as the *noumena* of Kant. Kant's noumena seek to express themselves through phenomena; the libido of Jung seeks to express itself through consciousness. Likewise, Jung considers the visions of Sri Aurobindo as the superconscious manifesting itself in the form of mind, life, and matter. Thus the visions of Sri Aurobindo involve actual entities, while the archetypes of Jung (including his *anima* and *animus*) are only forms or modes, not any particular character, by which the libido wants to express itself in a particular situation.

Sri Aurobindo divided visions into three distinct classes: the subtle physical, the vital, and the mental. The first class deals with the subtle causal form where future events of universal nature are revealed. These events concern the gross physical world visible to the external eyes. The second class deals with an intermediate zone that concerns the beings of the vital world. These beings appear in different forms, including those of gods and goddesses or demons, and create problems for practitioners that they will transcend in order to proceed further on the spiritual path. These beings may be called teachers or guides. The third class deals with the mental world, to which the practitioner qualifies after transcending the physical and vital worlds.

During mediation, beings of the mental plane may appear as the gods and goddesses of the Vedas or any other spiritual or religious belief. These visions are actual manifestations of the superconscious, parallel to the beings existing factually on the mental plane in the consciousness of the practitioner. These beings are capable of manifestation in any of the lower worlds.

Sri Aurobindo considered manifestation of the Mother as the emanation from the consciousness force (the kinetic form of God, or *Shakti*), the primary source of the creation. The Mother can manifest on any of the lower planes. Likewise, *saccidananda* (the potential form of God, or *Shiva*) is the Lord Krishna of Sri Aurobindo, who also embodied the historical Krishna on earth, still existing on a higher plane in the same form. The practitioner can contact the Mother or Lord Krishna. One can see them and talk to them on the appropriate inner plane of higher consciousness. Various saints have had such experiences. I have described my own experiences elsewhere.[7]

Jung also talks of these three classes of visions in the form of the future element of visions, Jungian gods and demons, and the Jungian archetypes of Mother and Mandala. Sri Aurobindo received confirmation of his visions in yogic practices and through myths and scriptures. He was left with no doubts about their reality. Jung, on the other hand, drew inferences from dreams and psychotic fantasies. However, he had real visions himself in later life.

The Ego

Jung defined *ego* as the result of "the collision between the somatic factor and the environment; it goes on developing from further collisions with the outer world and the inner."[8] Ego is the center of mental consciousness. It has its roots both in the conscious personality and in the inner being. Jung's "particular ego-sense" and "general ego-sense" correspond to Sri Aurobindo's "manifest" and "unconscious" substrata. The ego thus represents the concentricity of both the inner and the outer being. It is essential for the functioning of the sense organs and hence for the action of the individual and adjustment to the environment.

At the same time, the ego is the source of all suffering in humans, causing them to indulge in inhumane acts. This is a case of the slave becoming the master. It is like an anchor that is necessary to hold the ship near the shore temporarily and then, at the right time, release it to move freely. In another example, the earth may be erroneously said to be the center of the universe. Ignorance must be encountered, the anchor must be removed, the proper center must be found, and the ego must be displaced.

The ego is not monolithic; it is both subjective and objective with respect to its own knowledge, and thus suffers with its propensity to divide the personality into two disparate elements, as is obvious from the phenomena of dreams. Accordingly, the ego cannot be the center of the conscious being, and more so, of the whole psyche, which is vast and varied in its fullness. Thus, there is some other principle in the individual that is responsible for the unification of the disparate elements of the personality into a whole.

Sin and Suffering

The erroneous belief that one is the perpetrator of an act causes sin and suffering. One may think that he or she is carrying a bag on a flight from London to New York. In fact, the airplane is carrying the bag. Someone out of work may accuse others for his unemployment; but if a careful analysis is carried out, it would be found there are several reasons interwoven. No single factor can be held responsible. Similarly, any particular act on earth is the result of the whole machinery of the universe, and not any single factor. "There is no such thing as chance."[9] Things are happening by themselves; we wrongly think that we are the cause of a particular event; so sin and suffering have been invented unnecessarily. This is one of the most important teachings of the Bhagavad Gita. One who has assimilated this wisdom is a liberated person. Sri Aurobindo observes:

> The sense, the idea, the experience that I am a separately self-existent being in the universe, and the forming of consciousness and force of being into the mould of that experience are the root of all suffering, ignorance and evil. And it is so because that misunderstanding falsifies both in practice and cognition the whole real truth of reality; it limits the being, limits the consciousness, limits the power of our being, and limits the bliss of being. This limitation again produces a wrong way of existence, wrong way of consciousness, wrong way of using the power of our being and consciousness, and wrong, perverse and contrary forms of the delight of existence.[10]

Thus, believing oneself to be a separate entity other than absolute God consciousness, and thus thinking that one is the doer of deeds, limits one's potential on one hand and delivers one into the arms of karma on the other.

Cosmic and Higher Consciousness

The higher levels of consciousness—higher mind, illumined mind, intuition, and overmind—of which the individual is normally not aware was called by Sri Aurobindo the inner, or subliminal, consciousness. This inner, or subliminal, consciousness is part of the universal nature and coexists with matter, life, and mind.[11] The characteristic of the illuminated mind is simultaneity of comprehension, that of intuition is abrupt illumination, and that of overmind is the steady state of intuitive knowledge. At the fall of the wall between the outer and inner consciousness, a new consciousness dawns in the practitioner, called cosmic consciousness. The individual becomes directly aware of a universal being, universal states, universal force and power, universal mind, life, matter, and lives in constant relations with these things.[12]

Dr. Richard Maurice Bucke has presented detailed accounts of the lives and achievements of persons who were endowed with cosmic consciousness.[13] There are persons who achieved a consciousness higher than cosmic among the subjects described by Bucke, but he has not made any distinction between them and others. Its entanglement in the affairs of nature affects cosmic consciousness. Sri Aurobindo calls the state higher than the cosmic spiritual or supramental consciousness, a state that is characterized with the oneness and freedom of the absolute saccidananda. In this state, the subject and object become one; in other words, the seer, seeing, and seen become one. Here, he observes: "We enter into the awareness of Self, the Spirit, the Divine and are able to see in all things their essential reality and the play of forces and phenomena as preceding from that essential reality."[14]

There is a conscious personality representing the inner world, having a sense of wholeness and unity of both the conscious and unconscious minds. It must be a greater principle than ego, which unifies only the conscious mind. It is this conscious personality that is called the "supraordinate personality" and given the name of "Self" by Jung. Thus ego is only a derivative of the Self and it is related to the Self as the object to the subject. Both Jung and Sri Aurobindo found the real center to be the Self, which has a unitary nature and represents the inner reality in its totality. Both of them found that the Self is indivisible and, because it is the complete representative of the psyche, omnipresent. According to Jung, it is the common center of both the conscious and the unconscious. Sri Aurobindo considers it to be the original center of pure consciousness, and a finite representative of the infinite. In his view, it is the real "I," the Atman, the highest *purusha*, the secret soul. It is transcendent (combining diversity and unity, individual and universal) and eternal—at once wheel and motion, center and circumference.[15] It can both be inferred logically and realized in meditation, "extending itself upward into a transcendence of which the limits are not visible."[16]

According to Jung, "Under certain conditions the unconscious spontaneously brings forth an archetypal symbol of wholeness."[17] Referring to India's theory of the Atman, which unifies the complementary elements of consciousness and the unconscious, he said, "Atman on one hand embraces the universe and on the other is 'not bigger than a thumb' dwelling in the heart."[18]

Jung observed that one first disclaims the Self due to the arrogance of the ego, but soon becomes desperate in search of the same. Yet, one must keep a balance between the ego and the Self, in accordance with the law of opposites, which states that everything requires for its existence its own opposite or else it fades into nothingness. "It is only separation, detachment and agonizing confrontation through opposition that produce consciousness and insight."[19]

God

When we talk about God, perhaps we are touching the most important part of our discussion. In several religions, including Christianity, Hinduism, and Sufism, the archetype of Self has been called God. According to Jung:

> Christ, who is a typical manifestation of the Self, is regarded as the central figure in the Divine Trinity. In Hinduism, it is represented by Atman which is regarded as identical with Brahman.[20]

According to Sri Samkaracarya:

> Brahman and Atman which are designated by the terms "that" and "thou," respectively, are fully proven to be identical when investigated by the light of Vedic teaching.[21]

In the words of Aldous Huxley:

> Based upon the direct experience of those who have fulfilled the necessary conditions of such knowledge, this teaching is expressed most succinctly in the Sanskrit formula, tat tvam asi (That thou art); the Atman, or immanent eternal Self, is one with Brahman, the Absolute Principle of all existence; and the last end of every human being is to discover the fact for himself, to find out Who he or she really is.[22]

Merwan Sheriar Irani, a Sufi Muslim saint of the twentieth century, popularly known as Meher Baba, said that the human psyche has two parts: one falls within the range of consciousness, the other falls beyond it. According to him:

> The unconscious part, in its full extent, is identical with the power which is behind matter. It is referred to as God by the orthodox religions. The Ultimate Reality which is symbolically represented through such concepts can be known fully only by bringing the unconscious into conscious.[23]

Sri Aurobindo calls the ultimate reality saccidananda—*sat* (existence), *chit* (consciousness), *ananda* (bliss). He calls the creative power of saccidananda consciousness force. Thus consciousness is the inherent nature of God and his creative energy. Psychologically, neither Jung nor Sri Aurobindo could conclude whether it was consciousness or unconscious that came into existence first. Sri Aurobindo took refuge in metaphysics and declared that saccidananda went into self-concealment for evolution to take place. The highest stage of evolution is man, the level at which unconsciousness is thrown completely into the background and consciousness becomes preeminent. The moment the unconscious is brought into conscious, Self-realization, and hence God-realization, takes place. Sri Aurobindo describes Self-realization in these words:

> The status or action in us of an inherent, intrinsic, self-existent consciousness which knows itself by the mere fact of being, knows all that is in itself in the same way, by identity with it, begins even to see all that to our mind seems external in the same manner, by a movement of identity or by an intrinsic direct consciousness which envelopes, penetrates, enters into its object, discovers itself in the object, is aware in it of something that is not mind or life or body.[24]

In less complicated language, this can be summarized as follows: Behind the conscious mind lies an unlimited psychic region that is the unconscious. The unconscious mind has two divisions: personal and individual, or collective and universal. The individual part stores suppressed material from this life, which appears in dreams. The universal part is formed in the process of evolution over innumerable lifetimes. It is the infinite human heritage holding the past and reflecting the future. The conscious mind is a very small part of the unconscious. The unconscious is the source of paranormal phenomena such as telepathy, clairvoyance, and precognition. Ordinarily, it is unapproachable by the conscious mind. The unconscious is called the soul, Atman, psyche, or God. It is permanent and accessible to the conscious mind through meditation, *sadhana*, or the awakening of kundalini.

Visions belong to three categories: subtle physical visions that reveal the events of the future, vital or intermediate visions that reveal the beings of the vital world who may be called gurus or guides (or minor gods or goddesses), and mental, actual manifestations of superconscious such as Mother, Krishna, or Christ (one can feel their presence, see them, and talk to them).

Ego is a result of the interaction between somatic factors and the environment. Initially, it is like an anchor that holds the ship and connects it to the phenomenal world for normal functioning. However, it should be released, otherwise it will become the master. Sin and suffering exist due to the misunderstanding that one is the true initiator of actions or events and that one has an existence separate from the whole.

Sri Aurobindo suggests seven levels of existence in the universe. The physical group he calls vital and mental consciousness, or "outer consciousness"; the higher mind group is illumined mind or intuition; the overmind is called the "inner consciousness." When the wall between the inner and outer consciousness falls, a new consciousness emerges that can be called cosmic consciousness. At this stage, one develops an awareness of and a relation to the universal being. However, a person with cosmic consciousness still has some attachment to materialism and will suffer in proportion to that. Growing further, one develops a consciousness higher than cosmic, in which the seer, seeing, and seen merge into one. Sri Aurobindo calls this supramental consciousness.

There is a conscious personality representing the inner world that is whole and greater than ego. It has equal command over the conscious and unconscious. This personality is called Self, or Atman. It is a finite representative of the infinite. The law of opposites requires that a balance be maintained between the ego and the Self. According to the law of opposites, everything requires the existence of its opposite, or else it fades into nothingness. In a sense, the ego takes care of the horizontal aspect of our existence, while the Self takes care of the vertical. The horizontal and vertical aspects of existence are discussed at length in the next chapter.

Chapter Nine

THE JOURNEY TO THE SOUL

Many great thinkers have chronicled their journey to the soul through poetry, prose, and song. Although their experiences have differed in many ways, they all share the key characteristic of Self-realization. Jung and Sri Aurobindo experienced peace, bliss, stupendous silence, infinity of release and freedom, and the ecstasy of a nontemporal state. For them, past, present, and future appeared to be one. People have reported similar experiences while out of the body, for example in near-death experiences. These are therefore the experiences of the soul. Jung describes perceiving the physical world as in a box. William Wordsworth claims that living on earth is like being in a deep sleep, having forgotten the real home of soul, which is far away. Asaramji says that, as soon as one receives awareness or knowledge of soul, even for a moment, one is liberated from the falsehood of the physical world and there is no need for further incarnations.

In this chapter, we will share some of these soul journeys, and then explore the horizontal and vertical "axes" of the universe to better understand the reality of the soul.

Sri Aurobindo

Sri Aurobindo describes his three-day soul journey in 1907 thus:

> The first result was a series of tremendously powerful experiences and radical changes of consciousness which I had never intended and which were quite contrary to my own ideas, for they made me see with a stupendous intensity the world as a

> cinemagraphic play of vacant forms in the impersonal universality of the Absolute Brahman. . . . It threw me suddenly into a condition above and without thought, unstained by any mental or vital movement; there was no ego, no real world. . . . This was no mental realization nor something glimpsed somewhere above, no abstraction; it was positive, the only positive reality. . . .What it brought was an expressible peace, a stupendous silence, an infinity of release and freedom. [While confined to a solitary cell in jail for one month in 1908]: I looked at the jail that secluded me from men and it was no longer by its high walls that I was prisoned; no, it was Vasudeva who surrounded me. I walked under the branches of the tree in front of my cell but it was not the tree, I knew it was Vasudeva, it was Sri Krishna whom I saw standing there and holding over me his shade. I looked at the bars of my cell, the very grating that did duty for a door, and again I saw Vasudeva. It was Narayana who was guarding and sending sentry over me. Or I lay on the coarse blankets that were given me for a couch and I felt the arms of Sri Krishna around me, the arms of my friend and lover. . . . I looked at the prisoners in the jail, the thieves, the murderers, the swindlers, and as I looked at them, I saw Vasudeva, it was Narayana whom I found in these darkened souls and misused bodies.[1]

In the words of his host, Satprem, a student of Sri Aurobindo:

> One felt when he spoke as if somebody else was speaking through him. I placed the plate of food before him; he simply gazed at it, and then ate a little, just mechanically. He appeared to be absorbed even when he was eating; he used to meditate with open eyes. . . . Without falling into ecstatic trance, with eyes wide open, Sri Aurobindo found himself precipitated into the supreme Light.[2]

Sri Aurobindo fasted, slept very little, experimented with the principles of spiritual life very methodically. Finally, he put them into words: "I have been testing day and night for years upon years more scrupulously than any scientist with his theory or his method on the physical plane.[3]

His jailers mentally subjected him to all sorts of torture for fifteen days and he had to look upon pictures of all sorts of suffering before the final transformation of the consciousness took place. From 1910 to 1950, his life was devoted to confirmation, expansion, consolidation, and the practical application of the spiritual experiences he gained. In 1920, Madame Mirra Richard of France was entrusted with the charge of the

Ashram in Pondicherry. After considering his writings as sufficient, he discontinued the journal *Arya*. Freeing himself from all tasks, he devoted himself to the practice of yoga more intensively. He attained complete *siddhi* on November 24, 1926. He then withdrew into complete seclusion; only the Mother and a few selected people could see him. He left his physical body on December 5, 1950.

Carl Jung

In his later years, Carl Jung had experiences that fall into the category of spirituality as described in the previous chapters.[4] Jung was very conversant in both yoga and meditation, as one can see from this dream:

> I was on a hiking trip. I was walking along a little road through a hilly landscape; the sun was shining and I had a wide view in all directions. When I came to a small wayside chapel the door was ajar and I went in. To my surprise there was no image of the Virgin on the altar, and no crucifix either, but only a wonderful flower arrangement. I then saw on the floor in front of the altar, facing me, sat a yogi in the lotus posture, in deep meditation. When I looked at him closely, I realized he had my face. I started in profound fright, and awoke with the thought: "Aha, so he is the one who is meditating on me. He has a dream, and I am it."[5]

According to Singh:

> Jung treats this dream as a parable and understands himself, the dreamer as the ego, and the yogi as the Self. According to him, assumption of the human form, by the Self, is indicative of its entering into three-dimensional existence. The thought arising immediately after the dream, is taken to reflect the relationship between the Self and the ego, the later being treated as meditation within the former along with the understanding that the ego would evaporate into nothingness as soon as the meditation comes to an end.[6]

Savitri

When Savitri turned inward in search of the soul, the last part of the journey in the spiritual consciousness, she realized the Self ultimately, and gave the following account of the experience:

In the last chamber, on a golden seat
One sat whose shape no vision could define,
Only one felt the world's unattainable fount,
A power of which she was a straying Force,
An invisible Beauty, goal of the world's desire,
A Sun of which all knowledge is beam,
A Greatness without whom no life could be,
Thence all departed in silent self,
And all became formless and pure and bare.
Then through a tunnel dug in the last rock,
She came out where there shone a deathless sun,
A house was there all made of flame and light
And crossing a wall of odorless living fire
There suddenly she met her secret soul.[7]

William Wordsworth

Realization of the Self (soul) for William Wordsworth is rendered in the following passage from his book *Intimations of Immortality*:

Our birth is but a sleep and a forgetting;
The soul that rises with us, our life star,
Hath had elsewhere, its setting,
And cometh from afar.
Not in entire forgetfulness,
And not in utter nakedness,
But trailing clouds of glory do we come
From God, who is our home.[8]

Saint Asaramji

Saint Asaramji describes his journey thus:

> Paramatma is the source of cosmic energy which activates our consciousness. That consciousness makes the world of dreams in Hita nerve. That consciousness in a paralytic state is converted into deep sleep. Attainment of Atma-Paramatma, awareness or knowledge of It for a period of even three minutes by someone will not let one suffer the agony of being in the womb of a mother again, one becomes a liberated soul.[9]

The Horizontal and Vertical Axes of the Universe

The horizontal aspect of living is concerned with life as a physical being in the material world. Here, development at an acceptable level is essential to a satisfying life.[10] Establishment of one's identity, development of meaningful connections with others, achievement of a certain level of security and recognition (enough for the continuation of one's development) are all necessary first steps.[11] Dr. Annie Besant finds it natural to play with the toys—pleasure, money, power, honor—for satisfaction and for the development of the human will, mental power, and emotional strength. When the toys break, it opens the way for the expansion of the higher faculties and values.[12] The transition from horizontal to vertical aspiration takes place when the psychic needs of everyday living are in balance and an individual feels secure enough, free enough, to give attention to a new set of values.[13] In our current time, the word *process* has taken on an expanded meaning. Process is the amount of time we give ourselves to feel safe enough to admit what we already know is true. Jiddu Krishnamurti repeatedly asserted in his lectures that an inner order is a prerequisite to an outer order.

Jung defines the totality of psychological principles, fields, and functions in an individual as psyche. According to Jung: "The lower reaches of the psyche begin where the function emancipates itself from the impulsive forces of 'instinct' and becomes amenable to the will." The psyche for Jung has two parts: the conscious and the unconscious. "The subjectivity of the conscious psyche," he reminds us, "lies in its being subject to the operation of the ego while the objectivity of the unconscious psyche consists in its being autonomous."[14] Although the conscious and unconscious are assumed exclusive to each other, he did not rule out the possibility that "unconscious psyche is at the same time conscious."[15] Accordingly, we have to consider both the conscious and the unconscious simultaneously, without giving priority to one over the other, if we are to understand the psyche in a full way. "To these are to be added the ego and the self as centers of the conscious and unconscious respectively."[16] This suggests that the horizontal is represented by the conscious ego, while the unconscious Self represents the vertical.

Psyche is universal, collective, eternal, and unique—a cosmic principle and existence in and of itself. Although constituted of disparate elements, psyche functions as a whole. During sleep, consciousness disappears, yet we remember dreams. This, together with the paranormal phenomena—telepathy, telekinesis, precognition, and levitation—experimented with at Duke University and other centers shows the universality of the psyche. It contains the history of organic evolution due to the principle of hereditary transmission, which in turn shows its collectiveness. Because of its nonspatial and nontemporal character, Jung regards psyche as eternal and describes it as "a mathematical point and at the same time as a universe of fixed stars."[17] Because it is a source of consciousness, Jung calls it a "cosmic principle"; because of its transspatial, transtemporal, and causal properties, he regards it as unique and probably capable of constituting another dimension of the universe beyond the temporal and the spatial.[18] Because of all these properties, Jung regards the psyche as a miniature universe in itself. The interdependence of psyche and matter is obvious from his following statement:

> Psyche cannot be totally different from matter, for how otherwise could it move matter? And matter cannot be alien to psyche, for how else could matter produce psyche? Psyche and matter exist in one and the same world, and each partakes of the other, otherwise any reciprocal action would be impossible.[19]

According to Singh:

> In fact Jung regards psyche and matter as co-ordinate entities, each constituting the pre-condition of the existence of the other. If psyche without brain is inconceivable, the external world without consciousness is a virtual non-entity. Hence Jung characterizes the psyche not only as existent but also as "existence itself."[20]

We thus find two virtually opposing contents in psyche—matter and spirit. They give rise to animals or subhuman entities as a requirement of instinct and biological need on one hand, and to archetypal divine entities for the satisfaction of spiritual needs on the other. The pull of the two against each other creates friction and generates psychic energy, called *libido* by Jung. Freud was the first to use the word *libido* to describe the sexual drive creating energy for all psychological purposes. Jung called libido a general life instinct originating from the Sanskrit word *lobha*. According to him it is "an energy valve which is able to communicate itself to any field of activity whatever, be it power, hunger, hatred, sexuality or spirituality, without ever being itself a specific instinct."[21] Jung compared psychic energy to physical energy and tried to govern it by the formula given by Einstein, with the difference that physical energy is related to a quantity of mass, while psychic energy is related to a quality of spiritual force. Jung observed: "As we rise higher in the psychic sphere, the hold of instincts goes on lessening gradually until at last the psyche achieves complete autonomy and 'attains a so called spiritual form'."[22]

Jung divides the personality in two parts—inner and outer—that counterbalance each other. The inner personality, including the inner attitude, is the character turned toward the unconscious. It is the manner of one's behavior toward the inner psychic processes. He calls the outer personality the *persona*, while the inner one is called *anima/animus* or soul.[23] His way of defining soul differs from the traditional Christian view. However, it is the psyche that he defines as "the totality of all the psychic processes, both conscious as well as unconscious."[24] Thus, it is the psyche that corresponds to the traditional definition of soul in various religions, and to the Atman of the Hindus.

The coexistence of things may be taken as the horizontal part of the world, while the intensity and tangibility of things can be regarded as the vertical part. Thus, something that appears to be out of place may be the index of some universal activity. Both Jung and Sri Aurobindo admit the existence of worlds beyond the physical. On "the hypothetical possibility that the psyche touches on a form of existence outside space and time," and the validity of this possibility through the "relativization of the space category by modern theoretical physics," Jung is inclined to believe in existence beyond space, time, and the law of causality.[25]

Sri Aurobindo divides the existence into two parts—concentric, or outer, existence and vertical, or inner, existence. Outer rings are made of "our ordinary exterior mind, life and body consciousness," while the inner rings are made of "an inner mind, an inner life and an inner physical consciousness."[26] The inner mind preserves the entire history of evolution in condensed form and sees the future as clearly as it sees the present, unlike the outer mind, which depends on approximation through inference. It is also the source of predictive dreams. Sri Aurobindo believed in the coexistence of horizontal and vertical lives, and hence in the existence of a world of the mind, a world of life along with the world of matter, based on the law of continuity in nature. He calls the "psychic existence" of the group of inner mental, inner vital, and inner physical forms subliminal—forms of which a person is normally unaware. The subliminal is vindicated for its vast consciousness through dreams and yogic experiences, and through abnormal states of mind that provide solutions to problems otherwise not easy to solve.

Sri Aurobindo calls ego the center of the surface mind and psychic being the center of the subliminal, located just behind the heart—unlike emotions, which emanate from the front part of the heart.[27] The psychic being is also called the "*purusa* in the heart" or "*chaitya purusa*," referring to *sat-chit-ananda*, originating from the third cosmic principle, *ananda*, "the delight-soul in the universe."[28] Although it is the center of the subliminal, it lies beyond the inner mental, inner vital, and inner physical; it is the permanent referee of these three forms. It has "a direct touch upon truth" and one meets it as the profound mystic light at the fourth center of energy, called the *anahat chakra*.[29] *Jivatman*, Atman, or soul is an eternal fraction of the divine and it dwells always in the knowledge or Self-awareness of saccidananda. At the initial stages of involution of saccidananda, the soul remains dormant; however, when it asserts itself, individuality evolves from within the soul and is manifested as the psychic being. Thus, "the soul-form or Soul-personality develops through this evolution."[30] Growing as the personality of the soul, it controls all the factors of the subliminal and serves as the "central being in the evolution."[31] As a direct representative of Atman, it has all the knowledge of the universal reality inherent in it, and is gradually becoming omniscient.

Self is the center of our being in totality that continues from birth to birth, supervising and supporting us in every way. It manifests itself in two forms—jivatman and psychic being. While the jivatman remains unaffected by birth and death, the psychic being is quite involved in them. While the jivatman, as a portion of the divine, is universal as well as individual, the psychic being narrows itself down to sheer individuality. It indeed is the carrier of experience from life to life. Sri Aurobindo, as well as the Upanishads, states that there is a personal formation on each plane of our being, the physical, the vital, the mental, and the supramental. These formations are known as *purusas*. Thus there is a physical, a vital, a mental, and a psychic purusa each forming the center of its own plane. "When the soul or spark of the Divine Fire" begins to develop a psychic individuality, observes Sri Aurobindo, "that psychic individuality is called the psychic being. When the psychic being gains dominance over the mental, the vital and the physical, it makes use of them as its instruments." Sri Aurobindo described this as psychic transformation.[32]

The horizontal is thus concerned with life as a physical being establishing one's identity and developing meaningful relations with others. Interest in pleasure, money, power, and honor is likened to playing with a toy. When the toy breaks, expansion of higher faculties begins, which is the vertical. The horizontal is represented by conscious ego, while the unconscious Self represents the vertical. The pull of the two against each other generates friction that gives rise to psychic energy called libido, or sex drive.

Personal formations of our being, called purusas, exist on each of the physical, vital, mental, and psychic planes. Eventually, the soul develops a psychic individuality, called psychic being, that dominates all the purusas.

The psyche of Jung or the Atman of Sri Aurobindo is seen to be universal, collective, eternal, and unique—a cosmic principle and existence in and of itself. It is the soul of all the orthodox religions and is described as having similar properties by various scriptures. Details of the universe presented in chapter 5 further suggest that the soul has all the paranormal properties—telepathy, clairvoyance, telekinesis, and levitation. There are various biographies and autobiographies that evince these properties of the soul. For example, Paul Twitchell, the former spiritual head of Eckankar, could come out of his body at will and exhibit some of these properties.[33] Some of these properties are possessed by the quantum atom as stated by physicist Amit Goswami: the wave property, collapse of the wave, the quantum leap, and quantum action-at-a-distance.[34]

Two quantum properties—Heisenberg's uncertainty principle and the principle of nonlocality—are also possessed by souls. The first principle means that either the location or the speed of a quantum object can be measured at one time, but not both. The second principle means that one body can influence another, whatever distance they may have between them, and without an apparent exchange of force or energy.

True-life experiences have taken place around the world from time immemorial that suggest the soul possesses all the above properties. Accordingly, I hypothesize that the soul is not only nonlocal and quantum in its full content, but it has a large number of properties that are yet to be proved by quantum physics. I present some of these true-life cases from India in the next chapter. The authors of these writings, which have appeared in the Hindi magazine *Manohar Kahanian*, were still alive at the time of the writing of this book and can be contacted easily for verification.

Chapter Ten

ILLUSTRATIONS OF THE POWER OF THE SOUL

Following are three cases reported in recent issues of the Indian magazine *Manohar Kahaniyan* that illustrate the power of the soul.

Case 1[1]

An assistant professor in the Department of Ancient History at the University of Delhi accompanied Mr. Samarendra Singh and his sixteen-year-old daughter, Sarita, to study an old statue of Mr. Singh's ancestor situated in the backyard of an old palatial building a few miles from the city of Banares in northern India.

The professor was stunned to see that, while the statue was of an Indian warrior, it carried an impression of medieval Italy. He had not seen such a beautifully intact statue for a long time. Sarita, staring at it with wide-open eyes, simply whispered "marvelous." Leather sandal lacings wrapped around the legs in the Roman style. In his right hand, the figure held a sword, its scabbard in his left. He wore a pointed turban and mustachios, and his large impressive eyes appeared as if he were about to attack the enemy. Mr. Singh told his daughter that the statue portrayed one of their ancestors whose name he could not recollect. "How brave and attractive were our ancestors. I will never get tired looking at him," said Sarita, looking at the statue with great admiration and respect. She bent her head very respectfully to salute the statue and touched its feet with her hands. The professor and Mr. Singh were surprised to see this. She advised them, as if they were small children and she an elderly person, "Papa, he is our ancestor. It is our duty to pay respect to him." The two elders were ashamed to hear this and they too touched the feet of the statue with their hands.

The statue was a rare one, and the professor and Mr. Singh were thinking about how to protect it from bandits. Wanting to study it in detail and publish his work at the university, the professor suggested it should be transferred to the museum in Delhi. Meanwhile, the housekeeper, Raghu, told them the infamous bandit, Madho Singh, was very active in the area. Mr. Singh asked Raghu if the matter had been reported to the police. At this, Raghu smiled and sarcastically told them the bandits were so strong, even the police were afraid of them. Mr. Singh then said it was his responsibility to look after the safety of the area and he would do something about it.

That night, the bandit appeared and entered the room of Sarita with ten heavily armed men. Madho Singh was more than six feet tall, with an athletic body. He picked up Sarita and carried her away with him. All the others were bound with ropes and the bandit leader told Mr. Singh he should arrange for a 1,500,000-rupee ransom to be paid within ten days if he wanted his daughter back, otherwise she would be chopped into four pieces before her return.

Everyone was upset and imagining the worst. Suddenly, they heard a sound, as if someone were moving with very heavy feet in the backyard. The sound moved away and disappeared.

Just coming from the village, Raghu's nephew opened the door looking quite upset. He told them the bandits had looted the village and were headed for the jungle. Suddenly, a shout from the back of the house brought everyone running to see that the statue had disappeared from its resting place. Everybody assumed Madho Singh had taken the statue along with Sarita and would sell it to smugglers for several hundred thousand rupees. Everyone, especially Mr. Singh, was thinking about Sarita and the cruel treatment she must be enduring at the hands of the torturous bandits. Obviously, the police were not capable of action, so Mr. Singh began planning the arrangements to pay the ransom.

The sound of distant shooting was heard. A few moments later, the sound of someone walking with heavy feet in the backyard was heard for the second time. Raghu, surprise on his face, ran into the room shouting for everyone to come into the backyard and see the miracle. Rushing to the back of the house, they saw someone lying on the stairs in the dim light of early morning. It was Sarita, motionless and unconscious. As Mr.

Singh lifted her into his arms to carry her into the room, he saw the statue standing in its original place in the same graceful manner as before, to the amazement of everyone.

Coming to her senses, Sarita described her experience in the following words: "I do not know anything, Papa. I simply remember those people carrying me to the jeep and driving toward the jungle. Sometimes the moon would come out and sometimes everything was dark. I was very much afraid, but I did not cry. A fat bandit sat by my side as he drove and another bandit sat at my other side. Since the road was bad, the jeep bounced along slowly. Suddenly the jeep stopped with a lurch. The fat bandit, though trying his best, could not drive the jeep forward. He shouted at the people in the other jeep, asking them what was wrong. Papa, the jeep started moving backward. The fat bandit screamed at the other one, demanding to know if someone was pulling the jeep."

"Very surprising," said Mr. Singh, and he asked her to continue.

"Papa, the bandits in the other jeep got out and ran toward our jeep. Just then, our jeep tilted to one side, spilling the fat bandit out. Because it was nearly dark, I could not see everything. I was very afraid now. Shouting with fear, the bandits started shooting. Suddenly, I felt someone lift me up and we flew off. After that, I cannot remember anything. I first opened my eyes when you woke me up," said Sarita.

Suddenly four or five people came running from the side of the village; they appeared confused, and one of them said, "Sir, the bandits are all lying dead in the jungle."

"What?" all of us shouted at once.

The man continued, "We went for a walk in the morning toward the jungle, and we saw the bandits lying dead, their jeep turned over." All the people rushed to the jungle as the sun was dawning. On reaching the scene, they found the jeep was badly smashed, like a matchbox crushed underfoot. One of the dead was recognized as the bandit leader, Madho Singh.

Madho Singh's withered body was a ghastly sight. His hands and legs were severed, his eyes were wide with fright, as if he had seen something horrible, and blood was flowing from the side of his open mouth. The professor appeared sick as Mr. Singh said, "No living person could do this." Madho Singh was holding something in his right hand. The professor removed a triangular piece of stone from the hand and put it in his pocket. The other jeep was lying upside down nearby. The dead body of every other bandit lay scattered around. They died of deep wounds with terror in their eyes. Their weapons and ammunition were scattered all around. Everyone was surprised to see this and believed it was an act of God, since no human was capable of this. A man was sent for the police.

On their return to the building, Mr. Singh and the professor inspected the statue. The sword in the statue's hand was half covered with dried blood. There were scars where bullets had struck the statue's body and, most amazing of all, tracks from what appeared to be the statue's own sandals appeared in the soil and on the grass around the base of the statue. The triangular piece of stone, earlier removed from the dead bandit leader's fist by the professor, fit perfectly into a space left on the statue's hat.

After the two men speculated on what might have happened, the professor advised that the statue should remain where it was. It apparently could take care of itself. Mr. Singh agreed and announced he would repair the house, erect high walls around the statue for further protection, and convert the area into a temple. Both men agreed that it was Sarita's perfect faith in her ancestor that produced this miracle. In my opinion, two things are clear from this story: full faith, surrender, and sincere prayers can invoke a soul on the higher plane, and the soul possesses all the paranormal powers that are used by its manifestation.

Case 2[2]

Kabiruddin Sahib was born in Rangoon, Burma. He completed grade seven or eight in a Rangoon school, but was not interested in studying. He used to begin reading the Namaz (a Muslim holy scripture), but would leave it unfinished and run away to play with local vagabond boys. These boys were bad characters, committing thefts and other petty crimes. Kabiruddin worked in his father's hotel, where he was also caught stealing. His father gave him good beatings. His mother advised him not to get involved in bad things and to read the Holy Scriptures. According to Kabiruddin, his mother loved him very much and used to call him Heeria. She wanted him to become a doctor, but he was a confirmed thief at the early age of twelve or thirteen. Smugglers and other bad characters frequenting his father's hotel may have influenced Heeria's attitude. His pious mother was regular in her prayers and very graceful, but his father used to beat her as well. Naturally, Heeria did not like his father.

Heeria was admitted to an English school, but was removed because he ran away. His father beat him and his mother embraced him with love. Burma had English rule at that time and Heeria saw the devastating Japanese bombing everywhere. Heeria's father wanted to go to India, but the Japanese made that very difficult. Despite the dangers, many Indians left their flourishing businesses and escaped back to India when the Japanese army entered Burma. Heeria's family was among them. On the way, bandits killed his father. Then the family suffered many problems in the jungles of Burma on the two-month journey to India. With his brave mother always protecting him, they finally arrived in Bengal, in the east of India.

His mother sewed clothing as a livelihood and acquired a small house. When Heeria grew up, he occupied a house left by a non-Muslim (after the partition of India) and ran a gambling house. This area became part of East Pakistan. His mother advised him against opening a gambling house, but he no longer cared for his mother and, one day, he slapped her. She never accepted money from his dealings. He married a prostitute, bought a car, and lived a life of material comfort. Then he started dealing with the drug Mafia. His mother prayed for a change in Heeria's heart toward goodness.

While dealing with a Mafia group, one of his representatives was caught at a foreign airport. He was carrying drugs worth ten million rupees. He lost the deal with the Mafia group and was lured into a trap laid by the other party somewhere far from home. He was hung with a rope thrown across the branch of a tree then tied to his jeep. His body, resting on the soft mud, gradually sank. Naturally, this would be a long, agonizing death as his body sank and the rope pulled taut. He was intended to die, hanging waist deep in mud, while having the opportunity to watch his death slowly arrive.

In the words of Kabiruddin Sahib, alias Heeria, himself: "Just then, I saw a human shadow approaching me from the side of a small hill. The sun had set, spreading the twilight all over. Though my head was turned away, I could see a human shadow coming toward me. I felt it was a woman who had covered herself with a white sheet of cloth from top to bottom.

"The woman moved toward the jeep very fast. The first thing she did was to untie the rope from my jeep. This resulted in my neck coming down. The whole weight of my body fell once again on the soft mud, which began to swallow me gradually. The woman wore a white sheet and her face was half covered. She threw the other end of the rope toward me and said, 'Heeria! Catch hold of the rope.'

"I was shaken to pieces. That woman was my mother. Where did my mother come from? How did she come? At the time, I could not think of these things. I caught hold of the rope, even though my hands were tied.

My mother began to pull the rope. God knows where she got so much strength. She pulled me out of the soft mud. As soon as I came out, I fell at the feet of my mother and began to cry and sob like a child. My mother was moving her hand over my head with love and saying, 'My Heeria! My Heeria! Now you must be regular in reading the Namaz.'

"Supporting me, my mother carried me to the jeep. I cried bitterly, out of control, as she untied the ropes from my hands and arms. I asked her how she came to me. She lovingly said, 'Heeria! When you began to travel toward this area, I knew about it. Right from that time, I began to follow you. I knew you would not listen to me. Whatever you want to do, you will do it. Yet my heart is a mother's heart. How can I watch you suffer in any way? I was afraid of the place you were going; those people were against you. But on the way, you disappeared from my sight.'

"I asked, 'Mother! I cannot believe it. How could you come so far alone?'

"Mother replied, 'Now do not ask this. The maidservant you had hired for me, she helped me a lot. It is good that I forgot the way to Dera, and came this way toward the hill. If I had not have come here, God knows what would have happened to my son, who is like a jewel. Now let us reach home quickly.'

"I kissed my mother's hands and said, 'Mother, I take a vow never to return to the world of crime. I will lead a pious life. I will read Namaz five times a day and I will serve you for the rest of my life.'

"Mother was smiling lovingly as I seated her by my side in the jeep. Starting the engine, I hastily drove away. On reaching town, I did not turn into my gambling house, but rather drove on toward our old home. When our house was still a short distance away, my mother put her hand on mine and said, 'Heeria! Stop the car.'

"I stopped and asked, 'What is the matter, Mother? Why have we stopped here?'

"Mother opened the door of the jeep and stepped out. She said, 'You go home. I will meet Sister Aisha and come later. I have something important to tell her.'

"I said, 'Well, Mother, please come home soon. I am very hungry. Today I will eat food cooked by you.' Mother smiled. In her smile, I sensed a desire, and a disappointment. I did not think more about it and began driving home. On reaching home, I found the lights were on, the door was open, and people were sitting on cots. An elderly person came and said, 'This was the wish of God.' I did not understand. On entering the house, the housemaid began to cry and said, 'Mother has died. She took a little food in the afternoon, complained of a pain in her chest, and lay down on the bed. She called you by name once, remembered God, asked blessings for you, and then she was no more.'

"My mother had died, the same mother who was with me a short time ago, who pulled me out of that fatal trap and brought me to the door of her home. I entered the room. Women were reading something around the cot where my mother's dead body lay wrapped in white cloth. One of the women said, 'The nice woman remembered you before dying.' I screamed, lost my senses and fell down on the ground. I am describing the facts and telling you, when my mother came to the deep forest to help me escape death, she was already dead. You may not believe me. You may be saying in your heart I am telling a lie, but I have no need to convince you of the truth. I know I am telling the truth. When my mother came to me, her dead body was lying on a cot in her house. What is the truth? What is the secret? Neither you nor I will find it. Let the secret remain a secret."

These were the events narrated by Kabiruddin Sahib, his old face bent on his chest, tears flowing from his eyes. He did not want to live in that town any more. His eyes searched for his mother everywhere. He lost two legs because of infection. Yet, he crawled to the mosque five times a day to read the Namaz according to the desire of his mother, although he was rich and had helpers to support him. In the end, he said, "Maybe God might take mercy on me this way, he might forgive me and then Mother might also forgive me."

Details have been omitted from the original text, yet enough material is retained to show the relationship of the mother to her son, especially her unconditional and deep love for him, which resulted in the related events. The following things are notable in this case: Heeria's mother knew telepathically her son's intention to go to the Mafia dealer, that the dealer turned against her son, and that her son would need her help to survive. Her desire to help her son was so strong, she left her body. After leaving her body, his mother wore an astral body, which was exactly the same as her physical body on earth. Her son believed his mother to be alive when she was helping him. His mother's astral form had paranormal powers and she could interact with physical objects.

Case 3[3]

In this case, the experiences of a person who traveled back two hundred years in time, from 1997 to 1797, are described in his own words:

Leaving behind my friend, Dileep, who was still engaged in prayers, I came out of the temple of Sankatamochan Mahavirji at 11 A.M. After a morning of meditation, prayers, and receiving blessed food, I went for a stroll. I was not sure how much longer Dileep would take for his prayers.

A desire to go into the jungle suddenly popped up in me. I had heard that, several hundred years ago, there was a deep forest here. When Goswami Tulsidas established the temple nearly four hundred years ago, the local environment would have been quite different. Thinking about this, I walked deep into the forest, which called me to come further into its depths. Fresh and full of energy, the more I walked, the further I wanted to go. I looked at my watch and it was 11:45. I was under a magic spell coming from the forest and did not feel like going back. It would soon be noon and, thinking of Dileep, I turned around to go back. Suddenly, I heard the sound of lightning as a strong wind began to blow and the trees started shaking. I found it difficult to stay on my feet. This was very unusual weather for October. After running a distance, I suddenly realized I had lost my way back to the temple, but had found the heart of the deep jungle as it existed four hundred years ago.

The windstorm stopped and the sounds of the monkeys and birds became strangely quiet. The sunlight filtering through the trees was red and the air smelled wonderfully pure, which I could not understand. The time was now 12:10. I had become lost in only 10 or 15 minutes. Looking through the dense jungle, I saw a temple. I thought I heard someone call my name. Entering the temple, I discovered a life-sized statue of the goddess Kali with a long thick rosary of flowers around her neck, her red tongue sticking out, her lustrous eyes shining, and a sword and shield in her hands. Fresh flowers were scattered around. A heavy sword hung on the wall. I bowed to the statue of the Mother. Suddenly, I heard a deep voice, "Have you come, my son Ram Prasad?"

Amazed, I thought the statue was speaking. But the voice came from my side, "Look here, I am here." A *sadhu* sat in *padmasana* (lotus posture) on a deerskin in the dimly lit temple.

On asking the sadhu how he knew me, he replied, "Ram Prasad, I have been waiting for you a long time. I knew you would come today. Would I not know you?" I asked for direc-

> tions back to the Sankatamochan temple. The sadhu replied, "Going to the Sankatamochan temple was just an excuse. You had to come here. Today is the full moon, the dark fortnight begins tomorrow."
>
> I was worried now. The sadhu appeared to be a Tantric, six feet tall, strongly built, dark complected, with long and jumbled hair, a red-colored spot on his forehead, big eyes under thick eyebrows, and a rosary of beads and small bones around his neck—even his ears were pierced with small bones. He had iron bangles on his wrists and a deer skin around his waist. I was bewildered, but the power of his personality commanded my obedience.

The sadhu said he was now in the time of the *raja* (king) Chet Singh and Warren Hastings. The year was 1797 and not 1997. The sadhu was performing the rites to attain *trikal siddhi*, which would give him the power to travel into the future; he already had the power to travel into the past. Ram Prasad was going to be sacrificed on the altar to please Mother Kali, and it was for this purpose that he was brought back two hundred years in time. He was commanded by Mother Kali to do this. Ram Prasad saw Anand Narain, the minister of the kingdom, and others wearing clothes in the style of that period. He saw a beautiful young girl named Bhairvi. She was a virgin used by the sadhu for tantric purposes. The sadhu, for a few rupees, had purchased her when she was only a small child.

Ram Prasad was tied to a tree with ropes so that he could not run away. He was forcibly served a special wine, so that he would not create problems for the sadhu. Ram Prasad had lost all hope for his escape from the sadhu's clutches. However, the girl Bhairvi, who was herself a captive, was also looking for an opportunity to escape. She took this chance to kill the sadhu with a sword. Cutting Ram Prasad loose she said, "Run away fool."

As Bhairvi cut the ropes that bound him, a sort of lightning appeared to Ram Prasad. He had the feeling a strong thunderstorm was raging outside. The lamp blew out, and he lost his senses.

"When I opened my eyes," Ram Prasad reports, "I found myself alone in the heart of the forest. Alarmed and astonished, I could not see Bhairvi, the sadhu, nor the minister Anand Narain. There was no temple, only the forest all around. I came out of my trance saved by a miracle. I closed my eyes and saluted Sri Sankatamochan. Undoubtedly, his blessings saved me. I started to run. Fortunately, I was running toward the Sri Sankatamochan temple. The tale continues:

I met Dileep on the way. He appeared confused. He asked me, "Where did you go, Ram Prasad? I have been searching for you since I left the temple."

What could I say? "Brother, I was trapped in a mystery. Somehow, I have been saved: Have you been searching for me since yesterday?"

"Why do you say since yesterday? You were in the temple only a little while ago."

Surprised, I said, "since yesterday, I have been the captive of a Tantric. He was going to sacrifice me on the altar."

"What nonsense are you talking?" Dileep looked at his watch and said, "It is barely ten minutes since I came out of the temple after the prayers."

I also looked at my watch. What a surprise! The day and date were the same as when I left Sri Sankatamochan temple, 12:20 P.M. What is the answer to the mystery? Did I see a dream?

Dileep said, "Where did you get this rosary of red flowers?" I was astonished to find a rosary of red flowers around my neck. The Tantric had placed the rosary around my neck before offering me for sacrifice. With a jerk I threw it away. "Oh, oh, do not throw it away," said Dileep, and he rushed to the place where the rosary had fallen, but he could not find it. "What is this game?" He was so surprised. "It fell in front of me, and now it has disappeared."

Then I understood everything. I said, "That rosary belonged to a time two hundred years back. It has returned there on its own. As long as it touched my body, it could stay."

"I think your mind has gone," Dileep said as he caught my hand. "Let us go. We have to go back to Dharmshala."

"Wait," I said, "Let me see if the temple is on this side." We entered the forest. After a long search, we found an open place. On a heap of broken stones and bricks, we found the remains of a wooden cistern. It was stained with dried blood, how old, we could not know. "The temple was here, my friend," I said. Two hundred years! I did not see a dream. Certainly, that Tantric was a siddha (adept). I traveled back in time two hundred years. But the poor fellow could not complete his sadhana. It was interrupted by his own Bhairvi. "Have some hot tea, maybe then you will come to your senses," I thought. The intoxicating beauty of Bhairvi still moved before my eyes.

This case shows us several things: There is a particular mental condition and environment under which time travel can take place. A long time experienced in antiquity is proportional to a very short time in the present. It is difficult for others not involved to believe in the event—even relatives and close friends treat it as fantasy. An object from the past remains visible as long as it is connected with an object of the present. As soon as that association is broken, the object from the past disappears.

Hundreds of thousands of events of this type have been reported in India for thousands of years. These three cases suggest that the soul possesses all known paranormal powers identified in earlier theoretical findings.

Chapter Eleven

SCIENTIFIC EVIDENCE FOR THE SOUL

The phenomenon of the soul is infinite in nature. For this reason, orthodox science may not be able to accept it, as it cannot be reproduced and tested in the laboratory, although it is a repeating event. In the twentieth century, with the advent of quantum physics, some scientists have come to believe in the physical existence of the soul, especially those who have had their own spiritual experiences. The soul is a quantum entity, and quantum entities can only be experimented upon in their effects, not in their essence, since that essence has no measure.

Four hundred years ago, Descartes divided the world into two clear parts: the scientific and the religious, science being objective and religion subjective. This division has continued. It is the yogi, and others of similar spiritual understanding, who experience the merging of the objective and subjective, when the seer, the seen, and the seeing become one. This is the condition under which one experiences oneself as soul. The level of soul may never be touched by science, even after intergalactic travel becomes a reality, since the infinite may not be encompassed by the finite. However, quantum physics has the potential to discover the effects, and thereby the energy, of the soul. Thus have spiritual masters influenced the physical world of science.

There are two sets of properties that are common to quantum and spiritual entities.[1] The first is a set of four properties:

1. The wave property—A quantum object (for example, a photon) can be in more than one place at the same time.

2. Collapse of the wave—A quantum object cannot be said to manifest in ordinary space-time reality until we observe it as a particle.

3. The quantum leap—A quantum object can cease to exist here and simultaneously appear elsewhere, without passing through the intervening space.

4. Quantum action-at-a-distance—A manifestation of one quantum object, caused by our observation, can simultaneously influence its correlated twin object, no matter how far apart they are.[2]

The second is a set of eight major characteristics:

1. There is no deep reality (from the Copenhagen school of Niels Bohr).

2. Reality is created by observation (a second part of the Copenhagen interpretation, supported by John Wheeler and Fred Wolf).

3. Reality is an undivided wholeness (the view of Walter Heitler, Fritjof Capra, and David Bohem).

4. Reality consists of a steadily increasing number of parallel universes (from Hugh Everett and Paul Davies).

5. The world obeys a nonhuman type of reasoning (in the mathematical logic of George Boole).

6. Neorealism: The world is made of ordinary objects (defended by Albert Einstein, Max Planck, Louis DeBroglie, David Bohm, and Erwin Shrodinger).

7. Consciousness creates reality (from Walter Heitler, Fritz London, Henry Stapp, Eugene Wigner, and John von Neumann—an outlandish theory with distinguished supporters).

8. The world is twofold, consisting of potentials and actualities (Werner Heisenberg).[3]

According to Herbert, there are too many guesses about the nature of quantum entities, and all of them may turn out to be wrong. Still, an answer is worth seeking.[4] And Claire Walker adds yet another question: "Will psychic sense be involved in finding it [the naure of quantum entities], as it is most certainly involved in comprehending the discussion?"[5] This I will endeavor to answer.

I assert once again that science follows spirituality, knowingly or unknowingly, without orthodox science recognizing spirituality. Almost all the points stated above have long been exploited by the major religions. Scientists, having lost their proofs of accepted reality, fall back on spirituality for clues.[6] In my opinion, a day will come when science will merge back into spirituality. Science has always revised its fundamental views—from Galileo and Copernicus to Newton, and from Newton to Einstein—and a further revision is coming by way of quantum theory. As science takes clues and guidance from spirituality, more mysteries will be clarified.

The onus of proof that the soul is quantum does not lie with science, because science has not invented the mystery surrounding the soul. Rather, it is religion that has been preaching its views of the soul from time immemorial. Furthermore, it is not only orthodox science looking for such proof, nor is it spirituality, since spirituality does not need proof, as it has full faith in its own validity. Who else, then, is looking for such proof? Parapsychology is looking, because it wants to act as systematically and objectively as science does. Orthodox science does not yet recognize parapsychology as a science. Our concern is to show that the soul is quantum, and the mode of proof cannot be scientific; rather it will have to depend on inferences and circumstantial evidence.

Several millennia of information are available by way of religion, spirituality, and philosophy.[7] When Lord Jesus Christ says he and his father in heaven are one, he refers to his Higher Self, which is the index of his soul, a permanent element and the mediator between him and God.[8] This indicates the quantum nature of the soul. Likewise, Gautam Buddha's concept of God was the "Clear Light of the Void," which he described as having quantum attributes.

The philosophy of the Upanishads was developed and enriched in the Bhagavad Gita and finally systematized in the *Vivek-Chudamani* (The Crown Jewel of Wisdom) by Shankara in the ninth century A.D. Shankara observes:

> Realize, thou art "That"—Brahman is that which is untouched by the six human infirmities (hunger, thirst, greed, delusion, decay, and death); this is realized in the hearts of yogis (i.e., in *Samadhi*), it cannot be perceived by the senses, it is imperceptible by intellect or mind.
>
> By known logical inferences and by intuition realize thyself as Atman, just as a meaning of a word is understood; the certainty of this truth will be established without doubt just as water (held) in the palm of the hand.[9]

Quantum physicists have several clues to test and establish the further properties of the quantum. In the hierarchy of planes of the universe, when the individual upgrades to the next intuitive plane after the mental plane, even the subtle body is left behind and one lives as the "formless soul," and then still higher properties of the quantum nature are encountered.

My Personal Experience of the Soul

In chapter 10, we compared the study of the ego and Self through dreams by Carl Jung, and the study of Atman or sat-cit-ananda through yoga and meditation by Sri Aurobindo. Carl Jung argued that the ego is the center of the phenomenal world, while Self is the center of the whole psyche. In Jung's model, ego takes care of the outer personality, while Self takes care of the inner personality. According to him, Self is a subset of psyche, which is "whole." Psyche is universal, collective, eternal, unique, a cosmic principle, and existence in and of itself. According to Sri Aurobindo, ego is the center of surface mind, while the psychic being is the center of the subliminal. He divided self into two parts—jivatma and psychic being. While the jivatma is a portion of the divine, it is universal as well as individual, and the psychic being narrows to mere individuality. The Sufi saint Meher Baba also said that, when the unconscious is brought to the conscious, it is the realization of the eternal element that can be called soul. Orthodox religions call it God.[10] Thus, the psyche of Jung, the Atman of Sri Aurobindo, and the soul of Meher Baba are all quantum in nature, having many more properties than quantum theory has discovered so far.

The three real-life cases presented in chapter 10 demonstrate the soul's quantum properties. Innumerable yogis from all over the world have reported being on higher realms, in their soul bodies, exhibiting quantum properties.[11] Here, I will give a brief account of one of my own experiences, which I had soon after witnessing my own awakening of kundalini:[12]

> I found myself standing in front of a translucent fortress with a canal of clear blue water running through its center. There were gates on both sides. People moved slowly in a queue, entering through the left gate and coming out the right. People were in the form of invisible points, having semi-circular auras of light around them; the aura was what could be seen or recognized. I was floating in the sky and could see three people on the ground

> talking to each other. After a while, I received mental instructions from one of the three telling me to move forward. The instant I decided to move, I found myself in another location with green meadows, trees, and lakes, with a pleasing bluish-green light illuminating the area, although the light had no obvious source.
>
> I was fully conscious of being there. Suddenly, I thought to look at my body. I saw that I had no hands, legs, or even a physical body. I was simply there. I could see in all directions simultaneously. Filled with happiness and bliss, I was slowly moving toward a large, clear-blue river, so wide it looked like an ocean. Traveling in a straight line, I was having a wonderful experience until I crossed the water and came to the opposite bank. From there, a group of mountains rose up, but as soon as I approached them, I awoke in my physical body, back on earth.

I had many such dreams, visions, and out-of-body experiences, especially in 1987. I can confirm by my own experiences that the soul is an invisible point of existence. It can disappear at one place and appear simultaneously at another by way of thought. It can communicate with other souls telepathically and we recognize each other through intuition. These are quantum properties possessed by the soul. Perhaps other properties of a quantum nature can be discovered through a review of other experiences—my own and others.

Analyzing Reality

There is overwhelming evidence that Atman, or soul, is fully quantum in nature, not just a nonlocal aspect of human beings. Spiritual experience, psychology, parapsychology, and individual case studies have all testified to this fact. However, this proof is based on circumstantial evidence and intuition, not on controlled laboratory tests, because the soul can only be observed through intuition or spiritual experience. In fact, the burden must be on quantum physics to prove that it has the properties of the soul, and not the other way around.

But alas, scientists, even though they may follow guidance from spirituality, knowingly or unknowingly, usually do not pay it enough respect. For this reason, despite the tremendous achievements made by science, technology brings no peace to the hearts of humanity. Even though galactic colonization appears a realistic prospect in the future, as well as other feats like teleportation of a person from one site to another, competition, fear, jealousy, and unhappiness will still prevail in society. This is because spiritual realities are not respected. People are turning to meditation and looking inward, not by choice, but by compulsion. In my opinion, the best answer is a synthesis of science and spirituality, since both are necessary for evolution and the all-around development of humanity. This is happening now.

The second part of the Copenhagen interpretation of Niels Bohr's work suggests that reality is being created by observation. This appears to be correct, in that consciousness creates reality. Remember the bottle that illustrated the seven divisions of the universe? Just as that bottle will appear to have only stones if the viewer has only a solid physical viewpoint of observation, it will have only water if the observer has only the test for liquid in his mind.

Everything in the world exists, and perceived reality will depend on the consciousness of the observer. A man sitting in a restaurant simultaneously eating food and reading a book may not be aware of the food's taste if he is deeply absorbed in the book. A car horn in the street, the smell of roses in the garden, and the bite of a mosquito may be nonrealities for him, because he is not conscious of them, although they exist. Suddenly, a loud horn may distract his attention from reading and eating, and the noise becomes the only reality he perceives. Similarly, a worldly person only lives and assumes the reality of the perceived physical world. A man practicing contemplative meditation may be living in the reality of the astral world, although the physical world exists around him. Likewise, a saint or a prophet may be living the reality of the soul's cosmic bliss, although both the physical and astral worlds are around and available to him. Even in the affairs of the world, someone with a happy disposition will find happiness in the world, since beauty attracts his attention. A person with a gloomy disposition may conclude that everyone in the world should be unhappy, since what is wrong, in his judgment, attracts his attention. The world appears as we judge it to be.

I do not fully agree with the first part of the Copenhagen interpretation, that there is no deep reality, since knowledge is endless and there will always be one more step to discover. God is infinite, and Hinduism says that, even if the whole surface of the world were used as paper and the whole ocean were used as ink, the total attributes of God cannot be listed. Niels Bohr may have been right if his concern was with the realities known to humanity so far, but he is wrong if he talks about realities in general, since the unknown is infinite while the known is definitely finite.

The third point of the Copenhagen interpretation claims that reality is an undivided wholeness. All religions have been teaching this, and this is also the spiritual experience of saints and Self-realized persons. The fourth point, however, requires careful assessment. Reality has an infinite number of parallel universes. This is true in the sense that, every day, a new universe is being discovered. But the total number of universes as a whole may already be created. We may only come to know this truth gradually. A new star being discovered adds to the library of physics, but there may be an infinite number not known to physics. However, some religions hold that new universes are created and destroyed continuously by the ultimate reality, so there may not be a fixed number in this regard. Spiritual experience suggests all things are in a constant state of change.

The fifth point of the interpretation is seemingly correct. Human reasoning is finite (as the whole of reality is not known to us) and laws beyond human understanding govern the universe. Paranormal events such as telepathy, telekinesis, precognition, and levitation are perhaps beyond human understanding. Maharaj Nisargadatta also makes an interesting point when he says, "The part of you that thinks of itself as human, is not human."[13] Likewise the sixth point, that the world is made of ordinary objects, may be true as far as the physical world is concerned. Underlying this, however, is the question of what is the fundamental composition of ordinary objects.

That consciousness creates reality (the seventh point) is valid and covered earlier, as is the eighth point, that the world is twofold, consisting of potential and actual. In fact, ultimate reality has two divisions, as pointed out by spiritual reasoning: the potential and the kinetic. Potential energy corresponds to the static state of saccidananda, the sleeping storehouse, and kinetic energy is responsible for the creation of the universe and its objects, Hinduism gives it the name kundalini.

However, psychic senses will certainly be involved in finding the answers related to quantum reality. When one wants to have direct intuitive knowledge, then one may speak, if one wants to do that, with an experienced authority and seek that experience for oneself. Otherwise, one will draw inferences after much research and still not have confidence. That is why Herbert said that all eight views on quantum reality that make up the Copenhagen interpretation could be wrong. This uncertainty is due to most scientists not experiencing reality intuitively; they are postulating theoretically, hence the necessity of experiencing psychic sense.

The views proposed of quantum reality are not in conflict with each other; rather they appear to exist simultaneously. They are guesses based on observation. The details of life on the seven divisions of the universe, as presented in chapter 5, can give constructive ideas for research to physicists and other scientists in general. However, there are many properties found to be associated with quantum objects. I would suggest that, parallel to the soul, a quantum object may have the following properties:

1. Self-existence: Quantum objects are the most basic unit of existence and not the product or result of any process. Every other thing is made of it; there is nothing that is not made of it in the universe. Hence a quantum object, as consciousness, has no cause and is self-existent. This property is suggested by the "perennial philosophy," stating that God is the only doer. Its kinetic energy, which is of a quantum nature, is the creator of everything existing in the universe (see, for example, the Bhagavad Gita). In the Bible, we read, "In the beginning was the Word, and the Word was with God, and the Word was God, everything that was created was created by the Word, there is nothing that was not created by the Word." (John 1:1–5) Thus, the unstruck sound, or Word, is the quantum energy of God.

2. Fundamentality: The basis of existence is the quantum object.

3. Omnipresence: The first and third properties named by the physicist Amit Goswami combined in one property mean that a quantum object can be in more than one place at the same time, and may cease to exist at one place and reappear at another without going through the intervening space. This is the property of omnipresence attributed to God alone. But, since soul is contained in or one with God, the soul also has this property. The second from the lowest in the hierarchy of seven divisions of the universe shares this property. This may explain how you see dead relatives around you a few days before your death. On the astral plane, the moment you think of being with someone, you are with them, instantly. These are quantum properties. This property is also present on the mental plane, whose lower division is called heaven in orthodox religion, since the mental body is composed of yet more refined vibrations than those of the astral plane. Hence, the mental body, also a quantum object, is omnipresent.

4. Omnipotence: Astral beings can instantaneously create the food they enjoy just by thinking about it—or, for that matter, clothes, vehicles, houses, flowers, or any other thing they wish. They can call any person to them, go anywhere within the astral and physical planes, and can, in fact, create a world of their own. Are these not properties of omnipotence? Beings on each of the successive planes have this faculty increasingly more defined. The tremendous energy produced by the disintegration of an atom is given by the formula: $E = mc^2$, which is an example of action at the quantum level.[14] More uses of quantum energy are being developed by science. Ultimately, I believe physics will conclude that a quantum object is omnipotent.

5. Omniscience: Beings on the astral and higher planes have the capability of instantly knowing what is happening anywhere on their plane or on any plane lower than theirs. Thus a being on the mental plane, the plane known as the abode of saints and seers, will know instantly about anything happening anywhere on the mental, astral, or physical planes. The quantum nature of beings belonging to the mental plane is more free of ego-pollution. Thus God, who is higher than the highest imaginable plane, is, no doubt, fully omniscient. The degree of omniscience increases from the lowest plane upward in a gradual manner. This suggests that quantum objects are omniscient as well.

6. Identification: Each of us contains the soul's infinite potential. But we are confined by our belief in the narrow limitations of the physical body, which most of us consider as our only reality. Thus, our identification with the body limits us. While driving a car, we can move faster by utilizing the properties of the car. And when flying in an airplane, we move faster still, as we have aligned ourselves with the properties of the airplane. If, however, we can identify with the Self within, or the soul, we can move with the speed of thought, because then, as souls, we have reunited with our quantum properties. Utilizing a car or an airplane is easy, while identification with the soul is difficult, but not impossible. This identification with soul is called "individuation" by Jung, "transformation" by Sri Aurobindo, and Self-realization by most saints and some orthodox religions. Regardless of one's spiritual faith or religion, the process of identification with soul awakens a sleeping power within the individual. Or perhaps it is correct to say that the awakening of this sleeping power brings identification with the soul. The most popular name for this sleeping power is kundalini. In the next section, we will explore various methods of transformation and be introduced to this power.

PART THREE

Unity in Diverse Approaches

Chapter Twelve

INNER REALITY AND INDIVIDUATION

Sri Aurobindo divided inner reality into the following planes of existence, from highest to lowest:

1. **Existence:** consciousness and bliss (sat-chit-ananda), Brahman.

2. **Supermind:** real center of the totality of our being.

3. **Overmind:** direct descent of the supermind, intermediary between knowledge and ignorance, "a superconscient cosmic Mind in direct contact with the Supramental Truth-Consciousness, an original intensity determinant of all movements below it and all mental energies."[1]

4. **Intuition:** a special formation of the overmind, a sudden and intimate flash of self-existent knowledge, truth-vision, truth-thought, truth-sense, truth-feeling, truth-action.

5. **Illumined mind:** vision, truth-sight, and truth-light; "It illumines the thought-mind with a direct vision and inspiration, brings a spiritual light and energy into its feelings and emotion."[2]

6. **Higher mind:** just above the conscious mind, "spiritual parent of our conceptive mental identity . . . an unitarian sense of being with a powerful multiple dynamisation capable of the formation of a multitude of aspects of knowledge, ways of action, forms and significances of becoming, in all of which there is a spontaneous inherent knowledge."[3]

7. Conscious mind: pure consciousness descended from above, mixed with ignorance, its purity, comprehension, and force gradually diminished. Conversely, when this evolution takes place, individual consciousness passes from the lowest level of conscious mind to the higher mind, and is refined to a higher purity, comprehension, and force in the ascending order of the planes.

One can compare these seven planes with the seven planes of Table 1.

Divine	Saccidananda
Monadic	Supermind
Atmic	Overmind
Intuitional	Intuition
Mental	Illumined mind
Astral	Higher mind
Physical	Conscious mind

A natural hypothesis for the parallels between the two models would be that, as the consciousness of the individual becomes higher, he or she belongs to the next plane. Thus, an individual with only a conscious mind is a person of the physical type living on the physical plane. A person with a higher mind belongs to the astral plane, although living on the physical plane. This class may include people who exhibit paranormal powers while living on earth. A person possessing an illuminated mind belongs to the mental plane, yet lives on earth. One can proceed like this into the uttermost division.

According to Sri Aurobindo, the various divisions, which correspond to the energy substance of the spirit, do exist and there are worlds corresponding to all of them. Saccidananda (sat-chit-ananda) is itself the potential energy, while its kinetic energy substance, which he calls consciousness force, assumes different forms of energy on different planes of existence. Thus, it is the psychic energy of the psychic being, mental energy of the mind, vital energy of the vital body, and physical energy of the physical body. With its descent into the lower planes, the subtlety of this force converts into grossness and loses its purity, comprehension, and universality. It is the will of the transcendent spirit, called *tapas*, that brings the manifestation of the individual onto various planes. However, in the inner subtle form, the force is universal, while in the outer gross form, it is individual, with all appropriate limitations. The inner being is relatively unchangeable and "knows itself in time, past, present and future, all at once with an undivided view, which embraces all the mobile experiences of the Time-self."[4] In the opinion of Sri Aurobindo, desire is the deformation of will in the dominant bodily life and physical mind. "The essential turn of the soul to possession and enjoyment consists of a will to delight."[5] Thus, delight is the pure form of requirement by the soul, while desire is the deformation of this requirement, which manifests in the form of worldly pleasures.

Spiritual Dynamics and Kundalini

The inner reality has two poles: the lower, which is exterior, instinctive, surface, or conscious mind, and the higher, which is interior, archetypal Self, or spiritual psychic being, according to Jung and Sri Aurobindo, respectively. The exterior center is personal, individualistic, and a product of the outside world, while the interior center is transpersonal, universal, and fundamental. The exterior center is formed by the dynamics of the interior center, on the pattern of the latter. "But there is another side of the structure, which Jung makes wild guesses at, while Sri Aurobindo presents a well thought view. It is the vertical elevation of the inner reality."[6] The inner reality elevated vertically has a height; Sri Aurobindo calls it "Self," which is a fundamental entity in itself, represented by the psychic being. Jung, on the other hand, considers Self to be only a part of the psyche.

The words *energy* and *force* have been used by both thinkers as both the physical and spiritual parts of the reality. However, Jung calls the intuitive side energy and the physical side force, while Sri Aurobindo calls the spiritual principle of creation consciousness force and the evolutionary process energy. Jung has extended the scientific concept of energy into the field of inner reality, with the difference that quantity is replaced by quality. Sri Aurobindo, on the other hand, makes use of the term *force*. According to him, consciousness is inherent in the consciousness force, wherever it manifests itself. Moreover, before manifestation, the force undergoes a process of involution. It is the pull of the Self exerted on its own involved forms, or the psychic being, that results in the manifestation of various psychic forces during evolution.

Jung also has invariably maintained that consciousness is a part of the unconscious, and hence consciousness and energy are the two fundamentals of the inner reality. Then, according to him, it is the residue of experiences by the organism that forms the collective unconscious and the psyche. These experiences, which would have been conscious at the time of their taking place within the organism, are now lying dormant in the unconscious and constantly trying to reemerge. Jung says this attempt at reemergence is the main source of psychic energy, while, according to Sri Aurobindo, the involution began from the monotheistic saccidananda. Finally, Jung considers the psychic force to be emerging from the tension between the instinctive and the archetypal parts of the psyche, while Sri Aurobindo claims it is the pull of the Self on the psychic being that results in the formation of the psychic force.

According to Sri Aurobindo, the spiritual dynamic is the consciousness force, which is inherent in saccidananda as the source of all creation. The same force is inherent in the Self and its representative psychic being, which emanated from saccidananda. The consciousness force, which may now be called the psychic force, goes into hiding behind the veil of the mental, vital, and physical, and then lies dormant. This situation has its parallel in Jung's findings when he says that the residue of experiences is lying dormant in the unconscious.

The dormant consciousness force of Sri Aurobindo or the residue of experiences of Jung is the kundalini of Tantra lying dormant in the root center called *muladhara* chakra. The upward surge of the psychic force with the evolution of the world is the rising and ascension of the kundalini force in Tantra. As the psychic force in evolution passes through the physical, vital, mental, and supramental planes, the kundalini force passes through the various centers of energy, called chakras. It is important to note that, corresponding to the seven planes of the universe of Sri Aurobindo, there are also seven chakras through which kundalini has to pass. They are the *mooladhara, swadhishthan, manipura, anahata, vishuddhi, ajna,* and *sahasrara* chakras, in ascending order. Here, one can see the truth of the statement, "as above, so below." There are seven planes in the universe, and there are seven chakras in the human body, from the base of the spine to the crown of the head. As kundalini rises from the first to the seventh center, the individual consciousness rises from the lowest physical plane to the highest plane of saccidananda. Humans are a replica of the universe, and so the macro-process of the universe is also going on as a micro-process in the human body.

Orthodox religion teaches that the soul is a universal entity and it is not concerned with the individualistic side of the person. But both Sri Aurobindo and Jung believe that soul is both individual and universal. According to them, external individual behavior is connected with the core of the subconscient, or unconscious. Universality, according to Jung, is due to the collective unconscious, developing since the beginning of organic life. Hence, all humans inherit a "common property." Sri Aurobindo said universality is the essential attribute of all souls, since they have emanated from the same saccidananda. The soul is camouflaged by the ego; the moment ego is eradicated, the psychic being, which is the representative of the soul, displays universality. This is one point where the two geniuses agree with each other, yet differ from the orthodox belief.

Sri Aurobindo believed we live simultaneously on the various planes—physical, vital, mental, and supramental. Correspondingly, our supramental, mental, and vital growth is transmitted through the physical body, along with certain hereditary traits from birth to birth. This is because of the embodiment of psychic traits in the mental, mental in the vital, and vital in the physical. We have observed the causal body on its downward journey gather the mental, astral, and physical bodies in that order. This complete embodiment is called the personality of the individual. Thus, according to Sri Aurobindo, the total preformed personality, along with certain hereditary traits, is transmitted to the individual at the time of rebirth. He was very clear and confident about this theory. Jung, on the other hand, believed in heredity being the sole carrier and was puzzled by the idea that spirituality and universality could be transmitted through human genes, as they are only physical in nature. Heredity, in Sri Aurobindo's view, was only a subordinate factor. On the other hand, both researchers believed in the simultaneous existence of the physical and the psychic, without either of them depending on the other, as a set of coordinate entities. However, about the ultimate nature of the inner reality Jung was dubious and speculative, while Sri Aurobindo was certain. Sri Aurobindo believed matter and psychic being were the manifestations of existence and delight, of saccidananda itself.

The Method of Individuation

According to the models of both Jung and Sri Aurobindo, the whole has been separated into pieces and this is the cause of human misery. Reintegration is, therefore, required. Instinctive divisiveness can be overcome by the integration of the ego, resulting in the stability of humanity in the world. The ego has taken over the conscious mind and is overplaying its role. Egoistic divisiveness can be integrated, and conscious and unconscious combined into one whole psyche. Self is the higher principle, according to Jung, that can bring about this integration by the process called "individuation."

Jung's patients, suffering from diseases like neurosis and schizophrenia, dreamed of circular images such as coiled snakes when they were cured. Such images are called *mandalas* and Jung regarded them as stronger archetypes than *anima* or *animus* images of any kind. Since mandalas appeared in the state of unconsciousness and reconciled the problems of the ego, Jung said that they signified the wholeness of the Self. Individuation is, therefore, "the process by which a person becomes a psychological 'in-dividual,' that is, a separate indivisible unity or 'whole'."[7]

According to Dr. Chaturbhuj Sahai:

> When the ray of Brahmic power descends down from its abode for creation, it stops at five places in the universe and makes the mandala. . . . In these mandalas five elements—earth, water, fire, air and akasha—are present in variations, but one of the elements remains prominent as compared to the remaining others. Because of the presence of these five elements, every mandala has a distinct form, color, work, sound and light. Light and sound are one, but because of the interactions of the elements, it appears to be having different forms. Removal of these variations and bringing oneself to the unity in one is called "practice" or "sadhana." The same ray is called Kundalini by yogis, surati by saints and "rooh-va-tavajjah" by the Moslem Sufis.[8]

The conscious mind functions in the waking state, while the unconscious mind functions in the sleeping state. Accordingly, we all are dual personalities. And again, the unconscious has a personal and an impersonal unconscious, formed by the experiences of the individual and the race, respectively. The ego can take care of either the conscious or the unconscious because of their divergent nature. Hence, some unconscious formations cannot be taken care of by the ego, and this is one cause of the division of personality. The alternating of another personality with the normal one leads the individual to a pathological state. A large number of such cases are found in the West today. The balancing of such states requires the unification of the conscious and unconscious. Analyzing the dreams of his patients, Jung found a point located in the psyche that could unite the divergent elements. But "as opposites never unite at their own level, a supraordinate 'third' is always required for the two parts to come together."[9]

Since a total alteration of the ego may result in a chaotic condition, Jung recommends the maintenance of a strong ego that can withstand the impact of the unconscious, and a close contact of the strong ego with the Self, allowing the former to realize its subordinate position. Assimilating more and more of the contents of the unconscious by the ego may develop this contact. This serves two purposes: bringing the unconscious into the conscious, and shifting the ego from its place, bringing a change in attitude. Gradually, the personality is enlarged by the unconscious and the ego is reduced. The uncompromising and stubborn attitude of the ego shifts and accepts subordination to the stronger factor, namely to the new totality-figure, Self.[10] However, there is a danger that, if the ego is very strong, it may impersonate as Self after the shifting of the center. History is full with such people who exercise ego in the name of the Self and engage themselves in selfish acts. Another problem can arise if the ego is weak and unable to withstand the impact of the unconscious. In such a case, the ego goes back to "preconscious wholeness" and the confusion derails the person from individuation. The ego becomes weakened and "gives rise to a nebulous superman with a puffed-up ego and a deflated self."[11] Accordingly, Jung advises the maintenance of ego while searching for the Self, letting the former realize its relatively lower position in comparison with the latter in a natural way.

Anima and animus are the contents of the unconscious corresponding to the feminine and masculine parts, into which the ego is divided. Sentimental and intellectual aspects of the consciousness represent these feminine and masculine aspects of the ego. Thus, man's consciousness is dominated by intellectuality and his unconscious by anima; the woman's consciousness is dominated by emotionality and her unconscious by animus. Whenever a balance is reached between the female and male aspects of this nature, the woman or man becomes androgynous and individuation is achieved.[12]

Involvement in emotional ties loosens the grip of objectivity in life. Thus, emotional ties prove to be a big obstacle to individuation. According to Jung, "If we can visualize an undercurrent of objectivity, even behind the emotional ties, and disengage from the subjective projections, we would be on a sure way to individuation. The person, who has attained psychic wholeness, is immune to emotional disturbance and subjective bias."[13]

On achieving wholeness as a fruit of individuation, the person may see spiritual objects or beings in dreams and visions, which may indicate the completion of the process. Jung does not like to give a spiritual status to the person at this stage; however, he considers such an evolved person to be an ideal for society and the development of civilization as a whole. "Through the process of individuation, an individual first returns to the 'fundamental facts of his own being' and thus becomes 'conscious of his distinctiveness'."[14]

Jung considered humans to be of two types: extrovert and introvert. He held that human nature has four functions: sensation, feeling, thinking, and intuition. In combination, there are eight kinds of people, ranging from sensing extrovert to intuiting introvert. An extrovert is dominated by objective considerations, and sees subjectivity as a disturbing element. An introvert feels an object is only a representative of the subjective content and holds that Self and subjective psychological processes are above any object. Normally, both mechanisms work in an individual corresponding to outer circumstances and inner dispositions. Unbalance brings a pathological state, and ideal balance is a rare thing. Jung prefers introversion to extroversion, since too much interest in the objective world finally leads to ego-centrism and the person may exhibit behavior ranging from childish selfishness to wickedness and brutality. An introvert may also develop an incorrect attitude, but it is not as common. In a neurotic person, for example, the ego may start functioning as Self due to excessive subjectivity, which can bring chaotic results.

Chapter Thirteen

TRANSFORMATION AND COMPARISON

Sri Aurobindo divides evolution into three stages: ascension, integration, and *tapas*. Ascension is a radical development from one grade of consciousness to another—for example, from physical to vital, or from vital to mental. Integration is a consolidation of the quantitative change in one particular grade. Tapas is the concentration of a particular stage into the formation of the Self. Even after millions of years of evolution, Sri Aurobindo says, people are not yet free from physical, vital, and instinctive constraints.

> Physical incapabilities, habitual constraints, instinctive compulsions, emotional pressures and ideological conflicts pull him down or keep him in conflict. . . . Arrival of seer after seer, sage after sage, prophet after prophet is, at least, demonstrative of the will of man to formulate and reformulate certain basic ideas so as to make them more and more effective in improving the behavior of man. . . . The ideals of Buddha, Christ and others have been institutionalized. After the initial impact, of course, all institutions have degenerated into dead structures.[1]

The reason, he finds, is that inner reality is made of many inner states corresponding to various planes that actually exist and are connected organically with one another. One therefore needs an integral transformation of the complete set of states, not only the conscious mind, which is only the outer state. Accordingly, he observes:

> At present the Soul or Self in us, intent on individualization in Nature, allows itself to be confused with the idea of the ego . . . (hence) a deliverance from the limiting and imprisoning ego is the first elementary step towards the being of the gnosis. However, the ego is our rock of safety against the cosmic and the infinite. It is therefore small wonder that no sooner one gets rid of the ego one finds oneself "dissolved in a vast impersonality." This is by no means a welcome state of things. It does not only stand on the brink of eclipsing the individuality of the person but also makes him bereft of the "key to an ordered dynamism of action."[2]

Thus, on the one hand, the ego is to be eradicated and, on the other, it is required to save our individuality. So what is the way out of this paradoxical situation? One way out is to shift the center of personality from the ego to the Self. But the Self is not directly available; it can only be approached through its representative psychic being, itself trying to reach its originator transcendent Self. Hence the shift has to be in two stages—from ego to psychic being, and from psychic being to Self. The following steps are suggested:

1. Relieve the physical of its sense of limitation. This is achieved by the realization that the physical is nothing but the concretized form of the vital. This leads to the expansion of the physical into the vital.

2. Relieve the vital of its characteristic feature, desire. Desires have caused the formation of instincts. Furthermore, unfulfilled and suppressed desires have gone into the subconscious and formed a screen that is strong enough to appear erroneously as the center of personality. This screen is nothing but another form of ego.

3. Pierce the mental sheath, the result of selective outer experiences, and go behind it. Direct entry of the conscious mind into the subconscious is not recommended, however, since "it would plunge us into incoherence, sleep, a dull trance or a comatose torpor."[3] One should enter first into the subliminal or ascend the superconscient. This requires one to purify the surface nature and then explore all regions of the subconscient—physical, vital, and mental—through the enhanced power of one's knowledge. Suppression of the subconscious will not create the desired effect. One requires the illumination of the whole subconscious by a higher consciousness. Any part not transformed can nullify the transcendence. "Only when no part of the consciousness makes any response to the forces of the lower plane can the victory and transformation be absolutely com-

plete."[4] This establishes the individual fully in the psychic being and the subliminal as a whole.

Thus, psychic transformation is effected in two phases: purification of the physical sublimation of the vital and enlargement of the surface mind, and enlightenment of the subconscious by a higher consciousness of the psyche. The physical and the vital are transformed and the mind is universalized by illumination. Weaknesses are strengthened and life is charged with the consciousness force.The outer personality extends itself beyond its body and inhabits the body of the universe.

According to Sri Aurobindo, an important principle of the world is duality. He has defined the two poles as follows:

1. Outer physical (encompasses the everyday material world)/Inner physical (provides the substance not only of our physical but vital and mental sheaths).

2. Outer vital (involved in the physical body, bound by its past evolution in matter)/Inner vital (a subliminal force of life not confined between the narrow boundaries of vital being that we ignorantly take for our real existence).

3. Surface mind (our expressed evolutionary ego, the superficial mentality created by us in our emergence out of matter)/Subliminal mind (not hampered by our actual mental life and its strict limitations, the true mental being behind the superficial mental personality we mistake for ourselves).

4. Surface desire-soul (works in vital cravings, emotional aesthetic faculty, and mental seeking for power, knowledge, and happiness)/Subliminal psychic entity (pure power of light, love, joy; a refined essence of being, our true soul behind the outer form of psychic existence).

5. Complex of outer physical, vital, mental, and psychic (individuality that is operative in ordinary life with the ego as its central principle)/Complex of the inner physical, vital, mental, and psychic (characterized as our larger true individuality, which is psychic and touches our universality, the goal of our evolution in consciousness.[5]

Sri Aurobindo defined two systems of existence: concentric and vertical. The psychic being is the center of the concentric inner reality only, while the totality of our being, composed of several vertically superimposed planes, is circumscribed by the superconscient. His comparison can be interpreted as follows:

Egoistic consciousness	a flickering lamp
Psychic consciousness	moon
Superconscient	sun

It is the superconscient that illuminates the whole system. The "mind's formulas dissolve in a white flame of direct inner experience" when one reaches the supramental consciousness. The superconscient "may form itself as a spiritualized intuitive light and power in the mind itself." These are the signs of gnostic or spiritual transformation. Psychic transformation is achieved by concentration on the heart center with love, *bhakti* (devotion), and surrender, which remove the soul or psychic being from hiding to govern the body, life, and mind, and "open them fully to the Divine."[6] Sri Aurobindo tells us:

> The power of concentration above the head is to bring peace, silence, liberation from the body sense, the identification with mind and life and open the way for the lower (mental, vital, physical) consciousness to rise up to meet the higher consciousness above and for the powers of the higher (spiritual nature) consciousness to descend into mind, life and body. . . . For making these transformations possible, what we have to do is to take hold of the "exterior being" and make it an instrument of the Divine. Remembering the Divine constantly and at the same time by opening our nature upward to facilitate the descent can do this. This is to be supplemented by "constant faith and reliance on the Mother."[7]

The type of person is determined by the principle that lies at the center of the personality. The three types whose consciousness is related to the surface mind are described by Sri Aurobindo, in ascending order of consciousness, as follows:

1. Physical man: mainly occupied with corporeal life and habitual needs, impulses, life habits, mind habits, body habits; looking very little or not at all beyond that, subordinating and restricting all other tendencies and possibilities to that narrow view.

2. Vital man: concerned with self-affirmation, self-aggrandizement, self-enlargement, and satisfaction of ambition, passion, impulse, and desire; preoccupied with the claims of his ego, domination, power, excitement, battle and struggle, inner and outer adventure.

3. Mental man: tends to subordinate all to his mental self-expression, mental aims, mental interests, or to a mental idea or ideal, to the rest of his being; philosophers, thinkers, scientists, intellectual creators, idealists, and dreamers are representatives of this type.

None of these, however, represent the final stage, represented by the consciousness related to the inner physical, inner vital, and inner mental, which is much more comprehensive and powerful. When the subliminal is transcended, the spiritual is born. The fourth type, spiritual man, is nature's continuation after first creating "the spiritual sage, seer, prophet, God-lover, Yogi, Gnostic, Sufi, mystic," even after having already evolved "the mental creator, thinker, sage, prophet of an ideal, the self-controlled, self-disciplined, harmonized human being."[8]

It is worthwhile to note that Jung and Sri Aurobindo, having divergent approaches and having never met each other, arrive at similar conclusions. Jung is an empirical psychologist, while Sri Aurobindo is a yogi. Jung sees the inadequacy of ego to represent both the conscious and unconscious at the same time. He feels this is the cause of the division of personality and suggests the ego should be made strong and, at the same time, should be made to realize its subordinate position to Self. For Jung, ego and the Self should work simultaneously. Sri Aurobindo, on the other hand, does not recommend strengthening the ego. He suggests its complete replacement by the psychic being first, and then by the Self. Jung considers the ego to be the only representative of consciousness, and thus it is essential for him. However, for Sri Aurobindo, ego is only a stepping-stone that becomes obsolete. Self, for Jung, is only an archetypal representative of the inner reality. Consequently, although it may serve the purpose of integrating the disparate elements of the personality, it has no permanent base or strength to give to the personality of the individual. On the other hand, "as the Self in Sri Aurobindo's system is the Absolute, merely individualized, it is potent enough to give everything required to the personality, i.e., energy, unity, stability and purpose."[9]

Jung advises a duel between the conscious and the unconscious, which, according to him, is the way for the two to reconcile and finally harmonize. Sri Aurobindo's method is to subordinate the outer through the inner and thus become enlightened. Although both want the individual to come out of confinement, Jung's individuation does not come into Sri Aurobindo's purpose to illuminate the lower consciousness by a higher one and become governed by the law of hierarchy. Thus, he wants people to realize that the physical is under the vital, the vital under the mental, and the outer physical-vital-mental under the inner physical-vital-mental. This entire grouping is under the psychic, and the psychic is under the spiritual. Jung's individuation envisages a dualism between the objective and the subjective, or matter and spirit, that may finally churn out a higher principle. Sri Aurobindo's transformation believes that everything has descended from saccidananda, the eternal higher principle already in existence. "From this view point, the Jungian individuation theory is a pointer, a stepping-stone to the Aurobindonian transformation."[10]

The congruence of their findings can be seen as follows. The predecessors of Jung explained the division of personality by accounting for just one personality, but Jung worked for their integration by a superior and universal personality represented by the Self. Similarly, the predecessors of Sri Aurobindo have shown the way of recognizing one path only—this being the path of devotion, selfless service, or knowledge—and showing its relevance to the supreme being. Sri Aurobindo assigned a proper place to each one of them and has shown the path of transformation and integration of each one with the next higher one, finally leading to a well-balanced personality and recognition of a supreme being. Both thinkers have worked on the principle of unifying all the factors involved in the process, rather than choosing one and rejecting all others. Both individuation and transformation represent all parts of the personality and aim at unification leading to the wholeness of the individual. Furthermore, each of them has divided the individual into eight types. This division agrees on all points, except Sri Aurobindo's last type, which belongs to his classification system exclusively:

Jung	Sri Aurobindo
Extrovert sensational	Outer physical
Extrovert feeling	Outer vital
Extrovert thinking	Outer mental
Introvert sensational	Inner physical
Introvert feeling	Inner vital
Introvert thinking	Inner mental
Intuitive extrovert/Introvert (both types)	Subliminal
(Outside the scope of Jungian classification)	Spiritual type

One can see that all seven types of Jung correspond to the first seven types of Sri Aurobindo, while the eighth type of the latter is outside Jung's classification system. Another point of difference is that Jung considers his types to be abnormal persons because of the imbalance in different parts of the personality. This is not a happy conclusion, since it means a majority of people on earth are abnormal. Sri Aurobindo, on the other hand, considers his types to be dominated by one aspect relative to others on the ladder of evolution. On assimilating each lower aspect into the next higher, one reaches the finale in the spiritual type. This appears to be a clearer approach. However, Jung's preference of the introvert over the extrovert is a welcome departure from the usual Western thought, which gives preference to extroverts for success in the physical world. Clearly, introversion is a higher step toward evolution.

Both Jung and Sri Aurobindo advocate that the soul is both individual and universal. The physical and psychic exist simultaneously. Matter and psychic being are manifestations of the existent and delight parts of God. Delight is the pure form of existence by the soul, while desire is the corruption of this state, manifesting in the form of worldly pleasures.

The dormant consciousness force of Sri Aurobindo, or the residue of experience of Jung, is the kundalini of Tantra that lies dormant in the *mooladhara* chakra. Its rising through the seven centers takes consciousness to seven levels. In other words, the ray of Brahmic power that descends from its abode for creation is called kundalini by yogis, *surati* by saints, and *rooh-va-tavajjah* by Muslim Sufis.

According to Jung, psyche has two parts: unconscious and conscious. Self is the center of the unconscious; the ego is the center of the conscious. The whole is divided into two pieces: the ego and the Self. Their integration is the individuation that Jung says makes the individual whole. This is achieved when the female and male aspects of nature are balanced. On achieving wholeness as a fruit of individuation, the person may see things in dreams and visions, such as religious or cherished human personalities, crosses, circles, or other symbols with personal significance that may indicate the completion of the process.

Conscious and unconscious, when viewed as opposites, can never unite; a supraordinate third party is required to reunite the two parts. By assimilating more and more of the contents of the unconscious into the conscious, two purposes are served. The unconscious is brought into consciousness, the Self is enlarged, and the ego reduced. Ego reduction is a benefit, as fewer desires are created and acted on, allowing serenity.

Sri Aurobindo believed evolution takes place in three stages: ascension, integration, and tapas. Ascension is a radical development from one grade of consciousness to another. Ego is to be tamed and, at the same time, required to save our individuality. The shift from ego to Self is accomplished in two stages: from ego to psychic being, and from psychic being to Self. Self is the absolute, merely individualized and still potent. The superconscient illuminates the whole system.

Although these two thinkers began and proceeded differently, the convergence of their final results must prove to be the confirmation of truth or inner reality, which eventually will be the goal achieved by the people of the world, bringing improvement to society as a whole.

Chapter Fourteen

SCIENTIFIC WORLD RELIGION

The common findings of Jung and Sri Aurobindo are confirmed by the independent thoughts of Martinus, a contemporary of Jung and Sri Aurobindo, born on August 11, 1890, in the small village of Sindal on Jutland in Denmark. Martinus was born of an unmarried mother who died when he was a child. His maternal uncle and aunt raised him. He worked in the dairy industry until December 1922, when he left to devote himself exclusively to the creation of *Livets Bog* (*The Book of Life*). He had no desire to marry and make a home; rather he wanted to go as a missionary to Africa or the East. Martinus described the whole course of evolution, from mineral to vegetable to animal, where we are now. His conception of God differed very much from traditional Christian doctrine, although it is heartening to note that Martinus, along with Jung and Sri Aurobindo, divides the universe into seven planes of existence. Erik Gerner Larsson tells us that

> Martinus borrowed a small theosophical tract from a friend and meditated with his eyes closed by a kerchief. After a little while, sitting thus, he suddenly found himself enveloped in a glaring white light, and a number of cosmic experiences took place. . . . The process grew stronger during the following days. . . . He found himself in possession of new senses enabling him to see not only the world visible to everybody but, besides, all the real causes behind the misery of this world. . . . "The Great Birth," in the beginning gave rise to a violent awakening of psychic powers,

> now generally become latent in most people. . . . After his spiritual experience, it was impossible for him to relish the taste of meat, tobacco and alcoholic beverages.[1]

Martinus began writing *Livets Bog*," the first volume of which was published on July 11, 1932. In November 1932, circles for the study of *Livets Bog* were formed in the Danish cities of Copenhagen, Odense, Aarhus, and Aalborg. The first issue of the magazine *Kosmos* was published on April 1, 1933.

Scandinavian mythology relates the religious principle in two directly contrary forms. One impells individuals to consecrate their lives to war so that, by dying on the field of honor, they earn a life of bliss in the company of the gods. The second relies on charity and unselfishness for happiness after death. The first one is the "dark" form that "dominated humanity during its slow awakening and into the time when the three great cosmologic teachers, Buddha, Christ, and Mohammed appeared. Each one separately, gave prominence to charity as the only way to a life of complete happiness . . . a mode of living directly contrary to the one our ancestors regarded as the only salvation."[2]

Since everything that is perceptible by the senses, Martinus argued, can exist only in the form of vibration or motion

> . . . it naturally follows that no absolute "fixed point" is possible in the material world. However, as everything perceptible or observable is identical with vibration or motion, it is obvious that the fixed point can be only that which perceives the motion. The "fixed point" in existence, then, is identical with a "something" capable of perceiving motion. Motion being unable to perceive motion, it must be said "something" which experiences the motion and not the reverse. It accordingly makes its appearance as the master or originator of the motion. Thus, it is recognized that an absolute "fixed point" exists, around which all vibration or motion takes place; and the fact that this "fixed point" has experience of the movements makes it the most supreme "Something" in existence. This supreme "Something" is "God Eternal." . . . The divine presence, or highest "something" in the living being, is given expression in the concept of "I." . . . It has no tangible form, no potential capacity, it only is.[3]

This "I" is expressed as "X.1." Plants have consciousness—this has long since been proved by science. Creative impulses are at work even in minerals, although it is difficult to perceive through the physical senses. Only cosmic consciousness can perceive that every single atom is creating ceaselessly. This creative principle is named "X.2." These two eternal singularities could have not been known without the existence of the third one—the thing created, called "X.3." God is the aggregate of the triune principle: the I, the creative principle, and matter or the thing created, or X.1, X.2, and X.3. This analysis, according to Larsson, holds good for every living being and fully verifies the scriptural teaching that we are created in the "image of God."[4]

For Martinus, then, evolution is a process by which life is seen to migrate from vegetable to animal, to the human kingdom, and then to the higher realms, about which Christ said: "My kingdom is not of this world" (John 18:36). The third principle of the trinity—that is, the thing created, matter or energy—has six different primary forms. The lowest is the energy of instinct, as the sustaining factor of consciousness in the vegetable kingdom. The perennial sprouting and blooming of buds and a new flower unfolding the instant its predecessor begins to expire both represent the energy of instinct. The next is the energy of gravity. This comes into existence as "the killing principle," as the carnivorous plant wakes to life and takes possession of the plant consciousness urging it on to a new culmination—the animal kingdom. The beautiful petals of its flowers are transformed into teeth and claws, and we now see it as an animal and no longer recognize it as a plant. Thus, a carnivorous plant is at a transitional stage between the vegetable and animal kingdoms. The energy of spirituality is asleep at this stage.

Then, in the midst of the offending and suffocating situation of gravity, such as war, the energy of feeling, is born. It seeks disarmament, peace, and internationalism. Thus a longing to resume the peaceful life it had voluntarily abandoned begins to grow in its mind. This longing is

Table 5. Comparison of Planes of the Universe

Plane	Martinus	Chapter 1
1	Mother Energy	Divine
2	Memory	Monadic
3	Intuition	Atmic
4	Intelligence	Intuitional
5	Feeling	Mental
6	Gravity	Astral
7	Instinctive	Physical

spirituality. Thereafter, when the feelings culminate, the energies of intelligence, intuition, and memory come forward, in that order. All energies have their own zone. These energies are finally embraced in the highest energy: the Mother Energy.

The consciousness, and hence the existence of the individual, therefore passes through the following seven planes, according to the philosophy of Martinus. Notice in Table 5 on page 125 how the seven planes of Martinus correspond to the seven planes of the universe described in chapter 1.

Scientific World Religion

Our examination of Jung, Sri Aurobindo, Martinus, and others has shown us that there appears to be a common denominator in all faiths and traditions of the world. Although there seem to be differences in the procedures followed for Self- or God-realization, the steps are similar and the end results congruent. I therefore suggest that there exists a common scientific religion whose postulates are subsumed in all faiths and all scientific paradigms. Whether one is a Hindu, Muslim, Christian, Buddhist, or whether one belongs to any other religion by birth or adoption, everyone can also claim to have only one religion and one God, and just one community in the whole world. Perhaps we can call such a religion a Scientific World Religion.

Below, I give only a first approximation of the postulates of this faith. They are open to revision, subtraction, or addition. Comments and suggestions from readers are welcome.

1. Behind the conscious human mind, there lies an infinite unconscious psychic region.

2. Consciousness contains the history of events of present life, while the unconscious contains the record of all possible lives lived. The unconscious, therefore, possesses even the history of creation of the individual by its creator.

3. The center of consciousness is called the ego; the center of the unconscious is called the Self.

4. Ego and Self are two opposites that cannot be united; a transcendent third is required to bring the two together.

5. This transcendent third is called psyche, soul, or Atman; it has two parts, the unconscious and the conscious.

6. Bringing the unconscious into the conscious is called enlightenment, Self-realization, or achieving cosmic consciousness.

7. Cosmic consciousness continues to interrelate with nature.

8. There is consciousness higher than the cosmic in which one realizes one's identity with the creator God. One finds that soul is akin to God. Here one proclaims "Aham Brahmasmi" or "I Am That I Am." This is God-realization.

9. God absolute is sat-chit-ananda, or existence-knowledge-bliss.

10. On achieving wholeness as a fruit of individuation or transformation, the person may discover objects in dreams and visions, such as religious or cherished human personalities, crosses, circles, or other symbols of duality that may indicate the completion of the process.

11. Ego is necessary for establishing one's identity in the world, and for developing necessary relationships with others. Ego is required to deal with the phenomenal world for day-to-day requirements and for normal life.

12. Once the ideal of natural living is achieved, the ego should be transcended. It is like a ship's anchor and should be raised so the ship moves freely in the ocean again. If ego is not transcended after it has served its basic purpose, it can take hold of consciousness and make the individual live for desires and their satisfaction. Most inhumane acts are performed for the satisfaction of desire. If ego is transcended, desires are eliminated. Perhaps suffering would cease as well.

13. Matter and psychic being are manifestations of the existent and delight parts of God. Delight is the pure form of existence by the soul, while desire is the corruption of this state that manifests in the form of worldly pleasures.

14. There are seven levels of consciousness corresponding to seven divisions of the universe, which the soul travels on successive stages of evolution.

15. There are various methods of bringing the unconscious into consciousness or of achieving higher consciousness. Some of these methods, with some variations, are now in use in various faiths and traditions or religions of the world.

16. Most faiths and traditions have discovered that there is a dormant spiritual energy that requires awakening for achieving higher, or cosmic,

consciousness, or for Self- or God-realization. This energy is called kundalini in the East.

17. As kundalini passes through the seven chakras, the personality is transformed. One passes through seven levels of awareness, sees seven colors of VIBGYOR, and hears seven distinct sounds with the inner ear.

18. When kundalini arrives at the "center of command" between the eyebrows, the ego is fragmented into thousands of pieces, the chain of reincarnation is broken, and the gate to the kingdom of heaven opens.

19. There is one permanent sound heard internally, the sound of AUM, or Word, or KALMA-I-ILAHI. This sound is the manifestation of God. This sound takes the soul in "tow" back to the godhead.

20. The shortest method of awakening kundalini is the Integral Path, presented in chapter 25.

PART FOUR

Gateways to Higher Consciousness

Chapter Fifteen

KARMA YOGA— THE PATH OF SELFLESS ACTION

The knowledge gained by analyzing experiences that are supported by forces not perceived by ordinary physical senses is called spiritual knowledge. All human beings are at different levels of evolution. Just as some reasoning has supported modern science in its evolution, so there are beings whose thoughts are ahead of it, recognizing experiences as spiritual forces. Such people possess additional layers of consciousness at present unknown to science and most of humanity. These layers of consciousness are labeled "higher consciousness" by parapsychologists, "cosmic consciousness" by transcendentalists, and the "opening of the third eye" by Vedantists. In this chapter, we will explore means of attaining such consciousness.

We will discuss various methods, from the ancient classical to the modern scientific. Readers can go through all of them patiently and select one that suits their temperament. Just as no two people have the same fingerprints, so no two people will find the same procedure suitable. Even students of the same teacher may not have the same approach; they will differ according to their personal factors. Many people find more than one method useful. In such cases, they can act upon them simultaneously, skillfully combining them to make the process faster. I personally feel that a balanced combination of classical or basic methods is useful for two reasons: it can yield results in a single lifetime, and the side effects of misunderstanding a single method will not completely hinder progress. I have developed one such method through my own evolution and experiences; I call it the Integral Path, which is presented in the chapter 25. However, readers are encouraged to make their own choice.

Vedic Methods

These are the classic methods of Hindu philosophy developed by *rishis*, seers, or yogis over thousands of years. You find these methods taught in the Vedas, the Upanishads, and Bhagavad Gita. Lord Krishna advised his disciple Arjun to become a yogi by adopting these methods. However, modern citizens of the world may find them difficult or slow in producing results. They may wish to turn to faster methods described later in this chapter.

The goal of human existence is to achieve a state of liberation—that is, a cosmic mind, life, and matter, or a pure transcendental self-power in which the ego does not act. This is possible in three ways:

1. *Karma yoga*—the path of selfless action; requires renunciation of ego and desire, and personal initiation and surrender of the being to the cosmic Self or to the universal power called *Shakti*.

2. *Jnana yoga*—the path of knowledge; requires cessation of thought, silence of mind, opening of the whole being to cosmic consciousness, or Self, or supreme reality.

3. *Bhakti yoga*—the path of devotion; requires the surrender of the heart and the whole being into the hands of the all-blissful, adored master of our existence. This transformation unveils the secret master of our activities gradually. From the source of the supreme will and knowledge, he gives sanction to the divine *Shakti* working within us as a purified and exalted instrument for her use.

The rishis, experimenting with various methods and realizing truth in states of *samadhi*, found all individuals to be at different physical, mental, emotional, and intuitional levels. They consequently divided human beings into three groups:

1. Rational and intellectual beings, in whom the head dominates the heart.

2. Instinctual and emotional beings, in whom the heart dominates the head.

3. Harmonized beings, in whom the head and heart have almost equal influence.

Accordingly, the methods most suitable for their Self-realization are jnana yoga (path of knowledge), bhakti yoga (path of devotion), and karma yoga (path of selfless action). A fourth category was later designed for those in whom neither the intellectual nor the emotional level was sufficiently developed. A set of rules were originally prescribed and improved gradually over millennia. The name given to this kind of yoga is *hatha yoga*, who's greatest exponents were the saints Patanjali, Gorakh Nath, and Jyaneshwar of the Middle Ages. Kundalini yoga is an improvised form of this yoga and will be dealt with separately.

Of the four Vedas, Yajurveda is devoted to karma yoga, Rigveda is devoted to jnana yoga, and Samaveda is devoted to bhakti yoga. Below, I elaborate on the three basic methods, beginning with karma yoga, which received Lord Krishna's attention in the Bhagavad Gita, where the philosophy of liberation from falsehood has been comprehensively explained.

Karma yoga: The path of selfless action

The inner life of man, which depends mainly on the vital and physical natures, is not the entire real existence.[1] The present nature of man is only an outer appearance of the hidden Self. One has to understand Sankhya's distinction between the soul and nature—the power that knows, supports, and informs, and the power that works, acts, and provides different instruments, venues, and processes. The soul is the immutable omnipresent Self, or Brahman, while the nature of the soul is our mutable and dynamic being, which deals with the phenomenal world.

Nature acts through three fundamental modes, or qualities, called *gunas*: *tamasic*, *rajasic*, and *sattwic*. In tamasic action, an inert personality is subject to and satisfied with the mechanical scheme of things and is incapable of strong effort toward freer action or mastery. In rajasic action, the restless, active personality attempts to force nature to serve its needs and desires without understanding that, in doing so, it is only fulfilling the demands of nature itself and, in fact, there is no freedom. In sattwic action, the individual strives to live as an enlightened personality, working on reason and having the preferred ideals, truth, and beauty, which, again, are subject to the laws of nature. These ideals represent only the changing phases of personality, and do not lead to a definite rule or stable satisfaction. Those living in any one of the three modes continue rotating on the wheel of karma, obeying the power of ego, but not in communion with that power, let alone acting as the power. In this state, there is no real freedom, liberation, or mastery, only servitude.

To experience freedom, we must first allow our senses freedom from their grip of attachment to the external world—that is, relax the natural chasing of our senses after external objects and begin searching inwardly. Mastery of the senses will bring realization of the soul, which is clear of the mutations of the mind—self-existent, tranquil, self-possessed, and unaffected by the eager attachment to outer nature. Understanding that desire seeks to satisfy itself through the senses, whose only occupation is the play of passion, does this. With the release of old ego habits, by clearly realizing the true nature of desire, passions will fall into quietude. The illusory joy of possession, grief, success and failure, pleasantness and unpleasantness that used to entertain the passions will pass from the mind. Serenity prevails. Furthermore, since we need to live and work in the world, and our previous nature was to pursue the fruit of our work, we will bring the radical change in our nature to our work, but without attachment. Dissociating deeds from the ego and personality through reasoning that this is only the play of the gunas will bring about this change in the nature of the doer. This understanding will dissociate the soul from the play, by making it the observer of the workings of nature and leaving those works to the power behind the scenes. The only obstacle is the mind, whose nature is to chase after sense objects with its reason and will. Learning to still the mind will lead to awareness of the Self—calm, motionless, blissful, unaffected by events of the world, self-sufficient, and living in eternal satisfaction. Practical Formula 1 gives the steps in karma yoga.

PRACTICAL FORMULA 1: THE PATH OF SELFLESS ACTION

1. Consecrate all works as an offering to the divine in the world and in us. After initiating this attitude of mind and heart, remaining sincere and all-pervasive in our efforts will be a challenge.

2. Renounce attachment to the fruit of our work. The only desirable fruit is the divine presence, consciousness, and power in us. When this is achieved, all else follows. This is the transformation of the ego's will, desire-soul, and desire-nature. The second step flows from the first as a natural function.

3. Transcend the central egotism, the sense of being the worker or doer. This will flow from the first two steps. As the ego-sense is clearly seen, one knows one's true nature resting as part of the divine and renunciation follows naturally by focusing on divine power, or Shakti.

4. Release proprietorship of all material possessions.

When the Self is revealed within us, we begin to feel our peace and serenity. We grow into our fullness of calm, harmony, detachment, and all-pervading Self. Senses become still, ego dissolves into impersonal existence, and work ceases to be ours, or to bind and trouble us. Nature and her gunas continue to work, but our self-existent tranquillity is not affected. All is offered to that one united, universal Brahman.[2] "Once free, he/she has only to continue working in the sphere assigned to him/her by Fate and circumstances, until the great hour arrives when he/she can, at last, disappear into the Infinite."[3]

Chapter Sixteen

JNANA YOGA—THE PATH OF KNOWLEDGE

The path of knowledge is perhaps presently prominent, since it includes official science (which is also in search of truth in its own experimental way), and the Western approach, which includes the intellectual search for truth, including parapsychological and psychic research, as well as the work of Jung and others. The recognition of the potential in the human intellect by Vedanta will leave people amazed at their own incapacity to make complete use of their intellect in search of truth. Vedanta travels the path of pure reason and nurtures the "jewel of discrimination" between true and false, permanent and temporal, real and illusion, leading us to self-discovery, to the knowledge that Self and God are one consciousness. The path is also called raja yoga, meaning king of yogas. King Janaka, father-in-law of Lord Rama, was perhaps the first recognized raja yogi.

Raman Maharishi always focused on one thought: Who am I? One day, he arrived at the realization that Atman and Brahman are identical. Sankaracharya, Vivekananda, Socrates, Aristotle, Plato, Gurdjief, Rudolf Steiner, William Wordsworth, Richard Maurice Bucke, and many others were all thinkers who can be called raja yogis. The progression of steps on this path is more or less the same as in karma yoga and, of course, the final realization is the same. One goes on removing layer after layer of ignorance, just as one removes the leaves of a cabbage one-by-one, finally reaching the heart. Vast supportive literature is available on Self-realization both in the East and West, including the Vedanta.

Swami Vivekananda has written fifteen volumes on the subject, each nearly five hundred pages long.

This knowledge takes the individual to a certain stage of development or evolution in which the ego ceases to control and wisdom is received, giving direct perception of truth from beyond. Sri Aurobindo speaks at length of this path:

> Late, I learned when reason died the Wisdom was born; before that liberation, I had only knowledge.
>
> There are two allied powers in man: knowledge and wisdom. Knowledge is a partial truth, seen in a distorted medium, as the mind arrives at groping; wisdom is what the eye of divine vision sees in the spirit.
>
> When I speak, the reason says, "This will I say"; but God takes the word of my mouth and the lips say something else at which reason trembles.
>
> If mankind could see though, in a glimpse of fleeting experience what infinite enjoyments, what perfect forces, what luminous reaches of spontaneous knowledge, what wide calms of our being lie waiting for using the tracts which our animal evolution has not yet conquered, they would leave all and never rest till they had gained these treasures. But the way is narrow, the doors are hard to force, and fear, distrust and skepticism are there, sentinels of Nature, forbid the turning away of our feet from her ordinary pastures.
>
> What the soul sees and has experienced, that it knows; the rest is appearance, prejudice and opinion.
>
> They proved to me by convincing reasons that God did not exist, and I believed them. Afterwards I saw God, for He came and embraced me. And now which am I to believe, the reasoning of others or my own experience?
>
> Hallucination is a term of Science for those irregular glimpses we receive of truths shut out from us by our preoccupation with matter. . . . That which men term hallucination is the reflection in the mind and senses of that other reality, which is beyond our self-limited mental and sensory perceptions.
>
> Logic is a conceptually limited search for Truth, as self-righteousness is the ignorant imitator of virtue, for the one cannot see its own misunderstandings or the other its own arrogant self-judgment.

> The sign of dawning Wisdom is to feel that I know little or nothing; and yet, if I could only be open to my Wisdom, I would know I already possess everything.
>
> Knowledge is a child blinded with its achievements, he runs about the streets whooping, and shouting; Wisdom conceals the power of her clarity in a thoughtful and mighty silence.
>
> Spirituality and philosophy seek to rescue man from his ego; then the kingdom of heaven within will be spontaneously reflected in an external divine city.[1]

Here, the sage tells us that reason and knowledge take us to a certain stage, after which spontaneous knowledge and wisdom take over, leading to experiences of soul, which are permanent. We experience God directly, and have conscious knowledge of the permanent Self. Reflection in the mind and perceptions of that which is beyond our ordinary mental and sensory perceptions are called hallucinations by science. But the supernatural is merely that which has not yet been understood. Revelation is the direct soul experience of God, not God speaking.

Solitude is the place or state of being where the practitioner may listen to spirit and experience spiritual truth. True solitude exists everywhere, even in a crowd or battlefield, and is a measure of emotional maturity. When we tread the unfrequented ways, as Master Pythagoras said, we develop a love for solitude. In this manner, we rediscover God and our God-nature.

Sri Aurobindo points out two possible ways to approach God:

1. With faith and devotion, surrender to God, draw closer to Him and one day experience God.

2. A skeptical seeker who questions everything, continually asking the question, "Who am I," will also reach the truth.[2]

The first is the path of devotion; the second is the path of knowledge. One has to choose the path of his or her preference and go deeply into it. Others, who are uncommitted, may not master either process.

Most faiths and traditions have pronounced God as the only doer. Sri Aurobindo points out that the practitioner who has realized this fact and considers him- or herself as doing nothing, even when he or she may be achieving work of great importance, has mastered his or her ego and is now open to God. "If when thou art doing great actions and moving giant results," he argues, "thou canst perceive that thou art doing nothing, then know, God has removed His seal from thy eyelids."[3] This can be understood through a simple example. While traveling on a train, one may erroneously believe he or she is carrying a briefcase; in fact, the train carries the briefcase and the person. One erroneously assumes doership, and thus actions of one's own creation bind one to karma. The action creating events and doership cannot be ascribed to any single factor. A car runs because it has a motor, fuel to power it, and a driver at the wheel. If any single factor, claims credit for the car running, it is inaccurate. Similarly, daily events take place because of many known and unknown factors; any being ascribing doership to him or herself is mistaken. Understanding this frees us from creating karma and opens us to God.

Pain and suffering are concerns for most of us at some time or other. The average person may blame others, a particular circumstance, or God, and want escape as quickly as possible. Sri Aurobindo points out that "pain is the touch of our Mother, teaching us how to bear life and grow in rapture. She has three stages of her schooling, first endurance, next equality of soul, last ecstasy."[4] Pain is caused by a divine source for teaching lessons necessary to spiritual growth. If pain is borne with patience and courage and one stays open to the divine teaching coming through it, one finally reaches ecstasy.

An aspirant of God has the choice of two ways. Desire perishes either by complete renunciation or by total satisfaction; this is a prerequisite to experiencing God-realization. "Only by complete renunciation of desire or by full satisfaction of desire will the complete embrace of God be experienced," the sage tells us, "for in both ways the essential precondition is effected—desire perishes."[5] This is the basic and perhaps most important point on which two schools of Hindu philosophy are based. King Harish Chandra, like other yogis, transcended his passion and renounced all desire. He left his throne and lived an ordinary life. One day, he came to beg from his own wife and addressed her as *mata* (mother). For him, all women had assumed the form of the Mother Goddess, thus clearing the illusion of sexual attraction. This is the way of renunciation. The other way is to fully satisfy all desires and come out of them realizing their futility; this way is shown through Tantra. Kundalini is awakened by either of the two extremes. Water must be heated to the boiling point to convert it into steam. Likewise, kundalini, if left to simmer, may go a lifetime without bringing liberation, only another round on the wheel of karma.

Under destined conditions, just as water converts into steam, man converts into God. Hence, each of us will choose a path in this lifetime or another to achieve this unavoidable goal.

A saint, or avatar, may be a physical manifestation of God. Yet God absolute is the unmanifested infinite being behind the personality of the saint or avatar, who is the actual center of concentration and understanding. This is the final goal. Word or AUM represents God unmanifest.

Ramakrishna, Sri Aurobindo tells us, was "God manifest in a human being; but behind him is God in His infinite personality and His universal personality." And what was Vivekananda? "A radiant glance from the eye of Shiva; but behind him is the divine gaze from which he came and Shiva himself and Brahma and Vishnu and Om all exceeding."[6] Sin and virtue exist, we learn, only while the truth of the soul is dormant; as Self-realization occurs, the duality of sin and virtue fades. "We accept the double law of sin and virtue as binding because we do not realize the ideal of life and knowledge guiding our souls spontaneously and infallibly to its self-fulfillment. The law of sin and virtue loses its reality for us when the sun of God shines upon our souls with true, loving and unveiled splendor."[7]

Jesus Christ incarnated for his brothers and sisters to heal through his presence and push a step closer to God. Thinking one is a superior being will not and cannot save or liberate oneself or others. Even now, every soul serves his or her fellow beings by living these universal ideals, as best they can.

Mohammed enjoyed a rich full life, marrying several times. This indicates it is not necessary to renounce enjoyment of life and become a recluse to become realized. In living a full life outwardly, one may also be an inner renunciate, experiencing physical events in a detached way. King Janak of Hindu mythology also lived a full life of many pleasures. On a morning walk with a visiting *sadhu* (renunciate), a celestial guru, wanting to offer a lesson, created a *maya* (illusion), in which the whole palace appeared to burst into flame. King Janak was unmoved by this scene and said he did not bring these things into the world and was not worried about their destruction. But the sadhu exclaimed that his *langot* [saffron-colored underwear] and *kamandalu* [begging bowl] would be burned and ran toward the palace to save them. Who was the genuine renunciate? Cultivation of inner renunciation brings clarity. Outward appearance is never important.

When we examine the writings of various saints speaking about the signs of a true spiritual person, the unanimity of their views is interesting. From Sri Aurobindo, we hear:

> Live within; be not shaken by outward happenings.
>
> The Sannyasa [renunciation] wears formal garb and outer tokens; therefore, men think they can easily recognize it; but the freedom of a Janaka [father-in-law of Lord Rama] does not proclaim itself and wears the garb of the world; to its presence, even Narada [great sage] was blinded. . . . Unless thou canst see the Soul, how shalt thou say that a man is free or bound?[8]

Likewise, Dhammapada observes:

> It is not by shaving the head that one becomes a man of religion; truth and rectitude alone make the true religious man.[9]

And in the *Book of the Golden Precepts*, we read:

> Think not that to seat thyself in gloomy forests, in a proud seclusion, aloof from men, think not that to live on roots and plants and quench thy thirst with the snow will lead thee to the goal of the final deliverance.[10]

The Chinese philosopher Fo-Shu-Hing-Tsan-King agrees:

> Though the body be adorned with jewels, the heart may have mastered worldly tendencies; he who receives with indifference joy and pain is in possession of the spiritual life even though his external existence be of the world; nor is the garb of the ascetic a protection against sensual thoughts.
>
> Although the body be robed with the garb of the layman, the soul can raise itself to the highest perfections. The man of the world and the ascetic differ not at all from the other if both have conquered egoism. So long as the heart is bound by sensual chains, all external signs of asceticism are a vanity.
>
> A solitary man may miss his goal and a man of the world becomes a sage.[11]

The Bhuddist texts carry a similar lesson:

> He who practices wisdom without anger or covetousness, who fulfills with fidelity his vows and lives master of himself, he is indeed a man of religion.
>
> He who watches over his body, his speech, his whole Self, who is full of serenity and joy, possesses a spirit unified and finds satisfaction in solitude, he is indeed a man of religion.
>
> He who has conquered the desire of present life and of the

> future life, who has vanquished all fear and broken all chains, he is indeed a man of religion.
>
> He who punishes not, kills not, permits not to be killed, who is full of love among those who are full of cruelty, he is indeed a man of religion.[12]

Likewise, Saadi teaches:

> A gay liver, who spreads gladness around him, is better than the devotee who fasts all the year round. Fasting is a merit in the man who distributes his good to the needy; otherwise what mortification is it to take in the evening a meal you have abstained from during the day?

Chuang Tse exhorts the faithful that "to take neither wine nor meat is to fast ceremonially; it is not the heart's fasting which is to maintain in oneself the one thought." The Pastor of Hermes agrees, saying that "this shall be the true manner of thy fasting that thy shall be void of all iniquity."[13]

The man whose soul aspires to the eternal, Ramakrishna tells us, "cannot give thought to such silly questions as that of daivic food, that is to say, a simple vegetarian diet, and for him who does not desire to attain to the Eternal, beef is as good as daivic food." In the same way, Amaghanda Sutta teaches that "it is not eating meat that makes a man impure; it is anger, intemperance, egoism, hypocrisy, disloyalty, envy, ostentation, vanity, pride; it is to take pleasure in the society of those who perpetrate injustice."

Likewise the Pali Canon notes:

> Neither abstinence from meat and fish, nor mendicancy, nor shaven head or the matted locks, nor mortifications of the body, nor garments of a special color, nor the adoration of a god can purify the man who is still prey to illusion."[14]

Thus we learn from the masters that the outer appearance and outer life are without true substance; the inner attitude and inner life are what matters. A person may be vegetarian or a householder, may live in a forest or a palace, have a shaved head and wear saffron clothes, have beautiful hair and wear a suit and tie, walk or drive a car—it does not matter. If he or she has transcended ego and arrogance, neither kills nor supports killing, is humble and compassionate to all, receives joy and sorrow equally, has a heart not bound by sensual chains, is guided by wisdom, experiences serenity, and feels satisfaction in solitude, then he or she is a spiritual person. Such people may be living a full worldly life, yet they are close to reality and with God. Another person, lacking these virtues, may live in a monastery with shaven head and saffron clothes and still be separated from truth and God. Aspiring to become a yogi (inner renunciate) and not a pundit (one who is theoretically knowledgeable) is the goal. Naturally, a realized person will be a yogi and also a pundit. As is written: "He whose mind is utterly pure from all evil as the sun is pure of stain and the moon of soil, him indeed I call a man of religion."[15]

The following are quotations from various saints, identifying the soul with God. It is heartening to see saints from all over the world, confirming one and the same thing:

> Vedanta says, "Man, thou art of one nature and substance with God, one soul with thy fellow-men. Awake and progress then to the utter divinity, live for God in thyself and in others." This gospel which was given only to the few, must now be offered to all mankind for its deliverance.
>
> —SRI AUROBINDO

> Why should man go about seeking? He is in the heart-beats and thou knowest it not; thou wert in error in seeking Him outside thyself.
>
> God is my inmost self, the reality of my being.
>
> —VIVEKANANDA

> God cannot be recognized except in oneself. So long as thou findest Him not in thee, thou wilt not find Him anywhere. There is no God for the man who does not find Him in himself.
>
> The greatest joy man can conceive is the joy of recognizing in himself a being free, intelligent, loving and in consequence happy, of feeling God in himself.
>
> Man in order to be really a man must conceive the idea of God in himself.
>
> —TOLSTOY

> The supreme Brahman, the self of all, the great abode of the universe, more subtle than the subtle, eternal, That is thyself and thou art That.
>
> —KAIVALYA UPANISHAD

> Thou art That . . . not a part, not a mode of It, but identically That, the absolute Spirit.
>
> —CHANDOGYA UPANISHAD

> God is myself; we are one in consciousness and His knowing is my knowing.
>
> If I were not, God would not be.
>
> —ECKHART

The consistent message coming from teachers of diverse faiths and traditions is that man and woman, as soul, are identical and in unity with God. This is the highest truth to recognize on the spiritual path. There is a story in the Chandogya Upanishad that tells of two birds that sat in a tree loaded with alluring fruit. The fruit consumed one bird's attention; he devoured it and, although full to bursting, desired ever more and flew around to look for other fruit trees. Knowing only his desire, he eventually forgot his identity. The other bird, trusting nature would always provide for his needs, ate only to satisfy his hunger and retained his identity. The first bird is man and the second bird is God. The moment the first bird remembered his original identity, he also become God.

Following the path of knowledge may appear to be a slow process, yet it is a sure way and many have achieved enlightenment in this manner. Those who took it earnestly (i.e., Socrates and Raman Maharishi), found it pretty fast and easy. Wisdom can dawn upon you one day if the following steps are mastered.

PRACTICAL FORMULA 2:
JNANA YOGA (THE PATH OF KNOWLEDGE)

1. Travel the path of pure reason leading to self-discovery.

2. Continue removing layer after layer of ignorance by ceaselessly asking: "Who am I?".

3. A stage comes when the ego ceases to control and wisdom is reborn.

4. Recognize immortality as the awakened possession of the unborn and deathless Self.

5. Perceive nonaction in causing results and open the way to truth. In other words, remember, under all circumstances, that you are not the

doer, and remain free from creating karma. Serve others, without misunderstanding the true nature of doing.

6. Concentrate on suffering and discover that it leads toward intense bliss. Suffering teaches through three stages: endurance, equality of soul, and ecstasy.

7. Surrender dependence on external attachments and become vulnerable, thus making room for God to enter.

8. Either complete renunciation or full satisfaction of desire leads to the truth; in both cases, desire fades away, which is the required precondition. Choose one of the ways and master it.

9. Know that the inner renunciation of desire, ignorance, and egotism, and not monasticism, leads to truth. Through the state of renunciation, one becomes a jnana yogi. Acquiring knowledge and becoming a pundit is only the starting point.

10. Whenever you come to know that Atman and Brahman are identical, or that you and the Father are one, know you have realized the truth.

Chapter Seventeen

BHAKTI YOGA— THE PATH OF DEVOTION

Lord Krishna categorically declared to Arjuna that, of all the Vedas, the Sama-Veda, which deals with *bhakti* (devotion), is considered most important. In his words: "Of the Vedas I am the Sama Veda."[1] The paths of selfless action and knowledge bring the individual to the realization that the Self, or Atman, is identical with Brahman. But this, Lord Krishna proclaimed, is dry knowledge: "It is Rasa (Joy) and Rasa alone which surrounds it (bhakti) on all sides and permeates it. God Himself is Rasa personified and Rasa is the abode of supreme bliss. It is through Bhakti alone that one can perceive God, the embodiment of Rasa."[2]

According to Poddar, the practice of bhakti is the foremost Vedic discipline for the realization of divine love. As an end, bhakti manifests itself as divine love. The secret of the beloved can be known as a result of intimate, exclusive, constant, and unconditional love. In the words of Dr. Chaturbhuj Sahai: "In close proximity to God, when the love intoxicated practitioner begins to be absorbed in His consciousness, then this is called 'upasana', the deeper state is called 'samadhi'. Yoga or meeting oneself is possible in samadhi."[3]

Although innumerable people have plunged directly into the path of bhakti, or devotion, a faster and possibly more rewarding way is through selfless action (karma) and knowledge (jnana). Bhakti is not opposed to karma, and no competition exists between jnana and bhakti. In fact, those who possess real wisdom and knowledge of truth have obtained divine realization. Poddar wrote a commentary on the aphorisms of Devarsi Narada, which are devoted to the exposition of bhakti as directed toward a personal god. He discussed hindrances to the growth of bhakti, the means of attaining it, and the glory of bhakti and the bhaktas. Lord Krishna stated in the Bhagavad Gita that a devotee who is knowledgeable and wise is completely loved by him.

Maharsi Vyas, in possession of spiritual vision, divided the Vedas into four parts, then composed the Mahabharata, calling it the fifth Veda, and brought forth the *puranas*. Yet he was not at peace in his heart; something was missing. Devarsi Narada appeared before him and said the reason for his unhappiness was that he did not sing the praises of God or describe his glories to the same extent that he had described them in other aspects of dharma. Devarsi Narada, who knew the truths of the Vedas, placed bhakti (devotion) on a very high place.

In *Bhakti-Rasayana*, Madhusudan Saraswati divided bhakti into eleven stages. A practitioner of bhakti yoga, therefore, will wish to find a saint or a realized person and devote him- or herself to that person following the steps in Practical Formula 3.

PRACTICAL FORMULA 3: BHAKTI YOGA (THE PATH OF DEVOTION)

1. Personal service of *mahapurusha* (great men).

2. Acquiring of qualifications worthy of their attention.

3. Faith in the dharma practiced by them.

4. Hearing the divine glory with reverence.

5. Listening to and developing divine love.

6. Divine love leading to Self-realization.

7. Self-realization leading to the increase of love in the supreme embodiment of bliss.

8. Germination of supreme bliss through the increase of love.

9. Firm adherence to *bhagavata dharma* (duty toward God).

10. Development of the qualities of a *bhagavata* (realized person).

11. Attainment of the clearest realization of love.

According to the *Bhakti Sutras* of Devarsi Narada, bhakti, or devotion, is the development of unconditional love for God. This attainment opens one to God-realization, an understanding of immortality and peace. On realizing love, one becomes mad, silent, and serene in the Self. Love has no element of desire, being of the nature of *nirodha* (renunciation). Renunciation consists of relinquishing all forms of attachment to action, secular as well as spiritual; it may also be called an exclusive love toward God and indifference to everything seeming not of God, such as fear, anger, and greed. In exclusiveness, one experiences all things as God. Indifference to all that is not of God consists of conforming one's vision, both secular and spiritual, to God as creator of all that is. There is a stage when all activities, spiritual as well as mundane, cease as a matter of course; but until that stage is reached, both these forms of duty must be scrupulously performed. In reality, all activities are spiritual experiences and do not cease, even on the death of the physical body.

Different schools have different definitions of bhakti. According to Maharishi Vedvyasa, son of Parasara, bhakti means attachment to the worship of God and other allied practices. In the opinion of Garga, bhakti means fondness for hearing the stories of the various sports of the Lord. In the view of Sandilya, supreme attachment to God is not opposed to love of Self, as God is Self.[4] Narada has given examples of the devotion of *gopies* (milkmaids), who are always in eternal union with the Lord and do not require any yoga or meditation. Even in the state of forgetfulness, there is no absence of the divine glory in the gopies. Love limited by attachment, bereft of the knowledge of divine presence, is the love of a paramour; in this there is no joy derived from the beloved.

According to Narada, divine love is superior even to karma (action), jnana (knowledge), and yoga; it is an end in itself, thus encouraging some seekers of liberation to adopt this path of devotion.[5]

Regarding the methods of devotion, teachers and prophets have prescribed renunciation of worldly objects and attachments. Success is attained through ceaseless *bhajana* (religious songs to the glory of Lord). But the primary means is said to be the grace of a mahapurusha (a great soul who has realized God) or an iota of divine grace, after which other practices follow as a matter of course. However, contact with a mahapurusha is rare. Since God and his devotee are the same consciousness, it is recommended that one cultivate contact with a lover of God.

Evil company is said to be the main obstacle to realizing the divine love already within us, since such company encourages lust, anger, greed, and loss of wisdom. These appear as ripples on a pond in the beginning and, later, assume the dimensions of ocean storms.

Those who renounce all attachments, serve great souls, and do not regard anything as their own will cross *maya* (illusion). Those who achieve inner seclusion, cut all ties with the world, transcend the three *gunas* (modes of nature), and give up all thought of *yog* (providing for needs) and *kshem* (safety of one's possessions) renounce not only the fruit of action, but also the action itself, thus renouncing everything and becoming indifferent to all polarity. Those who totally renounce even the Vedas and attain ceaseless unbounded love for God will cross *maya* (illusion) and guide others across.

Divine love cannot be described in words. One who is in it does not speak, and one who speaks is not in it. Unconditional love reveals itself in rare persons who surrender to it. This love is without desire, each moment increasing, yet subtler than the subtlest. On attaining this love, the devotee sees only love, hears only love, speaks only of love, and thinks only of love. Divine love being considered primary, the secondary love or devotion is of three kinds, according to the three gunas or modes of nature: *sattwic* (pure), *rajasik* (active), and *tamasic* (having inertia), as defined earlier in greater detail.

According to Narada, among all forms of spiritual practice, the practice of devotion is the easiest, which is a proof in itself that it is of the nature of peace and supreme bliss. After surrendering oneself and one's interests (temporal and spiritual) to God, the practitioner will not worry about worldly issues; however, worldly activities will not be abandoned until reaching completion in devotion, practicing devotion in a detached way, and renouncing the fruit of action. If, having offered all other activities to God, the practitioner is still haunted by lust, anger, and arrogance, these may also be surrendered to God and perhaps, being seen as the illusions they are, forgotten.

Dissolve the triple consciousness (worship, worshiper, and the object of worship) and cultivate love alone in the form of incessant service to the Lord. Supreme devotion to the Lord can be superior in effecting liberation, when compared to the five types of *mukti*, or liberation. These are:

1. *Salokya* (residence in the abode of the Lord)
2. *Samipya* (living in close proximity to the Lord)
3. *Sarsti* (enjoying the same powers as the Lord)
4. *Saripya* (having a similar form to that of the Lord)
5. *Sayujya* (absolute identity with the lord).[6]

When devotees speak with emotionally choked voices, body hair bristling with joy, and eyes wet with tears, they sanctify their race and the earth. They also enhance the inviolability of sacred places and lend authority to scriptures, because they are one with God. Among devotees, there is no distinction due to caste, education, appearance, birth, wealth, or occupation, since they are all the same to God. To discriminate against any man is an offense. There are said to be sixty-four kinds of offenses in general.[7]

Entering into competitive situations creates opportunities for excessive ego. Meditating upon scriptures that promote devotion and performing actions of devotion will engender clear devotion. Following the ten principles given in Practical Formula 4 constitutes the principal activities that aid in the attainment of divine understanding.[8]

PRACTICAL FORMULA 4: THE CAPACITY FOR DIVINE LOVE

1. Scrupulous observance of duties prescribed for one's *varna** and ashram; renunciatory conduct on the part of the *brahmachari*, *vanaprasthi*, and *sanyasi*, and on the part of the *grahastha*; maintenance of parents, spiritual partners, children, and other dependants with proper respect and affection in the spirit of understanding God; earning a livelihood through truthful and moral means; performance of charity and austerities as enjoined by the scriptures.

2. Practice of *sadachara*.

3. Attendance in *satsanga*; hearing and *kirtan* of divine glory and meditation on the same.

4. Practice of *japa* of the divine name, and remembrance and kirtan of the same.

5. Worship of God; prayer and obeisance.

6. Personal service to saints and devotees while carrying out their behest with reverence.

7. Residence in places of pilgrimage.

8. Compassion for distressed creatures and their service to the best of one's ability, through body, mind, and wealth.

9. Offering the fruit of all actions to God.

10. Observing God in every living being.

Lord Krishna described, in the Bhagavad Gita, the signs of loving devotees as follows:[9]

---

*For definitions of this and other terms, see the glossary.

1. One who is not envious, is a kind friend to all living entities, and does not see himself as a proprietor; one who is free from false ego, serene in both joyful and stressful times, tolerant, self-controlled, and determined in devotional service; one whose mind and intelligence are fixed on Me.[10]

2. One who puts no others in difficulty and is not disturbed by others; one who has equipoise in happiness and distress, excitement and anxiety.[11]

3. One who is not dependent on the ordinary course of activities, is pure, expert, without cares, free from suffering, and not striving for results.[12]

4. One who neither rejoices nor grieves, neither laments nor desires; and one who renounces both auspicious and inauspicious things.[13]

5. One who is equal to friends and enemies, has equipoise in honor and dishonor, heat and cold, happiness and distress, fame and infamy; one who is free from contaminating association, silent and satisfied, not preferring any residence; one who is fixed in knowledge and is engaged in devotional service.[14]

6. One who follows this imperishable path of devotional service and completely engages with faith; one whose supreme goal is realizing Me.[15]

One will not spend a half second without *bhajan* (repeating the names of God) while awaiting the auspicious moment when one would be free from pleasure and pain, desire and sense of worldly gain, since attention will be on perfection as a means and not an end. Every single breath will be as carefully devoted to the remembrance of God as a miser is devoted to his limited number of coins. One will scrupulously observe all aspects of *sadachara* (right conduct), like *ahimsa* (noninjury to others), truth, clarity (external and internal), compassion, and faith in the existence of God. A God-realized person cannot be accurately judged from external conduct; nevertheless, these qualities are bound to be present in him or her.

When you chant with love, God speedily reveals himself and blesses you with his perception. The saints, men of wisdom, *purana*, and Vedas all declare that there is no difference between *saguna* (divine manifestation of God with attributes) and *aguna* (the absolute). He who is absolute, formless, invisible, and unborn appears as saguna (with attributes), compelled by the love of the devotee. "That form of God is not a creation of Maya. It is wholly a Divine and Supernatural Form; drawn by the Love of the devotee when it manifests itself before him, making itself perceptible by raising the devotee to the Divine level."[16]

Devarsi Narada taught that, among the three forms of truth practiced through body, speech, and mind, the path of bhakti is the surest. He repeatedly declares this, and his statement is corroborated by the Tripadibhutinarayana Upanishad in the following words: "Abandoning all other methods take recourse only to Bhakti. Be devoted to Bhakti, be devoted only to Bhakti. Through Bhakti, all forms of completion are easily attained. There is nothing which cannot be attained by Bhakti."[17] Other disciplines bring realization of God in other forms. He is also realized as the beloved through the path of devotion.

Sri Aurobindo speaks often in ways that reveal truths of the highest order. Here are just a few out of many:

> When I was mounting upon ever-higher crests of His joy, I asked myself whether there was no limit to the increase of bliss and almost I grew afraid of God's embraces.

> Monogamy may be the best for body, but the soul that loves God in men dwells here always as the boundless and ecstatic polygamist; yet all the time—that is the secret—it is in love with only one being.

> The joy of God is secret and wonderful; it is a mystery and a rapture at which common sense makes mouths of mockery; but the soul that has once tasted it, can never renounce it, whatever the worldly disrepute, torture and affliction it may bring us.

> The skeptical mind always doubts what it cannot understand, but the faith of the God-lover persists in knowing although it cannot understand. Both are necessary to our darkness, but there can be no doubt, which is the mightier. What I cannot understand now, I shall some day master, but if I lose faith and love, I fall utterly from the goal that God has set before me.[18]

Likewise Dr. Chaturbhuj Sahai, a realized person himself, went personally into the city where the great saint Mira Bai lived some four to five hundred years ago. Mira Bai is reported to have lived in the fifteenth century, although there is some uncertainty. Nature or the divine plan pushed her to one circumstance after another that led to loving God. She lost her mother in early childhood, received the statue of Krishna at the age of ten, met a realized saint, was separated from her husband, and met with Guru Raidasji, who initiated her. Every event pushed her further toward God.

Obstacles became opportunities and means of achievement. Here are the signs of love that Sahai found in the story of the Saint:

> Bhakti (devotion), Jnana (knowledge) and Yoga are stairs leading to Love.
>
> Love comes with all these disciplines and as soon as it comes it bathes us with bliss.
>
> The moment one dives into the ocean of Love, God appears before the individual. Love has such a power of attraction that it not only draws near human beings, but even God is drawn close to the devotee. However, Love makes the person appear strange, one loses one's consciousness too. One forgets eating, drinking, sleeping and waking. The turmoil of separation from the Beloved makes one suffer in inner agitation. Home, family, relatives, everyone is left out. Joy or grief, profit or loss, all such thoughts run away. Such is the glory of Love. When the practitioner reaches the highest summit of bliss, Love comes into being at that time.
>
> Faith and devotion are lower stages compared to the stage of Love.[19]

Likewise, devotees like Prahalad and Dhruv, now remembered with reverence by all Hindus, loved God from early childhood and God manifested several times before them. Ramakrishna Paramahansa used to talk to the Lord every day. The well-known Swami Vivekananda saw and talked with the Mother Goddess in her full physical form. As a child, Namdev with his intense Love, found God materialized before him and ate food with him. Sri Aurobindo experienced the presence of the Mother Goddess as well as Lord Krishna and he expressed this confidently in his writings.

For myself, I saw the Mother Goddess materialize before me during meditation and place her hand on my head to give me her blessing. This occurred at least three times in a period of six months. Child Brahman materialized before me at twilight twice during January 1988 while I was in England. Several other times, I experienced myself as a "dimensionless being" on some spiritual planet. I experienced the "divine female kiss" on my lips in Delhi in moments of loneliness; these kept me blissfully happy for the whole day. These experiences may not be explained in a religious framework. But then, how can I confirm the findings of others or say for certain that God, who is the ocean of love and mercy, materializes before anyone?

Chapter Eighteen

THE VEDIC METHODS OF LORD KRISHNA

Lord Krishna summarizes the Vedic methods to his loving disciple Arjun, and suggests various alternatives he can use for Self-realization. The methods suggested may be suitable for philosophers and westerners. Practical Formula 5 gives those methods, in order of their effectiveness, in the words of Lord Krishna, according to Bhagavad Gita:[1]

PRACTICAL FORMULA 5: LORD KRISHNA'S SUMMARY OF VEDIC METHODS

1. Just fix your mind upon Me, the Supreme Personality of Godhead, and engage all your intelligence on Me. Thus, you will live in Me always, without doubt.

2. If you cannot fix your mind upon Me, without deviation, then follow the regulative principles of bhakti yoga. In this way, develop a desire to attain Me.

3. If you cannot practice the regulations of bhakti yoga, then work for Me, because by working for Me you will come to the complete stage.

4. If, however, you are unable to work in this consciousness of Me, then give up all result of your work and be self-satisfied.

5. If you cannot perform this practice, then engage yourself in the cultivation of knowledge. More useful than knowledge, however, is meditation,

and more useful than meditation is renunciation of the fruit of action, for by such renunciation peace of mind is attained.

If one cannot fix one's attention directly on Krishna, Jesus, Buddha, or any chosen representation of God, then the principles of bhakti yoga are recommended, or one may begin with renunciation of the fruit of action. Knowledge gradually brings one to the point of meditation, and meditation gradually helps one experience God consciousness. Thus, there are two processes: an indirect one, as described here (through the chain of karma yoga, jnana yoga, ashtanga yoga, and finally bhakti yoga, in that order) and a direct one, the path of devotion, to bhakti yoga only.

Vedic methods are, in reality, interdependent of one another. Karma yoga develops equanimity, jnana yoga brings knowledge of the existence of the supreme being, and bhakti yoga unites the practitioner with the supreme being. They can effectively be performed in that order. The final stage is bhakti (devotion), leading to love and the manifestation of God. Many scholars have commented on these methods. Their interpretations can be summarized as follows:[2]

1. Faith and devotion are lower stages when compared to the stage of love.

2. Bhakti (devotion), jnana (knowledge), and yoga are stairs leading to love.

3. A faster and rewarding way to bhakti (devotion) is through selfless action (karma) and knowledge (jnana), rather than plunging directly into devotion.

4. Jnana is dry knowledge; you need something more than detachment—that is *rasa* (joy) that surrounds bhakti (devotion)—and God is joy personified.

5. The secret of the beloved can be known through intimate, exclusive, constant, and unconditional love.

6. When the love-intoxicated practitioner begins to be absorbed into God's consciousness, he reaches *samadhi*, or union with God.

7. Bhakti, or devotion, is the development of exclusive love for God, sweet as nectar in character; its attainment gives completion, an understanding of immortality, and full satisfaction.

8. Renunciation consists of relinquishing all forms of action, secular as well as religious; it may also be called an exclusive feeling toward God and

indifference to illusions (leading away from God. In exclusiveness, one gives up attachment to everything except God.

9. There is a stage when all activities, religious as well as mundane, fade as a matter of course. Until that stage is reached, both these forms of duty will be maintained naturally.

10. Divine love cannot be described in words. One who has the experience does not need to speak of it, and one who is speaking of it, is not in it.

11. After having offered all activities to God, if the practitioner is still haunted by lust, anger, and arrogance, these may be also offered to God. Making God the object of one's passion, anger, and arrogance allows them to be forgotten.

12. Supreme devotion to the Lord may be a faster way to realization than the five types of *mukti*, or liberation: *salokya* (residence in the abode of the Lord), *samipya* (living in close proximity to the Lord), *sarsti* (enjoying the same powers as the lord), *saripya* (having a similar form to that of the Lord), and *sayujya* (absolute identity with the lord).

13. A God-realized person cannot be judged from his or her external conduct; nevertheless, there are certain qualities that are bound to be present, such as those mentioned in chapter 17.

14. When chanting is done with love, God reveals himself and the practitioner is blessed with his vision. The saints, men of wisdom, *purana*, and Vedas all declare there is no difference between *saguna* (divine manifestation of God with attributes) and *aguna* (the absolute).

PRACTICAL FORMULA 6: SYNCHRONIZED VEDIC METHODS

1. Develop equanimity through karma yoga (path of selfless action).
2. Obtain knowledge of the existence of supreme being through jnana yoga (path of knowledge).
3. Develop the stage of love through bhakti yoga (path of devotion).
4. When love intoxication comes, be prepared to enter samadhi and witness God's presence.

Chapter Nineteen

THE METHOD OF DREAMS

When weighing it in relation to other methods, I find the dream method to be very important. It extends from the Vedic period to the present-day scientific world, and has been referred to by almost all methodologists in some form. For example, Eckankar, called the "Religion of Light and Sound," is based on dreams and soul travel experiences.[1] Its present leader, Sri Herald Klemp, induces dreams in his disciples and takes them to various planes of higher reality in those dreams. A series of lectures, called *Dream Discourses I* and *Dream Discourses II*, provides monthly training and practice to students. Klemp has also produced several books in which he describes travel experiences to the remote past, such as the Mayan and Atlantean civilizations.

In his analysis of the living being, Martinus found three unshakeable realities: that which experiences life, the I's creative faculty (that is, "the I"), and the principle of "the created"—its experience or day-consciousness. These three principles are dependent; if one of them does not exist, neither do the other two. Martinus's "triune principle" is analogous to the Vedic triad of the seer, the seeing, and the seen, as described by Sri Aurobindo.

> As none of these principles can be identical with the result of creation, the immortality of the living being becomes thereby evident as a fact. . . . As these three principles constitute precisely the three conditions that must be fulfilled by a thing in order that it can appear "living," every living being thus becomes identical

> with "an eternally living thing." This in turn means that the living being constitutes a reality that senses, experiences and manifests in an eternally continuing existence or experience of life.[2]

The terrestrial human, however, has no conscious realization of this eternal existence. In humans, the ability to remember is in an almost completely latent stage in this cosmic cycle. Because we are unable to remember every event in this physical lifetime, it is only natural that we do not remember events experienced in other lifetimes. This is only evidence of suppressed memory, however, and does not mean that past lives do not exist. There are centers in the brain that are connected through nerves to the physical sense organs of taste, touch, sight, hearing, and smell. Physical experiences are always taking place, but if a nerve is cut, no input is received in the brain. No reception, no memory.

With the nerves intact, however, the mechanism of perception occurs as usual. Similarly, there are connections between the "I" and past-life memories. These memories are recordings of past lifetimes. It is possible to become conscious of these memories. The realization of immortality may be expressed as an impression, instinct, or intuition. This is a classical "spiritual experience." In this state, the awakened day-consciousness bound to the physical body is borne by one of its other energetic bodies. When such transference takes place, the sensory perception of the individual is ignored or not available to consciousness on the physical plane. Martinus believed this transference was identical to the transition occurring in death.

The type of transference described above can also take place in other forms, such as anesthesia, hypnosis, trance, or sleep. Day-consciousness is transferred from the physical body to the "body of feeling." When a person is still living, day-consciousness comes back to the physical body. The "body of memory" usually does not transfer experiences from feeling to day-consciousness; spiritual experiences perceived there primarily remain stored in the unconscious state.

At times, the transference of consciousness from day-consciousness to the spiritual state is not complete and, consequently, we find ourselves in a twilight zone between the physical and spiritual. Examples of such intermediate stages are situations involving high fever, disease, or drugs. Under such circumstances, spiritual memories merge with physical memories and enter into the day-consciousness when one is physically awake. Such a fusion of the spiritual and physical memories is called a dream. For the average person, these dreams may be difficult to understand. However, for a developed person, they are reliable conscious facts.

According to Martinus:

> To the developed cosmic being, who consciously, or by means of his will, can carry out these transformations of the day-consciousness from one body of manifestation to the other, and whose body of memory appears in a somewhat more pronounced constellation to the body of gravity and the body of feeling than that of the terrestrial human being, these spiritual experiences are not "dreams" but fully awake experiences and thereby conscious facts.[3]

The experiences of the "I" with life are determined by a general organ for each basic energy corresponding to that plane of existence (see Table 1, page 37). The six general organs, or "I" (corresponding to the six planes) will be identical, with one body for each plane of existence. On the physical plane, the physical body is most developed, while other bodies are less so; accordingly, "I" is most conscious of physical and least conscious of spiritual vibrations. The physical world is most real to him. Later in evolution, when the person reaches a higher plane, one vibrating with spiritual energy, the situation is reversed. One becomes most conscious of the spiritual plane of existence and one's physical perception becomes dormant. This transference of consciousness can be visualized in dreams; the spiritual experiences stabilize and one can trace one's origin back to the spiritual worlds.

Hindu philosophy has always given importance to dreams as a means of attaining spiritual goals. According to Swami Sivananda Radha, a German psychiatrist who adopted a Hindu name during her discipleship in India, we are able to contact our Higher Self, or *guru* within, in dreams.[4] Discipline comes with the understanding of dreams, bringing independence from the assessment of others, habitual self-criticism, and awareness of new dimensions. Swami Radha recommends the maintenance of a diary to record dreams immediately after waking, and advises keeping a pen, paper, and light ready. Just before going to sleep, repeat at least twice: "I will remember my dream." Write down as much of the dream as can be remembered, along with any events that took place before the dream, or any mental preoccupation you may have experienced. Pay attention to changing perceptions of time and space during sleep. Make your own dictionary of the symbols seen in your dreams instead of consulting a book or following a particular school on symbols. It is helpful to know the way your mind repeatedly expresses itself in symbols that are personal to you. Dreams occur on different levels and, gradually, one begins to understand them more clearly and directly.

In *Recovering Spirituality from Dreams*, Henry Reed talks about his article "Getting Help From Dreams":

> It was about my initiation into the higher power of dreams by alcoholism. A turning point was a dream encounter with an old wise man who pointed to a bottle of wine and indicated that it was soul bait. . . . The founders of Alcoholics Anonymous credit Carl Jung for the gift of the secret formula, spiritus contra spiritum, Spirit against Spirits.[5]

According to Reed, every adversity has within itself a spiritual teacher ready to initiate the sufferer. He advises everyone to find some attachment (any will do) from which they can recover a spiritual gift.

In *Your Dream of Recovery: Dream Interpretation and the 12 steps*, which has much in common with the material presented in *Edgar Cayce and the 12 Stepping Stones to Spirituality*, Shelly Marshall says that "the purpose lurking behind events, or hovering over them, can often be revealed in dreams."[6] She presents several examples, including her personal stories, beginning with the following prayer: "God, grant me the serenity to accept all guidance revealed through my dreams, the courage to change the things I'm asked to, and the wisdom to interpret according to your will for me." According to Marshall, religion is only a bridge to spirituality. Worshiping the bridge will not help; we must cross over it and live in spirit. She draws a special connection between dreaming and drinking. She points out that our interpretation of dreams is ego-heroic; we wish to conquer the dream with our interpretation. The dream is discarded and its interpretation kept. Respecting a dream on its own merits and focus will always lead one to find God. She suggests methods to find something usable in a dream. The presence of puns has been mentioned in many dream books. According to Marshall, pun-consciousness in dreams can reveal many secrets: "Alaska" is not the same as "I'll ask her"; "sober" is not the same as "somber"; "won" is not the same as "one."

In *Your Dreams: God's Neglected Gift*, Herman Riffel presents some useful information. In the seconds between the "tick" and the alarm clock bell, a story may be unraveled that takes a long time to tell, and much longer to write. By comparison, he observes, an hour-long dream can contain volumes of material.[7] He found many references to dreams (while asleep) and visions (while awake) that were in both the Old and the New Testaments. Abraham, Jacob, Joseph, Gideon, and Solomon were all led or encouraged by dreams. Joseph and Daniel saved their nations through the interpretation of their dreams. Prophets received messages through dreams and visions. God said to Moses: "Hear now my words: If there is a prophet among you, I the Lord shall make Myself known to him in vision. I shall speak with him in a dream" (Numbers 12:6). Major events in the Bible are decided based on dreams and visions. Riffel discovered that, in fact, about one-third of the Bible is related to dreams and visions.[8] In his view, God still speaks to us in dreams and visions, but the Western world has taken a negative and unbelieving attitude toward them, although the Eastern world accepted dreams and visions as a source of wisdom many centuries ago.

According to Plato, there are three valid sources of knowledge: the five animal senses (seeing, hearing, smelling, touching, and tasting), reason (which is above the animal), and the spiritual realm (which he called "divine madness"). However, Plato's successor, Aristotle, and his followers ruled out the validity of spiritual realms and "this humanistic philosophy was transmitted throughout the Western world."[9] On his travels to the East, Riffel found temple gods on every street corner and on every important building—gods closely related to their religion, indicating unity of the spiritual and physical worlds. To westerners, this seems farfetched and even ridiculous. Riffel's discoveries shook his secure evangelical Protestant foundations.

Riffel's dream interpretations are interesting for this reason. One day he dreamed: "Alone in my car I was following a bus down a dirt road, and the bus threw so much dust in the air, I could hardly see where I was driving." He had learned that a bus in a dream represents the crowd and dust indicates confusion. His wife, Lillie, said: "The Lord seems to be telling you to follow Him instead of the crowd." Riffel noted that, as he opened himself to this new freshness, his inner spiritual life quickened and God continued to press him harder. The turning point came, and he needed to decide whether he wanted to continue in the ministry of the church or open up to the mystery of healing independently. He was still unable to decide.

Then a local artist with a group of people seeking the guidance of the Holy Spirit had this vision: "I see a beautiful belt that has many fingers proceeding out from it and hairline projections from the fingers." A woman with the group believed this vision concerned Lillie and Riffel. They were not to be bound, even by a belt that was beautiful. They were to be free. Later, the artist said the belt was a Protestant denomination, the fingers were the churches, and the hairline projections from the fingers were people. In the words of Riffel: "God would let us be a blessing to many within the belt, but we were not to hold on to it. We were to let go in an attitude of humility."[10] This is how Riffel received evidence of God using dreams and visions to speak to people. Eventually, he was dismissed as pastor of the church. Although being fired from his job was a painful experience, both of them were now free and peaceful and were looking forward to the exciting new life God had promised.

God continued to guide Riffel and speak to him through dreams. One night, he had the following dream: He was pushing a baby carriage with a baby in it. When he came to the end of the street he did not stop, but pushed the carriage right up and over a two-story house. The house was like the one they were living in at the time. Once, he even lifted the carriage over his head and the baby fell out, but he caught it. His friend Francis Whiting explained that the dead end of the street represented the dead end of his ministry in the church. But he was not to stop; rather he was to carry the baby (new idea or concept) right up over the top of the traditional house in which his soul was then living. Even if the baby fell out, he would not lose it (the new idea). This was a very meaningful dream to him. He believed that the death and resurrection process spoken of by Jesus was also being pointed out to him in his dreams, after he had opened himself to the spirit.

Riffel found his desire to know more about dreams diminishing. Then one night, he dreamed that he was on a raft some distance from the shore where people were swimming. The water was deep. A young girl who was in his care fell off the raft and sank into the water. He dove in, grabbed her, and pulled her out of the water. The dream meant that the baby (new idea) had now grown into a young girl and he was neglecting her (the truth). He became more alert and paid attention. He remembered the Jung Institute in Switzerland, received a scholarship in a miraculous way, and he and Lillie attended the school to learn dream psychology. He was further guided in a dream in which he entered a castle by crossing the moat around it. The moat meant motherly containment. So he broke the strong, and perhaps dependent, ties to his mother, freeing himself to be more masculine and aggressive. Earlier, when he asked God for a wife, a thought came to his mind to look at the school yearbook. He did so and stopped at the picture of Lillie. He proposed to her and soon they were married.

Even short dreams can be very meaningful. A man in Switzerland came and told Riffel about two short pictures he had seen in dreams. In the first, he saw his left leg badly swollen; the veins were dark lines. In the second, a poisonous spider sat on his briefcase. Asked if there was a problem with his walking, his behavior, or his way of living, he admitted to a messy situation in life, but he thought it would remain under cover. When asked what he used the briefcase for, he said, "My profession." Riffel then told him his bad behavior might even affect his work. The man used to think his behavior was not that bad, but after the shock of the dream interpretation, he changed.

Riffel believed that, if properly handled, the interpretation of dreams could bring balance and wholeness to people.[11] He cited the example of King David of the Old Testament, whose masculine and feminine qualities became properly balanced. David was physically strong and defeated his son, Absalom, in battle when the son wanted to oust his father from the throne. David, weeping bitterly after killing his loving son, was about to lose the battle, but was aided by his wise general Joab's advice to fulfill his responsibilities as king. Study of the Gospels can reveal Jesus had a balance of authoritative strength and supportive gentleness.

Riffel gave many more examples of his own dreams that guided him, along with examples of others who later came to consult him. His work shows the importance of dreams and different ways of interpretation that can reveal the wisdom of God and provide guidance and help. In his opinion, there are three reasons why we do not remember dreams: we have been taught from the beginning that dreams are unimportant or irrelevant, we experience a mechanical loss of them as we plunge into the affairs of the world on awakening, and spiritually, if we want to keep God out of our thoughts, his guidance goes unused. However, dreams may continue in the form of nightmares. God, or our Higher Self, may be telling us something, if we dare to listen. The message is generally twofold: it may tell about the present situation of the dreamer, or it may tell what would happen if the dreamer continues in the present direction of affairs. The response received from dreams is proportional to the attitude shown toward them.

Carl Jung, perhaps the greatest exponent of dream analysis, said dreams depict the inner state of the individual and, if properly analyzed, they provide a real opportunity for growth. He writes, in *Man and His Symbols*, his wonderful theory of *anima* and *animus*, and the four stages of inner development.[12] Dreams cannot be taken literally, but they can be analyzed to know the context of outer circumstances.

Symbols and Their Meanings

One dictionary of symbols and their meanings cannot be accurately written for everyone. One should make one's own dictionary after writing symbols down regularly and reviewing them at regular intervals. Nevertheless, general guidance on symbols and their meanings can always be found. Following are some common interpretations.

Birds: Thoughts, ideas, and spirituality. Because birds fly in the sky, their appearance in dreams shows the exalted mental condition of the dreamer. One is peaceful, pure, and tranquil, especially if one dreams of a pigeon or a dove. One may be involved in philosophical or spiritual activities, or in some creative venture.

Animals: A parallel mental/emotional state of the dreamer, according to the characteristics of the animal. For example, a rat that is known for entering the kitchen as a thief may represent the entrance of the dreamer's thoughts at the lower levels of life. A cat may represent the destruction of ideas; a dog may represent faithfulness in one's life; a fox may represent cunningness in the thoughts of the dreamer; a bull may represent a hardworking nature of the person or the presence of hard work at the moment, according to the physical, mental, or emotional condition of the dreamer during the dream. I once dreamed of running down a street chased by a dog, which finally caught up with me and bit me on the leg. Those were days when I had some unpleasant arguments with my relatives on property matters, and sometimes there were embarrassing situations. The dream was a warning of such situations. Riffel once dreamed of spearing a fish, but he had no license. In real life, his ministry was growing privately, with some groups that were not officially sponsored by the church. The dream suggested that he had to use caution and not be assertive in accepting offers from churches lacking official authorization. Thus, there is no fixed rule; follow your intuition.

Snakes: Sexual energy according to one school of thought, wisdom according to another. I would say that both of them could be correct. In yoga tradition, repeated appearances of snakes symbolize the spiritual kundalini energy that corresponds initially to sex, and to wisdom after the transcendence of sex.

Houses: The inner psychological house of good or bad memories, according to the mood of the dream. Sometimes, one is taken to their childhood home. Often, we see a new house with many rooms, suggesting the development of newer levels of learning or consciousness, leading to gradual enlightenment. Old or broken houses may suggest a gloomy situation in life. A well-maintained house may suggest a happy situation in life.

Automobiles: An indication of control, or the lack of it. A new car suggests an expression of freedom in one's life. If one is driving one's own car, it may mean one is in control of one's own affairs. If someone else is driving it, it may be indicating the control of one's affairs by another person and a suggestion to achieve freedom for real progress and happiness.

Baby: A new idea or thought.

People: No literal meaning as such, but rather parts of our own personality. When seeing a known person who is aggressive by nature, it may suggest the dreamer is behaving aggressively in general, or perhaps to a particular person or situation in life. Dreaming of peaceful people or a saint may suggest the dreamer is internally turning peaceful or saintly. Seeing a police officer, a leader, or authoritative person suggests the dreamer has a part of their personality authoritatively taking charge of affairs or situations in their life. Seeing a person as a saint, sitting in meditative postures, or as a yogi may indicate that this person has actually crossed over the spiritual boundaries. I personally know of instances of this kind.

Beating/Killing: A suggestion that one is not happy with someone or with some situation in life and revenge is desired.

Loving: A loving attitude toward others.

Sex: A widely misunderstood dream symbol. It does not mean the dreamer is having sexual relations with someone. It probably means the dreamer is interacting with one's inner Self or creative side, and is approaching a balance between the masculine and feminine principles—intellect and emotion. When understood, a feeling of joy and fulfillment comes, rather than guilt.

Money: A twofold symbol. Receiving money, a purse, or treasure in a dream indicates energy or power in real life. Loss, on the other hand, is indicative of a weak situation in real life.

Clothes: Suggestive of how one likes to appear before others. The type of clothing worn in a dream is indicative of wearing such dress in real life.

Nakedness: Indicates exposure to others and possible embarrassment. It may also symbolize not hiding from God, yourself, or others.

Triangle, square, circles, or ball: An indication of inner wholeness in the dreamer.

Water: An important symbol appearing in different forms, such as a pool, river, or ocean. Clear water indicates clear consciousness in real life, leading to philosophical or spiritual perfection. Muddy or unclear water may suggest a messy or unclear situation in life; one may be looking for a way out of a confused situation in life. Crossing a river is a sign of no return—a crossing from physical to spiritual dimensions. Such a person may have graduated from the school of earth.

The Anima and Animus Symbols in Dreams

The female figure appearing in the dreams of males is called anima, while the male figure appearing in the dreams of females is called animus.[13] The purpose of the anima or animus is to guide the individual toward wholeness and balance. There are four levels to the role these symbols play in dreams.[14] For the anima, these levels are:

1: Primitive woman, symbolizing innocence, for example, Eve.

2: Romanticized beauty, such as Cleopatra or Helen of Troy, symbolizing sex.

3: The Virgin Mary, feeding milk to the Christ child through her breasts, symbolizing love.

4: Athena, the Greek goddess of wisdom; the Mona Lisa, wearing a mysterious smile; Sapienta, or Shulamite in the song of Solomon; Devi Durga or Shakti. They all point toward spiritual experience.

The four levels of the animus are:

1: The wholly physical man, Tarzan of the jungle, symbolizing primitivism and innocence.

2: The romantic man, for example, the nineteenth-century British poet Shelley; or the man of action, for example, Earnest Hemingway, war hero, hunter, symbolizing sex.

3: The bearer of the Word, for example, Lloyd George, the great political orator, symbolizing love.

4: The wise guide to spiritual truth, for example, Mahatma Gandhi, Jesus Christ, or Buddha, symbolizing spiritual maturity.

The fourth stage of either symbol is rarely achieved by people in modern times, but is possible for serious students of truth.

My Personal Dream Experiences

Although I have been remembering dreams all my life, there are a few from recent years that provided me with life-changing spiritual guidance. Sometime around 1980, I dreamed of flying through the sky until I reached the summit of a hill surrounded by beautiful lakes, meadows, and gardens. Reaching the top of the hill, I found a beautiful temple, purest white and shining with equal luminosity from every side. A feeling of happiness and bliss, and a longing to have more visits to such a place, instantly filled me. My love for God increased and led me to regular practice of yoga and meditation. This began a withdrawal of my interest from worldly affairs. I realize now that this was a visit to a temple on one of the astral planes.

I have enjoyed similar dreams ever since, flying over places similar to those on earth—lakes, mountains, rivers, gardens, fruits and flowers so lovely and nurturing that I cannot describe my happiness. I have flown over villages, stopped and descended to the ground, and, when I wished, flown off again.

The dream I described in chapter 2 of a translucent fortress gave me a firsthand experience of the higher spiritual realms under the guidance of an invisible helper, or guru, who may have been the Eckankar Master Sri Herald Klemp, or Pythagoras, or perhaps another. The next day, I was full of happiness and my faith in yoga and meditation increased. This was in 1987. The visits to these realms were a source of happiness and bliss on one hand and detachment from the world on the other.

I remember several dreams in which snakes were all around me in different forms, but I felt no fear. For a time, these were almost daily occurrences. In later days, I saw snakes with open hoods in different situations. Sometimes, a snake would look at me in a friendly way; at other times, they would crawl on my body; at yet other times, they would fly with me in the sky. These are dreams indicative of awakening kundalini.

In 1995, while in San Francisco, I dreamed of a large gathering where I saw a man with an outstanding physique and glowing face and eyes looking at me in a very affectionate way. He was moving and I read the name "Bapu" written on his chest. The next day, my mother told me that was the nickname of a present-day Indian saint, Asaramji. As I understand now, my Higher Self had come to initiate and bless me in the form of a guru.

In chapter 2, I mentioned speaking with my deceased father through a medium in 1995. Later, I dreamed of traveling with my father while both of us were in our light bodies, perhaps on some astral plane. The dream lasted almost an hour by earth time, and we shared ideas of common interest. He said many things for me to convey to my mother and other relatives in Delhi. We embraced each other and parted happily. In the dream, he told me he was taking a long rest and that he would soon receive a new body and be transferred to a different, "more lighted," area.

Practical Formula 7 summarizes the dream method. It can be used to acquire the knowledge of heaven and trace one's spiritual identity. However, on awakening kundalini, powerful dreams can become a regular feature. Conversely, maintaining a diary and analyzing dreams regularly can help trigger the awakening of kundalini.

PRACTICAL FORMULA 7: A SUMMARY OF THE DREAM METHOD

1. The ability to remember is at a latent stage at present. This does not mean that past lives do not exist.

2. When forgotten connections are revived, we experience bliss and direct experiences (memories) of past events. One then understands immortality. These are powerful spiritual experiences.

3. Sometimes transference of consciousness from day-consciousness to a spiritual state is not complete and one finds oneself in the twilight zone between the physical and spiritual.

4. Under such circumstances, spiritual memories become merged with physical memories and enter into day-consciousness on waking.

5. Many people may not rely on dreams. But a developed cosmic being, by means of his will, can carry these transformations from one body to another. His body of memories is more pronounced than those of terrestrial humans. For him, these spiritual experiences are not dreams, but conscious reality.

6. This transference of consciousness can be visualized in dreams; spiritual experiences can be stabilized and one can trace one's origin back to spiritual worlds. Once this is accomplished, liberation occurs—no more coming back to earth.

7. One is able to contact one's Higher Self, the inner guru, in dreams.

8. Just before going to sleep, one can repeat a few times: "I will remember my dreams." Then write them down. Pray to God to reveal the truth and provide guidance.

9. Maintain a diary and record dreams immediately on awakening, whether you remember them fully or only partially.

10. Make a note of the changing perceptions of time and space during sleep.

11. Make a dictionary of symbols seen in dreams; learn how the mind expresses itself in symbols.

12. Review dreams at regular intervals, noting similarities of pattern in a specific time period, and the message conveyed to you related to real-life circumstances or the questions you had in mind. God, or your Higher Self, is talking to you about your future. You may call it precognition.

13. You will begin to understand the different levels on which dreams occur. This understanding becomes more clear and direct over time.

14. Dreaming is a spiritual gift that can be recovered in many ways. Exploring your attachments to experience is helpful—for example, possessions, temples, the opposite sex, or children. Any one of them can trigger a series of dreams and broaden your spiritual horizon.

15. The unclear purpose of events taking place in life can be revealed in dreams.

16. Some think there is a connection between dreams and drinking. However, I would not lay any stress on this point.

17. A few seconds of dreaming may reveal a whole life story. Such is the balance of time between sleeping and waking states.

18. Dreams depict our inner state.

Chapter Twenty

NEAR-DEATH EXPERIENCES

We receive firsthand proof of life beyond death through a variety of near-death experiences, such as surgical operations, falling from a height, or any injury causing unconsciousness. In my opinion, getting a taste of the afterlife is like a visit to a foreign country with a visitor's visa that can be converted into citizenship through meditation, metaphysical practices, or any other method of Self-realization. Such an experience is not restricted to any religion or only to good people. After a near-death experience, most people become more spiritual or begin to believe in some form of God consciousness.

According to Atwater, some people find it difficult to adjust back to normal life because of the profundity of this kind of experience.[1] Negative reactions include fear of talking about their experience and depression at having to resume their lives. Positive reactions include ecstasy, the thrill of a wonderful experience, gratitude, awe, enhanced psychic abilities, and an enlightened, fearless understanding of death. According to Rosemary Ellen Guiley: "Ring, the philosopher Michael Grosso, and others have theorized that the NDE may be a form of enlightenment or 'gateway to a higher consciousness', and could have a transformative effect on the entire planet if enough people have similar experiences."[2] Similarly, Carol Zaleski writes that stories of near-death experiences can introduce a "religious sense of the cosmos" into the scientific or secular understanding of the individual.[3]

It is important to note that near-death experiences take place spontaneously; there is no specific method to induce them. Yet, there are factors in the psychological makeup of a person—abuse, neglect, or dissociation during childhood—that can make a person prone to these experiences. Take, for instance, the experience of Barbara Harris Whitfield:

> Then I separated from my body, just as I had when I was being abused as a child . . . I saw myself in a bubble, face down in my crib, crying just as hysterically . . . energy was wrapping around me and going through me, holding up every molecule of my being. It took me a long time to use the word God . . . in a cloud of bubbles . . . each bubble was another event from my life . . . I relived 32 years of my life . . . I could hear myself saying, "No wonder, no wonder. No wonder you are the way you are now. Look what was done to you when you were a little girl." I saw all the abuse . . . my mother physically abusing me, came from the abuse she received as a child.[4]

While out of body during her experience, Barbara Whitfield heard two nurses talking about her and noticed they did not change the pillows she had wet. After coming back into her body, she told the nurses, to their great surprise, all about their conversation and the fact that they did not change the wet pillows. This description and thousands others should convince skeptics who believe that near-death experiences are only dreams.

Whitfield defines spiritual awakening as an experiential opening to a power greater than ourselves.[5] I would say it is an experience of the greater power within us. Martinus defined spiritual knowledge as an analysis of experiences promoted by forces not sensed by the five physical senses.[6] Both are authors who achieved Self-realization through entirely different methods, yet, their conclusion is the same and is parallel to Eastern findings—for example, in the works of Sri Aurobindo. Whitfield evoked the spiritual energy "that can be called many things—kundalini, divine energy, holy spirit, *ruach ha ḳodesh*, or the holy wind that guides my life. When invited into your life, this energy will show you how to see from a higher point of view."[7] In her view, a mystic is someone who relates to God through a direct experience of communion with the soul or child within. One receives direct knowledge of reality, and one's journeys lead to this reality—an interesting confirmation of ancient Eastern beliefs and the findings of many seekers!

Diane Goble awakened to the reality of the spiritual world when she slipped under the waves of a raging river and breathed in the cold water (an experience described on the cover page of her book *Through the Tunnel*). She believed she was going to die and watched scenes of her death from above. Suddenly, she found herself speeding through a dark tunnel toward light. A being of light communicated with her telepathically and guided her through a library of books from which she accumulated knowledge. Being given an option to stay or return to earth to complete her mission, she reluctantly decided to come back and dragged her body back to the raft still caught in the waterfall. This is a model story of a near-death experience. The message she offers is: "We are all on our Spiritual Path back to our Source. Earth life is an education and a creative opportunity—its purpose is to enhance our spiritual growth as Children of a Loving God."[8] She concludes that "the pursuit of knowledge and wisdom should occupy our time—learning how to be in the physical world without becoming attached to its pleasures or caught up in its troubles. No matter what, as it is only temporary."[9]

Is this not what Gautam Buddha said 2,600 years ago, confirmed by his contemporaries Zoroaster, Confucius, Pythagoras, and others, and later realized independently by Jesus? We discover the same truth over and over, by different methods at different times.

Globe emphasizes that "the CLEAR LIGHT is what appears to everyone just prior to the moment of death, but few see it."[10] According to her, love, kindness, and compassion raise a person's energetic frequency. One will be drawn as close to the light as one has been open to it during one's lifetime. Recognizing the clear light and merging with it can achieve complete liberation from negative karma, but if one dies with a hatred-filled heart, one may not be aware of the light. One will not reach its frequency and will go on to experience the *bardo thodol* of Tibet, which says the chance of illumination is greatest at the moment of death.

Many scholars have commented on the significance of near-death experiences. Nils Bjorn Kvastad, in his *Problems of Mysticism*, points out that "the deceased sees a lightening, called the 'clear light of the void'. If he unites with it and consciously realizes it, he will have a mystical experience and be liberated."[11] Dr. Raymond Moody appears to be writing of the same light as the Bardo Thodol when he says:

> Mystical experience can then be a foretaste of life after death, a view the mystic and devotee of Isis, Apulejus, expressed when he described a mystical experience: "I have passed through the gates of death." However, if this light is realized and the after-life has become a continuous mystical experience, as the "Bardo Thodol" holds it can be, this is no individual, separate existence. The deceased will somehow be merged with the universe.[12]

Yogis, as they experience death while still living, see this light and then experience visits to higher realms.[13]

Near-death experiences take place when needed by the soul; they cannot be generated or forced. No practical formula can be designed to create one. However, when such an experience does take place, taking refuge in an organized direction to gain Self-realization can be helpful. The same is true of the sudden events described in chapter 21.

Chapter Twenty-One

CRISIS AND SUFFERING

Barbara Harris Whitfield noted that the Chinese symbol for crisis also means opportunity, and that ancient Eastern spiritual literature recognizes that the path of liberation is accelerated during crisis and suffering.[1] I agree with this and add that, whenever conditions become so difficult that a crisis appears, an individual can then open to spiritual advancement. Crisis is opportunity. Paul Twitchell and Harold Klemp have given similar statements in their books on Eckankar.[2] Crisis seems to be a catalyst for spiritual development. Once liberation or Self-realization has been achieved, it does not matter how one appears to live.

Childbirth is an opportunity for spiritual experience. During childbirth, some women report leaving their bodies to view the delivery from the ceiling. Some have reported the presence of deceased relatives, some visit landscapes on higher realms, and some experience unbelievable ecstasy followed by bliss for many days or even weeks. These spiritual experiences can be allowed to happen naturally through awareness, if women are prepared in advance. Christina Groff, founder of the Kundalini Research Network in California, is a brilliant example of this. Her kundalini aroused during the birth of her second child; later she took a formal initiation from Swami Muktananda in Honolulu.

Bereavement is a crisis in which someone who is excessively attached to a dying person can experience awakening. I know some people personally to whom this has happened. I can also cite the example of my father, who died on September 7, 1992. On that day, around 8 P.M., during my regular prayer and meditation, I went into an exceptionally deep state of concentration and peace for about an hour. During that time, I felt the presence of someone around me. My father had expressed his love for me more than I showed mine for him; he never wanted me to leave India.

Several days later, after my arrival in Delhi, I wept bitterly in my father's room. I retired late that night and awoke in the early morning hours with the feeling that my shoulder was being strongly shaken by someone. I sensed breathing around me and knew it was my father. For the next half hour, I said many things to him and assured him I would take care of my mother and see that the property left by him was equally divided. I then asked him to wake me up once again to give me proof of his presence. And he did wake me up one more time early that morning. The same night, my sister heard my father calling her name and saw him standing outside her window wearing the suit I had brought for him from London. He appeared as a much younger, smiling thirty-five-year-old man.

Three days before his death, my father started seeing deceased friends and relatives standing around him. There was the presence of someone in uniform writing on a notebook; he commented that this policeman could not harm him as he had not committed any crime. He also saw me wearing a white turban, involved in some ritual. This foresaw my official declaration as head of the family in a religious ceremony with a white turban on my head, which occurred a few days after his passing.

We all witnessed my mother increasing her mantra-chanting meditations, and going into longer periods of trance. Afterward, she told of seeing deceased people in her visions. She saw strange, partially understood writings on the wall and celestial beings in the room, especially when we were singing devotional songs and when I read from religious books. When offering food to Lord Krishna, she invariably reported his coming in an astral body and sharing the food. She became a completely changed person. My mother cried day and night, and continued to do so for weeks after my father's death. Eventually, I brought my mother with me to Fiji, where she stayed for a few months. The main point here is that my mother was very much involved in the process of my father's death and she received her awakening at that time.

Sharing the dying moments of his wife, Sally, English mystic poet P. J. Kavanagh experienced "revelation" at the hospital in Java:

> It was not a visual experience but it is best described in visual terms. It was though streams of connections of light were going from cloud to cloud. Everything seemed connected. It was not an

> aural experience either but if you can imagine choirs of angels, the music of the spheres, they were present. And what was really surprising about it was that there seemed enormous vats of consolation. Everything was all right, absolutely everything was all right. It was of immense warmth. This came as no surprise; it seemed as though one had always known that. And it was only afterwards that I realized that I hadn't thought, "My goodness! This is a revelation, an illumination!"[3]

After two months, he started seeing colors in a clear form, in a mysteriously vibrating way. He suddenly felt an overwhelming love for England—an emotion he had never felt before.

Kavanagh was in his early sixties at that time. While attending a party, he was suddenly filled with a bubbling well of silent laughter—an inexhaustible, Mozartian kind of laughter. It was undirected laughter, not focused on any one thing, and there was no Self in it. It was beautiful and subsided with an inner cleansing, like the feeling one has after a fit of weeping. It was a sudden release from the Self. According to Kavanagh, the heightened emotional state was responsible for dropping the barrier. He thinks every man and woman has his own moment. For him, these were the moments of literary inspiration containing light and warmth, when he felt human rather than personal. He does not believe these illuminations can be harnessed. However, some kind of formal concentration or social concentration, some form of prosaic habit was necessary for him. It led him to God. In his opinion, everybody has to find his or her own path.

Physical or emotional torture can also open one to the presence of God and induce transcendental knowledge from within. This happened to Dr. Sheila Cassidy of England in 1975, when she was arrested and brutally tortured by the Chilean secret police. On being asked about the moment when her belief became profound, she replied that there was no particular moment. She never experienced God speaking in words. The experience was more a knowledge from within. When they started to take off her clothes, she was completely incredulous, because she had always thought she had a measure of protection. But while it was happening, she did have a sense of God's presence, which never left her. In her own words: "At the time of the interrogation and my fear of rape, I was just surviving minute by minute and being absolutely terrified and not feeling any emotion for the people . . . after the torture I was more and more convinced of a loving God who knew and loved me personally."[4]

The Road to Damascus

According to Sir Fred Hoyle, scientist and astronomer, blinding revelation for scientists as well as for religious people comes through crisis:

> If we go back to the road to Damascus, St. Paul had been putting conditions on his thinking and suddenly they were removed. This is why it is an intensely personal experience. It can only happen if one has gone through a sort of crisis either of moral, mathematical or scientific thinking.[5]

In his opinion, everybody has to travel the road to Damascus. Hoyle says that Einstein summed up the whole scientific philosophy in his remark: "God may be subtle but he's not malicious"; it is just a feeling within oneself; it is a light on the road to Damascus. As pointed out earlier, Sir Alister Hardy, commenting on the phrase "road to Damascus" used frequently by Sir Fred Hoyle in *Revelation: Glimpses of Reality*, said that the phrase means a "sudden revelation," or something very important, that influences the whole outlook of the individual and to which he might give the name of God.[6]

The loneliness and agony of masturbation in front of men triggered a spiritual experience in British actress Sarah Miles. According to her, male directors cannot explain to a woman how to masturbate; it is something we all do in private. Shortly after doing a masturbation scene, she had her first revelation. On seeing the daily film rushes everybody said, "Well done," but Sarah was distressed because of the pain of the loneliness in doing the scene. Walking on the empty road back to her home, she experienced something new:

> It was quite beautiful. I had enormous heat coming from an area just above the solar plexus. It was a fierce heat from the center, like fire, hot fire, hotter even than fire. I also noticed that I was numb in my extremities, my feet were cold and I was icy but boiling in the center. My breath seemed to be coming from a place that I had never known it came from before. I felt fear because of this heat and then it changed. I was doubtless. There was no doubt; there was an aching of strength that passeth all understanding. I felt at that moment, not I, but something else that was me, yet was not me, was capable of just dancing across estuary. I felt that I could, through something else that was happening to me, do anything. It was a moment of utter doubtlessness and I think almost omnipotence. It was as if God was within and with-

> out and I was at one within and without with all things. It sounds terribly cliché'd, but it is so difficult to describe. Extraordinary doubtlessness. This was what was so strange—doubtlessness about everything and knowledge about everything.[7]

Since then, Sarah hears an inner voice all the time and follows it. She realized we are all eternal and decided to discover her spiritual body and eternity. As she looks back, the actual moment of revelation was perhaps a split second, while the actual journey was about five minutes. Trust, God's presence, and a strange new breathing pattern remained after the experience. She passed from being all-powerful to being a total puppet. Something else took over that was telling her to do things.

After reaching home, she was in a hot bath for almost three days, constantly renewing the hot water. She felt drawn toward death, but had no fear. Something happened to her and she took a handful of sleeping pills, then a realization came and she put the pills aside. She took a pen and paper and began writing, and continued writing for three years. This led her to meditation and yoga, both of which have served her beautifully over the years. In her opinion, meditation is a wonderful route for people to gain self-knowledge. Sarah put herself in the hands of fate, something she had never done before. She knew death was not the end. That was not a belief; it was knowledge—she knew it. But she feels that putting this knowledge into practice is extremely hard work. She received a mountain of correspondence in response to her revelation program and was happy her program helped to awaken the seeds of spirituality lying dormant in most people.

Hurtling downhill, being catapulted down head over heels, heading toward a long drop, Britain's best-known mountaineer, Doug Scot, thought: "Well, now I am going to die but it won't be a bad thing! A warm feeling came over me. Then I stopped dead in the snow."[8] He experienced what it is like being in an avalanche and having visions of snow and rocks. The episode left something permanent in him. He realized that, although he would not choose to die now, he was not afraid to die.

A few weeks later, he was walking with a woman who was suffering enormous grief for her dead boyfriend, another mountaineer named Dougal. Suddenly, he felt vibrations in the landscape and rushing energy at the periphery of his vision. The intense experience expanded his sense of compassion. He could understand people's problems and see a connection between everything. His heightened perception was hard to describe. Although it lasted for only a few seconds, it changed his whole outlook on life. He became involved with friends and acquaintances having problems and was effective in helping them with support, sympathy, understanding, and awareness. Earlier, he had been ineffective, but now, for the first time, he started doing something for someone else without expecting any reward.

The experience lifted him up to a new way of looking at the whole business of being alive. His new interest in literature on the topic calmed him down because of its profound nature. He started reading all kinds of esoteric literature—Tao, *I Ching*, and much more—in search of understanding. Although the effect was strong for only a few months, it remained a reference point for the rest of his life. Although nothing happened to him on the mountain, Doug Scot noted that one does not eat or sleep much there, and that might be a key to his heightened sensory perception. He could feel thoughts coming, and there was a space between the thoughts. That space contained calm and peaceful. Although he is not in that space all the time, he values the experience as a permanent reference point. However, he maintains that one does not have to go to the mountains to have such an experience; one can have it at the back of one's garden if one knows the technique and if one has the burning desire. I would agree with Doug Scot on this.

On being asked if he hopes to have one of those moments of revelation again, he said that it would be great if it happens, but one does not achieve it when trying too hard. It is only through letting go of the ambition to climb a peak that events often work to allow one to get there. It is perfecting the means and not the result that yields these moments. Doug Scott could control his body to such an extent that he could quickly heal himself. He would sense the needs of others by becoming calm, relaxed, interested, and sympathetic. He has realized the truth, in the words of Ouspensky, that "most of us are asleep." Likewise Gurdjieff observes that "most of us live in a state of sleep." Doug Scot was shocked when he awakened to his own faults and received a glimpse of the vast potential each of us has.

Harold Klemp of Eckankar describes a finding similar to that of Doug Scott in his *Letters of Light and Sound*. A female parachutist could not get her parachute to open, in spite of her best efforts. Seeing imminent death, she came out of her body and found she had forgotten to press the correct button. Quickly, she reentered her body, pressed the required button, and landed safely. Her heightened perception while out of her body changed her entire view of life; she was never the same person again. She eventually studied metaphysics and serious meditation, and reported spiritual improvement as time passed.

Knocked flat by a warrant officer in a Japanese prisoner-of-war camp, Sir Laurens Van Der Post suddenly heard a voice inside him saying: "Go back, and let him beat you again!"[9] He turned instantly and stood before the officer. The officer picked up the chair on which he was sitting and was just about to hit Van Der Post with it, when the thought came to his mind that he had just knocked this man down. The rhythm of something evil in him broke down; he threw the chair down and walked away in disgust. Sir Post is certain that, if he had not faced the officer once more, many people would have been killed that day, but he had no foreknowledge he was going to do it. He always felt there is something in us, whether we die or not, which is always just a jump ahead of death. He felt it was the voice of creation speaking at that moment. He wrote more than twenty books and has made several films including *The Story of Carl Gustav Jung*.

Sir Laurens observes that scientists fail their own calling when they forget Einstein's quote: "The spirit of science is devout." Science tends to reduce the spirit to rationalism, which in his opinion is wrong. He thinks this overall drive is in everyone and we can make ourselves receptive to revelation. There is something in life that tries to compensate if life goes too far in one direction. Spirit speaks to different people in different ways. One cannot explain the nature of an artist, priest, or scientist rationally. We cannot rationally discover the element behind their creativity; for example, something made Archimedes discover that the amount of water displaced by his body in a bath is equal to the mass of his body. Descartes said, "I think: therefore I am," which means that there is something that thinks through us. Germans call it *einfall*—inspiration—something that falls into us suddenly like a flash of light. Inspiration occurs when an unknown thought is suddenly recognized.

According to Sir Laurens, revelation is a flashing act of recognition. However, he thinks that revelation is continuous; it need not always be dramatic. He has more faith in steady evolutionary revelation than startling and dramatic ones. He observes that man has never felt so threatened, insecure, and frightened as at present because of the terrible fear of atomic war. It is a force created by man, but we do not know how to control it. This imbalance has produced insecurity.

An insult turned into a loving embrace evoked the revelation of the old proverb "Forgive us our trespasses, as we forgive those that trespass against us" in the heart of British actor and comedian Kenneth Williams. While serving military duty in Sri Lanka, he was thrown out of the British mess by Indian soldiers for being improperly dressed. He was later asked by his officer to return to their mess, now in proper uniform, and apologize to the Indian officer for his act. While doing so, he felt very ashamed and expected to be insulted in return. But the Indian officer embraced him, kissed him on both cheeks, and invited him to dine with them. When Williams expressed surprise, the Indian officer reminded him of the proverb. Williams reports: "I was thunderstruck and transfixed. It was a revelation for me because I'd said it a hundred times without any real concept of the import of the words."[10] It came like a bolt from a clear blue sky and he was helped to become aware of the real significance of the Lord's Prayer by a Hindu.

According to Williams, self-will has a purpose that science cannot explain. Science can tell us how electricity is harnessed or how lightning strikes, but it cannot explain why. Faith supplies the "why." In his opinion, comedy has a mystical content. A mysterious thing happens in an auditorium where laughter is created. One can convert a misery-making thing into an amusing and creative thing through comedy. In his view, happiness is an ephemeral thing and the most we can hope to achieve is contentment with our lot. Perhaps he forgot we are created out of happiness and through laughter, and that we momentarily transcend our separation by experiencing our true nature.

The sudden events described in this chapter are all spontaneous; the people concerned had no control over them. However, one can conclude that, when one is open to the "inner voice" at the time of crisis, the voice of one's inner guide or guru will speak. Moreover, following that voice or intuition can possibly lead one out of crisis. Receiving a revelation or glimpse of reality, and then studying an organized method of spiritual perfection can help one achieve liberation from maya and Self-realization.

Chapter Twenty-Two

THE SEX DRIVE

The sex drive is a powerful and natural—and perhaps the shortest—path to Self- or God-realization if understood properly. "The Tantrikas transformed sex into spirituality, but the preachers of morality in India did not allow the message to reach the masses."[1] Although practicing Tantra was banned thousands of years ago, its philosophy is immortalized in the monuments of Khajuraho and the temples of Puri and Konark in India. On seeing the images of naked couples engaged in intercourse on the outer walls of the temples of Khajuraho, one senses no vulgarity; rather, one is enveloped in feelings of sacredness and peace. On the faces of the statues, one finds the serene and peaceful impression of Buddha and Mahavir. Visionaries who knew spiritual sex intimately created the statues. Just as watching two men fight satisfies and dissipates the deeply rooted instinct for fighting, meditation on these images of intercourse releases wild sexuality from inside the watcher, who becomes calm and peaceful. Freedom from lust can be achieved through long sessions of concentration on these drawings. On entering the temple, one experiences the peaceful statue of Lord Shiva residing inside. This is the secret of Tantra.

Talking about *samadhi*, Jesus said, "There shall be time no longer." If one observes the process of copulation and orgasm closely, one finds that two things are created—egolessness and timelessness. These are precisely the characteristics of samadhi. In that brief moment of sexual climax, the individual tastes bliss and divinity. To have the same experience again, the person indulges in sex repeatedly and uses a considerable amount of energy and vitality. However, one has touched the subtler level of the sexual experience, which is spiritual in essence. What one can come to understand at this point is that sexual pleasure is not the end, but the means to attain the permanent bliss of samadhi. Normally, ejaculation accompanies orgasm. If one can know the secret of separating one from the other, one can enjoy the bliss of the absolute without losing energy or vitality. This is what happens to yogis. They are in a state of permanent bliss and full of energy. This is where meditation comes into the picture, and one is required to know the art of converting sex into meditation.

Muhammad Subuh, later known as Pak Subuh and nicknamed Bapak, was a Sufi Muslim and native of Java. According to him, interaction on the human level comes about through sexual intercourse:

> Act of sexual union gives man a chance to be influenced by the force which is properly human because, in the moment of orgasm, the inner most Self of the man or woman becomes isolated from the lower forces. At this instant, if a man can be free of desire, and of thinking, he will become aware of an inner awakening to his true nature."[2]

When one's consciousness is raised to a purely human level in the sexual act, one can become aware of the nature of the lower forces and detach oneself from them. Once their domination is over, the person becomes their master and can direct them into their proper paths.

According to Swami Satyananda Saraswati, spiritual energy passes through four different levels of existence: ignorance, sex, love, and spiritual experience.[3] In the process of yoga, when kundalini reaches the fourth center at the level of the heart, energy is converted from sex to love. When kundalini reaches the sixth center between the eyebrows, the energy is converted from love to spiritual experience. Thus in yoga, one endeavors to transform sexual energy into love and then into spiritual experience. Pundit Gopi Krishna expressed that it is the same energy that is at the two extremes of existence: at the lower level, it is responsible for erotic experience, while at the higher level, it gives rise to spiritual experience.[4] The two levels are so close to each other that they appear barely separable from one another.

Elisabeth Haich speaks in depth about sexual energy and shows the way to convert it into the highest consciousness through yoga. According to Haich:

> Sexuality and the highest consciousness are two different forms in which the one divine creative force, the Logos, is manifested. Sexual energy, the lowest form of the Logos, can in man become

> the highest form of Logos, divine consciousness. . . . Modern depth psychology can help us along a part of this path of development but only yoga and meditation can bring us to the goal.[5]

Freud also observed that sexuality can be converted into "spiritually creative power" and he called the process sublimation. Haich points out that the only fuel that is absolutely indispensable for the stimulation of the chakras is sexual energy. The whole process is equally valid for both sexes. The same sexual energy that has brought man from a spiritual to a bodily state can bring him back to his divine primal state of wholeness. Loneliness, not personal relations, pave the way to God. Yoga is the healthiest and shortest path to God. One cannot give up sex unless one has known fully what a healthy sex life means. The secret key to the philosopher's stone of the alchemists is one's own sexual energy.

According to Haich, individuals are nothing but their own sexual energy passing through various stages and assuming different forms. "As long as man remains unconscious, he experiences God within himself as sexual desire. When he has become conscious, he experiences God as his own Self, as his own true being, as I am! God is for man the absolute state of Self-awareness."[6] She calls the union of Logos and consciousness of the physical being a mystical marriage. Her book shows a picture representing God in ancient Mexico. At the base is a serpent, symbolizing sexual energy. On it stands a male figure that symbolizes the body-sustaining, emotional, mental, and intuitive manifestations; at the very top is the incorporeal, pure, spiritual, and radiant Self-awareness—God. She has noted that the same serpent in India is known as kundalini, and has described the manifestation of the energy at the seven levels called chakras.

Sexual energy alone brings us liberation from sexual energy itself. Sexual energy is the cause of inner unrest and continually goads us to find the inner path. In Haich's words:

> In an unexpected moment, among the animal impulses, in the "night," in the darkness of unconsciousness, our Self-awareness is born, just as the Holy Child was born in a manger, among animals, in the "night," in darkness. . . . He alone can reach God who has become thoroughly familiar with sexuality and tasted it and all its potentialities to the full, either in this life or a previous one.[7]

Sexual energy is the bearer of life, and God will remain beyond the reach of a person who is ignorant of sexuality. Full experience of sex can release one from its bondage and then the individual can exercise control over it and use it as a creative power.

Haïch observed that a person cannot serve two masters. One can direct the creative powers either to the higher or to the lower centers, not to both at the same time. This means there is a stage at which the individual stops using the lower centers and, from then on, concentrates only on the higher centers. By this time, sexual desire has fallen away like ripe fruit from the tree. Although the sexual organs are strong and healthy, as in any other normal person, potency goes into a dormant state. Their energy is spiritualized and used only in a divine creative way. Truly great persons have never lived licentiously; they have been role models to others on the path of liberation. These ideas are corroborated by the teachings of Pythagoras, who used the symbol ♈ to say that one can either go on the path of spirituality or on the path of worldliness, but not both at the same time. The thought is further confirmed by traditional Hindu teachings. However, it is difficult to find liberated people, since, from their outer appearance, they look the same as any others. Mainly those who are just below the level of the saintly person are able to recognize them.

After taking the journey from sexuality to spirituality and interviewing several men and women who also had successful experiences, Barbara Harris Whitfield wrote the book *Spiritual Awakenings*, in which she teaches that spirituality and sexuality are two sides of the same coin, our nature. Sexuality is the key and also the doorway to realms of transcendent consciousness. People confided in her that their spiritual awakening happened during lovemaking and that it was preceded by a rush of divine energy. Some participants and speakers told her of periods in their journey where they wanted celibacy, generally for a period of a year or two. For some, this becomes a permanent choice. Whitfield observes that the path of intimate relationship may not be for everyone. It may even be inappropriate for some or in some situations.

> Divine Energy makes itself known personally. Two then understand and experience the sacred three (God, you and me) becoming one . . . union with God is a direct personal experience. Sexuality connects us into a frequency of ecstasy that then connects us back to our Divine Source.[8]

According to psychoanalyst and natural scientist Wilhelm Reich, making love is humankind's attempt to return to the original, unimpeded flow of cosmic energy. Whitfield suggests the blissful moment involves three basic elements: transcendence of time, transcendence of ego, and being totally natural. These three things, which give us ecstasy, just happen naturally in sex. Once these three elements have been experienced in sex, one can experience them in meditation as well, or vice versa.

According to Whitfield, the science of sex cannot be grasped in a day. However, persistent efforts can bring results. Her method of spiritual sex is to prolong the act of coitus and remain in a relaxed state while connected genitally, simulating meditation. There should be no thrusting movements except when erection is being lost, and then gentle thrusting should simply maintain penetration. Full erection is not necessary. The two partners should be at right angles, so that the contact is purely genital. There should be no talking and the mind should only be used to sense what is happening. Just feel the flowing warmth, the flowing love and energy in the contact. There should be awareness without strain and a feeling of effortless floating. In a short time, the valley appears; you have a relaxed orgasm and transcendence happens. There is no sex anymore, only the meditation of peaceful ecstasy. Von Urban says the energy cycle becomes apparent and, within 28 minutes, the bliss sets in and continues for a long time. Whitfield's interviews with others showed that this occurs sooner and transcends time. Regular meditation and spiritual sex both last about 20 minutes. There is a feeling of being younger and livelier, and a renewal of energy. The key words are tension, letting go, and awareness.

I have elaborated elsewhere, through a variety of examples, that married persons have more success in their spiritual quest than celibates.[9] I have drawn cases from both East and West, and from saints to average householders. Many people have married more than once in order to find a suitable partner. It may be that people, in one way or another, have used tantric sex, either knowingly or unknowingly.

Osho Rajneesh spent his whole life perfecting the method of ecstasy, preaching it to others through centers round the world, and writing a large number of books on the subject. According to him, there is no deeper mystery, no deeper secret, and no deeper subject than sex—in the world and in life. An average person goes through the routine of coitus throughout life without knowing what it is. Those souls are rare who have fully understood the art of sex, passed through its intricacies, had rich sex lives in previous births, and are now in a position to attain the stage of real celibacy. Sex has become useless for them and, through complete celibacy, they reveal the truth about sex and divinity.

Osho has made some useful observations on the subject. An average man, he claims, lasts for about a minute and will desire sex again the next day. If the period can be prolonged to three minutes, he may not want it again for about a week. A prolongation to seven minutes and he may not need sex for three months; an extension to three hours may free a person for life. Such coitus is samadhi, resulting in contentment and bliss that lasts a lifetime. Perfect coitus leads to real celibacy. In an average person, this does not happen and one carries the passion of intercourse to a ripe old age without satisfaction. Osho suggests slow breathing. The faster one breathes, he claims, the shorter one lasts in intercourse. Deep breathing through *pranayama* is a way through. Regular practice can bring the stage of sex-samadhi that opens the door for realization.

During the act of intercourse, Osho notes, one should focus attention on the third eye, at a point between the eyebrows. The duration of climax will thus be prolonged one to two hours or more, and a state of samadhi leading to celibacy can be achieved. Attaining celibacy without a real experience of sex is very difficult. A successful celibate in this life owes it to a deep coital union either earlier in this life or in a previous life. "If during sex one has had an absolute revelation, even once, he is released from sex for the unending journey of life."[10]

One must give a sacred status to sex in life, Osho teaches. During coitus, one is close to God; as such, one's attitude should be that of a man going to a sacred place, a temple, a church, or a mosque. If one approaches sex with a pure mind and a feeling of reverence, one can gain a glimpse of the supreme, sublimating sex and achieving bliss. According to Osho, sex is a re-experiencing of the original unity. A glimpse of the eternal will convince one that sensual pleasures are meaningless. He gives the following steps to achieve spiritual coitus;

1. Develop slow breathing to stay longer.

2. Keep your awareness between the eyebrows.

3. Have reverence for creation.

4. Approach sex when you are cheerful, full of love and prayer.

The temples at Khajuraho, with their displays of sexuality and eroticism, were said to be built by the Chandela kings of medieval India. "Khajuraho temples are the juxtaposition of religion and sex. Erotic sculptures on the walls of the Khajuraho temples have religious sanctity and a philosophical background."[11] According to Dey, the sculptures symbolize yoga (divine unity) through *bhoga* (worldly pleasures). Tantric scholar Sir John Woodroffe says:

> The practitioner is taught not to think that we are one with the divine in liberation only, but here and now, in every act we do, for

> in truth all soul is Shakti. It is Siva, who as Shakti, is acting through the Practitioner. When this is realized in every natural function then, each exercise thereof ceases to be a mere animal act and becomes a religious rite a yajna. Every function is a part of the Divine Action in Nature.[12]

Likewise, *Brihadarnyaka Upanishada* states in a couplet: "In the embrace of his beloved a man forgets the whole world—everything within and without, in the very same way, he who embraces the Self knows neither within nor without."

Even when understood, the way from sex to Self or God, though straight and short, is not easy. When misunderstood and practiced improperly, Tantra may take years or more than one lifetime. Of course, there have been innumerable people who have achieved success in a single lifetime. I would say that sex combined with yogic practices and concentration between the eyebrows, which prolongs the duration beyond belief, and with reverence for God, can bring freedom from sexual dependency on the one hand and Self-realization on the other—within a few years or in a single lifetime. I call it regulated sex.[13] However, there are other ways, like the one suggested by Barbara Whitfield. And, of course, there are other techniques practiced over millennia.

The completion stage of freedom from sex is clearly known by the practitioner through dreams, visions, and direct feelings—for example, dreams of one's sexual organ being separated from the body like a ripe fruit being put away some place in the house. Although one may still desire the company of the opposite sex, the difference is like earth and sky. The desire may be for convenience, or for propagation of the teachings, and not for sexual desire as before. In fact, if only one of the partners is on this path, the other partner may complain about the irregularity of sex, since he or she still needs it as before.

Self-realization happens without warning; one may be in the midst of coitus or doing some routine work. One begins to hear the unstruck sound through the inner ears and see the divine light through the inner eyes, witnessing the soul and manifestation of God in many different ways. One may continue to live—eating, drinking, wearing normal clothes—all as before, but the inner transformation has taken place.

Geniuses in the past designed methods through which inner reality could be shown by outer physical symbols for understanding by the common person. For example, the seven chakras, which exist in abstract form on the spine, have been symbolized as temples in the Himalayan mountains, beginning from the temple of Kamakhya Devi in Assam, to the temple of Vaishno Devi near Jammu, and ending at the Amarnath temple on top of Kashmir. Similarly, the inner reality of God-realization that is achieved after the transcendence of sex is shown in the temples of Kjajuraho, where one sees erotic scenes on the walls outside and images of God inside the temple. Should not humanity pay respect and gratitude to those geniuses?

There has always been a controversy regarding sex after liberation. It is correct that truly great men have never lived licentiously. According to some, those who have achieved high spiritual levels and still have sex, although on rare occasions, have not yet become whole; they are on the path of becoming whole. Another view, however, is that if a saintly person once has a physical union with his loved one out of true love, with inner devotion and a healthy physical desire, he should not be considered on any account either a weak, fallen, or sinful person. After transformation of the energy, one experiences the union of "I" and Logos, or AUM; through faith and surrender one lives under the control and direction of the spirit, having given up self-will. The same spirit may, at some time, direct one to have physical contact with one's beloved, although the two may be living as celibates normally. After all, even sex is a manifestation of the spirit.

The Method of Sex

Following is a summary of how spiritual liberation can be achieved through the method of sex. You can use the techniques described in Practical Formula 8 on page 194 to bring yourself closer to this spiritual state.

1. It is a natural and short path to Self- or God-realization.

2. Tantrikas transformed sex into spirituality, but the preachers of morality did not allow the message to reach the masses.

3. We find the serene and peaceful expression of Buddha and Mahavir on the faces of the statues of naked people involved in sexual acts on the walls of the Khajuraho temples in India.

4. Meditation on these images of intercourse transcends vulgar sexuality from within, and one becomes calm and peaceful.

5. When entering the temple, one finds the peaceful statue of Lord Shiva engaged in eternal meditation. This is the secret of Tantra—gaining victory through sexuality leads one to peace and meditation.

6. The process of copulation and orgasm creates egolessness and timelessness, which are characteristics of samadhi.

7. During climax, one tastes bliss and divinity.

8. Through proper practice, the yogi separates orgasm from ejaculation, then there is no loss of energy and vitality. One experiences mental orgasms constantly and acquires a permanent state of bliss and peace.

9. One learns the art of converting sex into meditation.

10. During orgasm, the Self becomes detached from the lower forces. At this instant, if a man or woman transfers his or her attention from sensual pleasure to thoughts of God, or begins to chant a mantra, one day he or she will become aware of inner awakening and its associated signs—inner light and sound.

11. Conversion of sexuality into spiritual creative force is called sublimation, both in man and woman.

12. The same sexual energy that brought one from a spiritual state to the physical body can take one back to a divine primal state of wholeness through sublimation.

13. For alchemists, sexual energy is the secret key to the philosophers' stone.

14. Sublimation is best achieved through the regular practice of yoga, which is a healthy and short path to God.

15. Arousal of kundalini is the sign of sublimation.

16. Sexual energy alone can liberate one from itself, and then one becomes a natural celibate.

17. When one has mastered the art of sublimation, Self-awareness is born among animal impulses, in the darkness of the unconsciousness.

18. One achieves liberation from the cycle of death and rebirth.

Compared to other methods, the method of sex is perhaps the fastest way to realize the Self. The trick lies in converting "human" sexuality into "divine" sexuality, or spirituality. The following steps are suggested for achieving this goal.

PRACTICAL FORMULA 8: SPIRITUAL SEX

1. Through regular practice of yogic discipline, acquire the power of holding ejaculation and performing prolonged sex.

2. Chanting of the mantra "Kling Kling Kling Kamdevaya Namaha" for 30 to 60 minutes every day brings the power to retain semen.

3. One should copulate in a state of cheerfulness, love, and reverence for the creator.

4. Once penetration is achieved, minimize movement as much as possible.

5. Thrusting should be done from time to time only to maintain erection.

6. Develop slow breathing to stay longer.

7. Keep your awareness at the midpoint between the eyebrows.

8. Remember God in a way or form comfortable to you.

9. At the time of ejaculation, think that you are offering semen for a holy purpose.

10. When the right time comes, Self-awareness will be born suddenly and unexpectedly.

11. You will witness inner light and hear inner sound.

12. When this happens the goal of liberation has been achieved.

Chapter Twenty-Three

OTHER METHODS

The various methods described in this chapter will not have equal power to produce results. Vedic methods, for example, are very powerful and have the capacity to take the practitioner into the end-state of liberation and Self-realization. Near-death experiences and the methods described in chapter 20, on the other hand, initiate the person on the way to liberation by showing them a glimpse of reality beyond the physical. The individual is then inspired to adopt a more rigorous discipline, such as metaphysics or meditation, to complete the journey.

One may find that he or she is suited to more than one method. More often than not, this is the case. It is good to combine and synchronize as many approaches as one can, without confusion, to encourage progress. Most methods are not exclusive and can be practiced simultaneously. There are many other ways as well, including music, dance, or ritual performance. Let your heart guide you on the path to higher consciousness. You may not be led the way you want to go, but you will always be led to where you need to go.

The Method of Prayer

Prayer is one way of opening oneself to higher consciousness. The results of prayer may vary from passing an examination to a direct experience of God, depending on the intention of the person and the intensity of the prayer. Visions that open the gate to higher or cosmic consciousness may appear, especially to those who are more evolved.

Emotional intensity is very high during moments of grief, joy, fear, gratitude, and loss. At such moments, a prayer or sincere request made to God is always heard. One feels connected to a power, receives communication, feels secure, and may find a peaceful reality beyond the physical.

All religions since the beginning of time have advocated prayer. But is all prayer the same, or will some prayers bring different results? Most religions teach the law of cause and effect—we shall reap what we sow; what we send out we will get back. Prayer may be the most powerful symbol of this cosmic law. Following this truth, whatever thoughts I send out (my beliefs, both conscious and unconscious) will create an effect that will come back to me. This will mean that what I experience as my reality is the result of what I have been sending out. My beliefs, fears, and desires have also been sent out as prayers. How my prayer can be answered, and how every prayer is answered, will depend on what I believe in that moment. I want to be as aware as I am able of my desire, because it will be answered. Prayer can remind me of my constant connection to God, or I can experience separation by feeling that God does not hear me or answer me in the way I want. There is an old saying: Prayer is telling God what you want and meditation is listening to what God wants.

To touch the height of what prayer can do, consider the following event from ancient India. There was a boy from a poor family who went to school in a neighboring village. He complained to his mother that all the other boys had a security guard to escort them to and fro every day. That very day, there was a party at school in the evening and the boy felt afraid of the jungle in the dark. He asked his mother to arrange a guard for him. Needless to say, the mother could not, since they were poor. Being a wise and loving mother, she told the boy that his real brother, Kanhaiya (another name for Lord Krishna), lived in the very jungle he had to pass through and, whenever he felt afraid, he could call Kanhaiya sincerely and loudly and he would immediately come. The boy believed his mother completely and called for Kanhaiya that evening while going to school. And lo! There was Kanhaiya, clad in the traditional dress of that time and holding a flute in one hand. The boy held Kanhaiya's finger, and was led to school safely. Needing a gift for the party, the boy asked Kanhaiya for a small glass of milk as his contribution. Kanhaiya produced one for him.

The boy arrived at school happily and handed the glass of milk to the man in the kitchen. While the boy was enjoying the party with his friends, the headmaster came running to the boy and asked him about the glass of milk. He wanted to know who it gave to him. The glass was refilling itself; no matter how many times they poured the milk from it, there was more. The boy told everyone about Kanhaiya and that he would come to fetch him at the end of the party. Everyone waited but, when Kanhaiya came to escort the boy, only the boy could see him. The boy was smiling and describing the clothes Kanhaiya was wearing, the flute he was carrying, and the peacock feather he was wearing in his hair. But no one could get a glimpse of Kanhaiya in spite of their best efforts. On reaching home, he told his mother everything. She understood what had happened and thanked Lord Krishna from her heart. Even though she could not see him, she trusted in him. He is visible to the pure, innocent, and devoted. Many normally intelligent people with professional degrees and wealth can easily disbelieve the truth of this event, and others believe it completely. One is referred to the book *From Sweeper to Saint* by Baba Haridass, which contains ten such real instances from India.[1] Baba Haridass is presently the yogi at the Mount Madonna Yoga Center near Santa Cruz, California.

Evidence exists that prayers made to God in times of distress and with heartfelt sincerity are heard and answered in ways that are noticeable. The way is already given; only our desires block us from seeing it. Having the highest goal of liberation from falsehood and freedom from the cycle of death and rebirth in mind, one should pray and request help in seeing the way. This should be done a number of times, for a few minutes everyday, especially before going to bed at night. One may begin perceiving directions in dreams and visions, or through books and writings. The universe is programmed to answer all requests.

Freedom from Choice

Freedom from choice is a state of being that "Krishna called Moksha, that Jesus called Kingdom of God, that Buddha called Shunyata (Void), that J. Krishnamurti called Choiceless Awareness, the Awakening of Intelligence."[2] According to Krishnamurti, it is in that equanimity that the silent lake of our consciousness reflects the majesty of our conscious universe. The situation may be understood through a Sufi story.

There were two friends, one of whom always enjoyed good health while the other grew weaker and weaker each day. Finally, the weaker friend reached his deathbed. The healthy one always ate his food from one bowl, regardless of mingling the tastes of its different ingredients. The other one ate the sweet food from one bowl and the bitter from another. On his deathbed, the weaker friend asked his healthy friend to tell him the secret of his good health. His friend answered that he simply ate all foods from one bowl, without distinction between bitter and sweet tastes. The weaker friend then ate, for the first time, all his meal from one bowl and felt a little better. He began eating all his meals in in this way and, to the amazement of all, he soon recovered his health and began to live a healthy life.

This teaches us that truth is one, beyond all duality, such as good and evil. Totality and its divisions—such as associating oneself with one race, religion, sect, political party, or sex—is dis-integrating and results in likes and dislikes that fight with each other. This identification with separation enables the phenomenal Self to become master and the real unifying Self to be suppressed. Preference creates division; division creates choice; choice leads to conflict. A confused mind makes a distinction between this and that. A clear mind eats everything from one bowl and, from equanimity, creates no struggle, no dis-ease. In equanimity, the Self is realized.

As we know it, equanimity is the result of Self-realization. The converse is also true—that is, by cultivating equanimity in life, we arrive at Self-realization. By developing the habit of "choicelessness," we achieve equanimity. This means making a habit of being happy and content in whatever the situation. This is a way to higher consciousness.

Godless Karma

Godless karma is another way to achieve higher consciousness, a method advocated by the Jains, the sixth largest religious group in India (after the Hindus, Muslims, Christians, Sikhs, and Buddhists). In this atheistic religion without a personal God as creator-controller-destroyer of the universe, there is no agency to award favors and assign punishment. The doctrine of karma involves an automatically functioning mechanism. It stresses the supremacy of moral law. Prayers and worship are of no avail against the force of the karma.[3]

Whether living as a monk or a householder, a balanced individuality can be cultivated through the transcendence of passions like *krodha* (anger), *maana* (pride), *maya* (deceit), and *lobha* (greed). Renunciation consists in realizing the illusion of love and hate. Beyond *dukha* (misery, pain, or suffering) and *sukha* (comfort, happiness) is Nirvana or moksha (eternal bliss, emancipation), which is true happiness and the ultimate goal of Atman. True happiness results from the end of creating all karmas through cultivation of right conduct (*samyak-charitra*), which is based on right belief (*samyak-darshana*) and right knowledge (*samyak-jnana*). The ethical discipline (*achar dharma*) is prescribed for the fourfold community consisting of *sadhu* (monk), *sadhvi* (nun), *sravaka* (layman), and *sravika* (laywoman). The five vows to be taken by a disciple and followed rigorously are *Pranatipata viramana* (to desist from killing), *Mirsavada viramana* (to desist from telling a lie), *Adattadana viramana* (to not accept when not rightly bestowed), *Maithuna viramana* (to desist from sex), and *Parigraha parimana* (to fix the size of acquisition).

Meditation

Meditation deserves a separate article in itself because of its overwhelming importance to the world. But there are many ways meditation can be used and different systems of Self-realization adopt different techniques. For example, in Zen as well as in *Vipassana*, the focus is on the breath—the meditator watches the exhalation and inhalation passively, until he or she becomes the breath itself. A relaxed mental flow is established wherein there is no one breathing and no one watching. Thus, kundalini yoga has its own way of meditation that we are going to explore in detail in part 5.

At one level, a variety of meditative techniques are used as a way to increase awareness, which is distracted in our busy contemporary world. There are professionals using meditation as a tool to help manage stress, to increase their capacity for sustained work, or to maintain general good health. Being centered gives a feeling of freedom from frustration and concern.

At other levels, meditation becomes the art of "looking within," leading to cosmic consciousness and self-realization. Buddha has become synonymous with meditation over the past twenty-five centuries. He achieved a hat trick by being born, enlightened, and passing on the same day—by Tibetan reckoning, always the full moon in June, or May 11 by the Western calendar. Buddha used two words that are relevant in the modern context of one-sided development: sight and insight. "Sight with insight is wisdom. It is the bridge connecting one's life to the ultimate truth. The Buddha says the main, if not the only, means to receive insight is through meditation."[4]

Dr. A. Kasamatsu and Dr. Hirai conducted an experiment on Zen masters and pupils in 1960s. A preponderance of alpha waves, with some rhythmical theta waves, was found in the monks during meditation. "Alpha brain waves run 8 to 13 cycles per second and are connected with a relaxed yet alert mental state. Theta waves run slower, 4 to 8 cycles per second and are generally related to a state of drowsiness, intuition, creativity, and the REM dream cycle."[5] Likewise, a decrease in respiration rate, slower pulse, lower blood pressure, and a reduction in the need for oxygen, were some of the effects of meditation found by researchers at Harvard and California universities.

Regular and systematic practice of meditation for 20 to 30 minutes twice a day is recommended. Out-of-body experiences, in which one views one's body from an external vantage point, can give a feeling of expansion with the universe, visions of galaxies and stars, and visions of writings in Hebrew, Latin, or Sanskrit. Barbara Harris Whitfield used to hear her own chuckling and the sound seemed to reverberate throughout the universe.[6] I strongly recommend that you study and select a way of meditation for yourself.

Guided Meditation

Guided meditation, or creative thinking, is also used to achieve higher states of awareness. As an example, imagine yourself sitting in a dark cave, bound by chains you are unable to move. Feel a ray of light coming from somewhere and suddenly shining on you. With this ray of light, you receive the power to stand up and walk toward the cave opening; slowly, you walk out of the cave. You find light everywhere and you are full of energy. One by one, the chains break and you are free. You suddenly raise your hands and shake your whole body with great strength. You exclaim with joy and happiness: "I am free; nothing can bind me now, and I can do whatever I like."

As another exercise, imagine a large statue sitting cross-legged in front of you. Look at the face; you find that it is you. Now imagine your guru appearing with a shovel. He tries to move the statue with his bare hands, but he cannot since you are firmly rooted to the ground. Then he puts the shovel between your body and the ground and applies pressure to raise you up. He does not succeed. Your guru's friend now arrives with another shovel and applies pressure from the other side at the same time. Both of them keep trying, but you are so firmly grounded that they cannot succeed. After some rest, the two gurus try again to raise your statue from the ground and, with great effort, they succeed. Like two weight lifters, they lift the statue up and put it on their shoulders. Both are now smiling and you notice you are smiling as well. Slowly, both of them carry the statue to a raised platform and put it there. The statue comes to life, stands up, and raises both hands to the sky with a smiling face. With regular practice of about an hour everyday, you are likely to find your consciousness raised up in due course. This is an aid to Self-realization.

Zen, Martial Arts, and Pilgrimage

Zen can be called the inner art and design of the East, taken to China by Bodhidharman from India in the sixth century, and from China to Japan around the twelfth. Zen has been described as "a special teaching without scriptures, beyond words and letters, pointing to the mind essence of man, seeing directly into one's nature, and attaining enlightenment."[7]

The martial arts are more than a means of self-defense or fighting. Kaicho Tadashi Nakamura, Grandmaster and founder of the World Seido Karate Organization says: "Seido Karate is a way of life. It develops the spiritual being as much as the physical." Martial arts require a high degree commitment, dedication, and self-discipline. "The practice of the martial arts also enables one to keep one's cool under pressure, just like a manager needs to. The structured daily application of the art improves concentration through the practice of zen meditation."[8]

The pilgrimage, or Haj, is considered to be the highest form of Islamic worship. The rites of pilgrimage are called *sha'air* (symbolic objects) in the Quran. Pilgrimage symbolically represents the life of Abraham and his progeny. "Different stages of God's scheme are repeated symbolically in the pilgrimage rites, making pilgrims feel at one with the tradition of Abraham and his descendants."[9] Perhaps this is the way to open the door of higher awareness for them.

A pilgrim leaves his home and sets off for the holy land, Mecca, to commemorate Abraham leaving his native land of Iran for Hijaz; he exchanges his tailored clothes for two unstitched sheets, comparable to the simple dress worn in the days of Abraham and Ishmael. On reaching Mecca, the pilgrim walks around the house of God to commemorate Abraham and Ishmael walking around the same house to solemnize the covenant they made with its master. The pilgrim then walks seven times between the hills of Safa and Marwa in memory of Abraham's wife, Hajra, who wandered between those two hills in search of water. This rite is called *Saee*. Abraham performed this by first readying himself to sacrifice his own son, then completed the sacrifice by slaughtering a ram at the command of God. The pilgrim then stones the devil at Jamarat. The pilgrim keeps uttering the words, "Here I am at your service, Lord," throughout the pilgrimage. The holy journey culminates in the assembly of pilgrims on the plane of Arafat. At the end of this religious service, the pilgrims pledge before God to live their lives in the spirit of Haj.

Solitude

Pythagoras taught that treading the unfrequented ways, or solitude, was a way to self-discovery. The capacity to be alone is a measure of emotional maturity. "The capacity to be alone thus becomes linked with self-discovery and self-realization; with becoming aware of one's deepest needs, feelings, and impulses."[10] In the words of Edward Gibbon: "Conversation enriches the understanding, but solitude is the school of genius; and the uniformity of work denotes the hand of single artist."[11]

There appear to be two opposite poles of nature. The life of a normal or average person revolves around the hub of intimate relationships. The chief, if not the only, source of human happiness appears to be interpersonal relationships of an intimate kind, especially the ones with sexual fulfillment. Nonetheless, a creative individual's way of living seems to run counter to this assumption. According to Storr:

> Many of the world's greatest thinkers have not reared families or formed close personal ties. This is true of Descartes, Newton, Locke, Pascal, Spinoza, Kant, Leibnitz, Schopenhaur, Nietzsche, Kierkegaard and Wittgenstein. Some of these men of genius had transient affairs with other men or women; others, like Newton, remained celibate. But none of them married, and most lived alone for the greater part of their lives.[12]

According to Graham Wallas, a sort of re-ordering process takes place in the brain during creativity, which he calls incubation. A creative person develops interest in a particular subject, gathers supporting material, and studies everything possibly related to it. He calls this first stage preparation. After some time, the accumulated material reaches a boiling point and something incomprehensible goes on during the period of incubation that forms a prelude to the next stage, illumination. In three stages—preparation, incubation, and illumination—the creative person receives a new insight and finds a solution to the problem, or can rearrange the accumulated material to put it under an all-embracing principle.

Great spiritual and religious leaders have demonstrated that solitude promotes insight and inner change; they retreated from the world and, after illumination, returned to share their revelation with others. Buddha reflected upon the human condition and meditated away from the world under the Bodhisattva tree for seven years, culminating in his enlightenment. According to the accounts of St. Matthew and St. Luke, Jesus spent forty days in the wilderness and then returned to the world to give his message. Mohammed used to withdraw from the world to the cave of Hera during the month of Ramadan each year. Anthony Storr noted that St. Catherine of Siena spent three years in seclusion in her little room in the Via Benincasa, during which she underwent a series of mystical experiences before entering upon an active life of teaching and preaching.

Anthony Storr has collected information showing that many noted philosophers and writers produced their best work in solitude. The Roman philosopher Boethius was imprisoned in Pavia by the Ostrogothic king, Theodoric. He was tortured and put to death in 525 A.D. While in prison, Boethius composed *The Consolation of Philosophy*, for which he is still remembered today. Sir Thomas More, Henry VIII's chancellor in 1529, was imprisoned in the Tower of London, after which he was tried and executed in 1535. During imprisonment, he wrote the masterpiece of Christian wisdom known as *A dialogue of Comfort against Tribulation*. Sir Walter Raleigh was imprisoned in the Tower of London and, after trial, was executed in 1618. During imprisonment, he wrote his famous work *The History of the World*. John Bunyan was committed to Bedford County jail in England from 1661 to 1672. During eleven years of liberal prison conditions, he wrote his spiritual biography, *Grace Abounding*, published in 1666. Also, a considerable part of *The Pilgrim's Progress* was composed during the same period. Dostoevsky spent four years in a prison camp on his arrest in 1849. During this period, his repressed memories were released and he was relieved of psychic blockages and morbid fixations. Although never alone in prison, he was emotionally isolated and lacked companionship, which turned his attention inward and converted his preoccupation with the peasantry into a mystical belief. Pen and paper forbidden, he wrote in his notebook, resulting in the book *House of the Dead*, describing his prison camp experiences.

The perverse imagination of Marquis de Sade flourished in captivity; he eventually died in 1814 while confined in the asylum at Charenton. His famous works *Justine* and *Journées de Sodome* were written in the fortress of Vincennes and the Bastille. Adolf Hitler dictated *Mein Kampf* to Rudolf Hess while in prison for nine months after the failure of his *putsch* in Munich. In his own words: "Without my imprisonment *Mein Kampf* would never have been written. That period gave me the chance of deepening various notions for which I then had only an instinctive feeling."[13]

Anthony Grey, in China, and Arthur Koestler, in Spain, were put in solitary confinement; their experiences were televised and Koestler published transcripts in the magazine *Kaleidoscope*. Both men admitted that solitude triggered their feelings of sympathy for their fellow men and they found themselves in touch with a higher order of reality. They felt the abstract existence of something that cannot be defined or expressed. Anthony Grey found a new awareness and Koestler received a feeling of inner freedom in which he confronted the ultimate realities. On being shown the picture of a lotus growing in mud by a Chinese friend, Grey felt that a glimpse of heaven could be had in hell too. It is timely to comment here that Jawahar Lal Nehru, the first Prime Minister of India, wrote *The Discovery of India* while he was in prison, while Sri Aurobindo studied the Bhagavad Gita in prison, where he received repeated visions of Lord Krishna through his meditations.

I recall events in my life where I was repeatedly thrown into solitude by some design of nature. When less than a year old, my mother went for her studies in another town and I was left in the care of my grandmother. I used to weep at the separation from my mother. All my education, from nursery school to Master's degree, occurred away from my family, and I used to weep in loneliness. Coming to professional life, I was mostly away from my wife and other family members for several reasons, and I was often depressed. I have served in eight countries and I have lived mostly by myself; in the suffering of my loneliness, I felt like striking my head against the wall. Nevertheless, in my later years of loneliness, I took to meditation and reading scriptures seriously and I gained experiences with the spirit. Self-realization and the writing of several psychical papers and books helped me through this aloneness. Until middle age, I used to accuse solitude for my suffering; later, I had only praise for it. Perhaps it is in solitude that the inner Self grows to become the eternal Self.

The growth of the Self has been well documented in solitude. Occasionally, we should spend some time alone and perform our chosen spiritual activities—whether days, weeks, months, or years of living alone depends on various factors. Follow Pythagoras and tread the unfrequented ways. Truth may dawn unexpectedly as flashes of intuitional knowing.

PART FIVE

Exploring Reality through Kundalini

Chapter Twenty-Four

SECRETS OF KUNDALINI AWAKENING

History has recorded the reality, mystery, and importance of kundalini. Kumar tells us that

> Some people write inspiring prose or poetry and some compose beautiful music while others cannot; some students earn high marks with little study while others, in spite of long hours of study, score poorly; some fight on the battle field for days while others could not even do their normal work; some are known for wonderful discoveries and inventions while others live mediocre lives and die unnoticed.[1]

In the course of history, it has been found that there is a special form of energy within every individual. In most, kundalini energy is dormant; in some; it is slowly evolving; while in a few, it is fully awakened. Because this is energy of infinite capacity, having no form or dimension, it consequently has been identified as having many different forms, under many names, and in various traditions of the world. Perhaps Hinduism maintains the oldest records that name this energy kundalini and depict it in various forms for common understanding. Among all methods available for opening the gateway to higher consciousness, this method for kundalini arousal is the most dependable, taking the practitioner to Self- or God-realization and beyond.

To awaken kundalini, first desire an understanding of the secret of awakening and then find the most effective method for you. Where does this kindling of unusual energy originate? It comes from the storehouse of infinite cosmic energy; however, the event of awakening takes place only under certain circumstances. So the secret lies in creating those circumstances in a safe and steady manner, eventually awakening kundalini permanently.

There are two ways of creating these unusual circumstances: through *shaktipat* (receiving direct transmission of energy through a guru or a realized soul with awakened kundalini) and by creating the circumstances through perseverance. Although shaktipat appears to be the easiest way and many will be tempted by it, it still has difficulties and limitations. One difficulty lies in finding a genuine guru. People have sometimes delivered themselves into the hands of the unrealized and have used major parts of their lives creating undesired results. Genuine Self- or God-realized gurus are rare. Moreover, it is helpful to have prepared oneself through self-discipline and self-study to receive the direct transmission of energy. Whenever a person is prepared to receive this transmission of energy, the guru naturally appears at the right time. The old adage comes true: "When the student is ready, the master appears."

Lasting effects are received through one's own energy, rather than through shaktipat. What happens within oneself is most important, basic, and fundamental; it is one's only real wealth. World-famous spiritual leader Osho Rajneesh observed that: "Shaktipat will not add to your wealth, but it will certainly step up its capacity to grow. The effect of shaktipat is indirect, and therefore you need it time and again."[2]

The awakening of kundalini is like a flash of lightning illuminating a glimpse of the road ahead and showing the temple or the journey's destination. But once is not enough; it is needed a second time and a third. One can also reach the destination without shaktipat, although it may take more time. Nonetheless, one will certainly reach the goal. While shaktipat is helpful indeed, you must prepare yourself with innate wisdom and be ready to receive the direct transmission from a guru. The inner and outer gurus are of the same consciousness. By preparing for and receiving the grace of the inner guru, you establish the connection attracting you to the outer guru. Above all, shaktipat can be requested and obtained through the divine presence itself. In any case, indigenous efforts are always the source.

Two foundations of religion have evolved throughout the world—one based on meditation and another based on prayer. Through prayer, one experiences God to be above, in the skies. Through meditation, one raises consciousness up from within, sensing something asleep at our roots. This concept of above and below generates the experiences of prayer and meditation. Once again, words from Osho can show us the way:

> . . . by and by , religions of prayer have been loosing ground and dying out. There is no future for them; they have no future whatsoever. And religions of meditation are daily growing in potentiality, and they have an enormous future before them.[3]

It has been shown that most religions have been using practices similar to yoga and meditation under different names, and kundalini energy has been at the root of almost all faiths as the common denominator, to open the gate of higher consciousness.[4] The difficulty is, that every such school is not aware that others are doing the same thing in their own ways."[5]

Thus, yoga and meditation are the real innate wisdom to create the unusual circumstances to awaken the infinite energy called kundalini. The Integral Path, a name given by me to a scientific combination of all yogic methods, is proposed here as the "shortest path" to awaken the kundalini energy.

The Integral Path

The Vedic methods described in part 4 have three main branches: bhakti yoga (path of devotion, suited to people whose heart dominates their mind), jnana yoga (path of wisdom, suited to people whose mind dominates their heart), and karma yoga (path of selfless action, suited to people whose heart and mind vibrate at the same rate). Hatha yoga is the fourth category, introduced in the Middle Ages for people in whom neither the heart nor the mind is developed enough to use the other three methods. This branch of yoga became so important over the years that the word *yoga* meant only "hatha yoga." In the words of Dr. Rammurti Mishra:

> Yoga is mastery of mind. It is a process of dehypnotism. Yoga presents a scientific way and methodical effort to attain perfection through the control of the elements of the physical, metaphysical and psychical natures.[6]

For millennia, yogis and rishis observed postures a practitioner would automatically go into when kundalini awakened. They then advocated that, through regular practice of these postures, kundalini could possibly be awakened, reversing the process. Osho Rajneesh observed that:

> All the yogic asanas and mudras follow the patterns of our mind's

> different states; and they are the results of countless experiments and experiences. . . . After thousands of experiments it was found which kind of mudra is formed in a particular state of mind. Then the reverse process can also be worked out, in which you can attain to a particular state of mind by forming the mudra that corresponds with it.[7]

Thus, the first step on following the Integral Path is to learn and practice yogic postures (asanas and mudras) producing peaceful and thoughtless states of mind and concentration at the third eye, the point midway between the eyebrows.

Breath work is another process associated with producing different states of consciousness. Breathing creates or brings one into a state of silence. Having attained such a state of profound peace, other less peaceful states, like fear or anger, are not created. Pranayama (deep breathing) is one of several specific techniques used to achieve this. In addition to breath, we add three locks to concentrate spiritual energy to activate the chakras: root lock (*mool bandh*), navel lock (*uddayan bandh*), and throat lock (*jalandhar bandh*). These three locks are used to pressurize the chakras from the root center (*mooladhara*) to the eyebrow center *(ajna)*, or from the first to the sixth energy centers. The sleeping kundalini at the base of the spine is stimulated through the double power of deep breathing and the three locks, becoming one of the causes of awakening. Pranayama, together with the three locks, is the second step in the Integral Path.

Shashank asana is a special yogic posture used to regulate the breath through both nostrils to an equal flow, reducing breathing to a minimum. This brings the mind to a quiet state and lets you slip into meditation easily. You may recollect that, while sexually aroused, one's breathing rises to the maximum. Meditation is the opposite state, in which breathing is calmed to a minimum. Shashank asana is the third step in the Integral Path. Chanting AUM with a concentration on the third eye is the final step in the Path. This practice opens up the ajna chakra (eyebrow center).

With all this preparation, one is now ready to go into meditation. In order to leave no stone unturned, and to make the process more effective, the following four disciplines should be added to the Integral Path:

Prayer, invoking faith and surrender. God is invited in as light and sound.

Jnana yoga (path of knowledge), applied through the reading of scriptures and stories about realized saints. The layers of ignorance fall away one by one.

Bhakti yoga (path of devotion), the chanting of a mantra. Love of God and Self is developed.

Tantra yoga, the method of regulated sex. This acts as a catalytic agent and liberates the person from sexual attachment.

Prayer precedes meditation, while the latter three factors are practiced at other times.

Chapter Twenty-Five

THE INTEGRAL PATH AND KUNDALINI

The Integral Path is a way of life adopted by the practitioner. It can be summarized as a daily routine in the following way:

1. Two-hour morning practice, comprising yogic exercises for 45 minutes, pranayama with the three locks for 20 minutes, shashanka asana for 15 minutes, chanting of AUM with concentration on the third eye for 15 minutes. This is followed by prayer (shaktipat from the divine), which closes all the doors to the physical senses and invites white light as the personification of God. Feel it entering your body through the crown center. Feel it activating your kundalini and opening the seven chakras, one by one. Gradually, you will go into a state of samadhi, experiencing yourself as Atman and merging with the absolute in the ocean of bliss.

2. Two hours of reading scriptures and case histories of realized persons (path of knowledge), at any time of the day.

3. Two hours of chanting a mantra selected by you or given by your guru (path of devotion), at any other time of the day.

4. Practitioners should learn the way of spiritual sex, which expedites the entire process as a catalytic agent and liberates the person from sexual attachment.

Consider this. To obtain a professional degree, one needs to devote many hours each day for five or six years. God-realization is not less valuable than a degree. If you remember God or your own spirit on a part-time basis or half-heartedly, he will also reveal himself to you on a part-time basis or half-heartedly. We have had a part-time relationship to God and our own souls for innumerable lifetimes and our spiritual evolution has been slow. The formula presented here can bring liberation from the need for further incarnations. Those who cannot devote six hours to God-realization due to their involvement in the affairs of the world have not earned this privilege through their karmas in past lives. This is not a failure on their part, any more than a child in kindergarten is at fault for not reading at a college level. It is not yet their time. They have yet to understand many lessons in the school of earth before they can devote the necessary time in search of Self or God. However, there is always a way when determination is strong.

One can begin with one hour a day and gradually increase the time. It is a way of life practical for anyone with the desire. One can awaken the kundalini and achieve Self-realization in one lifetime, without the help of an external guru or shaktipat. On awakening, kundalini assumes the role of the guru. According to Swami Vishnu Tirtha: "To a yogi She is what Lord Krishna was to Arjuna, a guide and driver of his chariot on the battle-field of this worldly war for spirituality."[1] This is a method in which the personality of the individual evolves in an all-round manner—physical, mental, emotional, and intuitional—producing a balanced person.

PRACTICAL FORMULA 9: DETAILS OF THE INTEGRAL PATH

The postures described here take about 45 minutes to perform. Inhale before the beginning of the posture and exhale slowly as you disengage from it. This set of postures will produce calm, serenity, and automatic concentration on the third eye. It provides an all-round development of the physical body and transforms sexual desire into unconditional love.

1. Stand straight with your feet about one foot apart. Keep your hands on your waist and bend backward with your eyes toward the sky. Six to ten repetitions.

2. Stand straight with your feet two to three feet apart. Put your hands on your waist. Bend to the left and touch the outside of your knee with your left fingers twice. Do the same on the right side. This is one set. Repeat six to ten sets.

3. Lie face up, and yawn like a cat for a few minutes.

4. Lie face down, legs together. Raise one leg at a time, as high as you comfortably can, keeping it straight. Repeat seven times, alternating legs. Now raise both legs together and hold that position for a few seconds. Then lower them slowly to the resting position. Repeat three times.

5. Lie face down with your hands parallel to your body. Bend your legs up and reach back to grasp your ankles with your hands so that your body takes the position of a bow. Hold the posture from 30 seconds to one minute.

6. Lie face down with your legs together and your hands palms down beside your shoulders, parallel to your body. Pushing with your hands, raise your upper body like a cobra raising its hood. Bring your body into the shape of a cobra, touching the ground with your navel region and turning your eyes toward the sky as much as possible. Hold the position for 20 seconds and repeat two to three times.

7. Sit on the ground with your back straight, legs stretched out. Pull your heels in with both hands, pressing them against your body; keep your eyes closed and focus your attention on the third eye. Hold the position for about a minute.

8. Kneel on the ground with your back straight, knees together, resting on your heels. Slide your seat off your heels to the right so that both legs are now bent to your left. Lift your left leg over your right, placing your left foot on the ground, touching the outside of your right knee. Place your right hand on your left knee and hold your left foot with your right hand. Twist your body to the left as much as comfortably possible, and look toward the left. Hold the position for 20 seconds. Interchange the roles of the right and left parts of the body and hold the posture for 20 seconds.

9. Sit on your feet with your heels turned aside, making room for your hips. Keep your spine straight, with your hands on your knees and your attention focused on your third eye. Hold for five minutes. (This is perhaps the only pose that can be practiced for 15 to 20 minutes, soon after eating a meal, to produce quick digestion. This is known as *vajrasana*.) Then breathe out completely and push your stomach in and out 20 to 30 times while holding that exhalation. Repeat 4 to 8 times.

10. Lie face up with your back on the ground. Raise one leg, hold it at a 45-degree angle for a few seconds, and then slowly lower it. Repeat with the other leg. Repeat this movement with both legs seven times. Now

raise both legs together, hold them at a 45-degree angle for a few seconds, and lower them slowly. Repeat three times.

11. Lie face up with your legs bent and the soles of your feet touching the ground, arms parallel to your body. Raise your body from the middle as high as you comfortably can, making a bow between your feet and your shoulders. Hold the position for 5 seconds then lower slowly. Repeat 7 to 8 times.

12. Lie face up with your knees bent and the soles of your feet touching the ground, arms parallel to your body. Keeping the center of your body on the ground, raise your hips as high as you can and hold the position for a few seconds, then lower your hips slowly. Now keeping your hips in touch with the ground, raise the center of your body, making an arch for a few seconds and then slowly lower. Repeat 7 to 8 times.

13. Lie face up with your knees bent and your feet together with soles touching the ground. Place your arms out to the sides, slightly apart from your body. Slowly lower your knees to the right until they touch the ground, keeping your face looking up to the sky. Hold the position for a few seconds, come back to the original position, and repeat the exercise, lowering your legs to the left. Repeat 7 to 8 times.

14. Lie face up, back on the ground. Bend your legs, hold them behind the knees, and pull them into your body, getting your knees as close to your body as possible. Press your knees against your body twice, then repeat. This can be done ten times in two held breaths. Repeat the exercise with one leg then the other, and then with both legs together again. After the set is complete, lie face up, back on the ground, arms resting at your sides. Relax your whole body as completely as possible. All thoughts should be as relaxed as well. This restores blood circulation. Hold the position for one to two minutes. This is called *shavasana*, or death posture.

15. Sit cross-legged with one of your heels pressing the region of the mooladhar chakra, or root center. The heel of the other foot should rest on top of the first heel and press against the second chakra called swadhishthan, or the sacral center. This is *siddhasana* for men and *siddhayoni-asana* for women. Men should take care that their genitals are not crushed between their heels. Women should also take care as the lower heel has to press against the root chakra through the vaginal opening.

Rest your hands on your knees, palms up, and center your attention between your eyebrows.

This is a favorite posture of yogis because it keeps the spinal column straight, which quickens the awakening of kundalini and facilitates its upward movement.

16. Sit in the posture described in step 9 (*vajrasana*). Bend forward from the waist until your forehead and nose touch the ground and your hands and arms are stretched out on the ground in front you. Breathe in a relaxed way. This is *shashankasana*; it brings balance in breathing through both nostrils to produce equanimity and readiness for going into meditation. The posture should be held for 15 minutes.

17. *Shirshasana* (headstand): This is a very special yogic posture recommended to men for speedy spiritual growth, since it helps by reversing the direction of flow of the seminal fluid. One can do it for any amount of time, ranging from one minute to a half hour. Place your forehead on a cushion on the ground and cup your head between your interlocked palms. Set your elbows firmly on the ground forming a tripod with your head and elbows. Raise your whole body up slowly, with your weight on your forehead and both elbows. Hold your body and legs straight, with the soles of your feet facing the sky. This posture should be held at least one minute or for as long as you can. In case of difficulty, this posture can be held against a wall. With regular practice, one can become *urdhvareta*, or the one in whom the flow of semen has been reversed.

18. *Sarvangasana* (shoulderstand): This is another special yogic posture recommended to men for speedy spiritual growth, since it helps by reversing the direction of flow of the seminal fluid. One can do it for any amount of time, ranging from one minute to a half hour. Lie face up with your back on the ground and your hands parallel to your body. Raise the lower portion of your body upward so your weight is placed on the tripod of your elbows and shoulders. Place your hands on your waist to support the weight of your body. Stretch your legs straight up. Your head should be resting on the ground and your breathing relaxed. Hold the posture for at least a minute or as long as you can. It is an alternative to shirshasana and has similar benefits.

To perform pranayama with three locks, sit in the posture given in step 15, called siddhasana for men and siddhayoniasana for women. Press the heel of your lower foot, right or left, against the root center (mooladhar) in your body—under the reproductive organs in men. Press the heel of your other foot against the pelvic center (swadhishthan) just above your reproductive organs. Care should be taken not to squeeze the organs between the two heels. In women, the heel of the lower foot should be a little inside the vagina and pressing this point in the body; and the heel of the other foot should be above the lower one, pressing the point just above the clitoris. This is to awaken the first two centers in the body. Your spine should be straight, like a stick set in the ground. Place both hands on your knees.

Close your right nostril with the thumb of your right hand and inhale through your left nostril for a count of 4. Hold your breath for a count of 16. This is called inner *kumbhak*. Now close your left nostril with the small finger of the right hand and exhale slowly through the right nostril for a count of 8. Hold this position, closing both the nostrils for a count of 8. This is called external *kumbhak*. This represents one set of deep breathing, with a count of 4-16-8-8. Repeat the process, inhaling through the right nostril for a count of 4 and, after retaining the breath for a count of 16, exhale through the left nostril slowly for a count of 8, and then hold the exhaled position for a count of 8. Keep on repeating the process with alternate nostrils for 20 minutes. This is *pranayama*.

The three locks are introduced during pranayama as follows. While inhaling, squeeze the muscles of your anus and pull them upward; your genitals are automatically pulled in and up. Hold this position for the complete duration of each set of breathing. This is the root lock (*mool bandh*). Squeeze your navel area simultaneously, pull it inside, and hold this position for the duration of each set of breathing. This is navel lock (*uddayan bandh*). When inhalation is complete at the count of 4, press your chin against your body and hold it for the complete duration of each deep breathing. This is the chin lock (*jalandhar bandh*). At the count of 16, when you begin exhaling, release all three locks at the same time. Pranayama and the three locks activate the sleeping kundalini, stimulating it to wake up. It also pressurizes the first five chakras, from root to throat, to open them up. An automatic concentration on the third eye is produced.

Next, hold the posture shown in step 16 (shashanka asana) for 15 minutes. You will find that the speed of your breathing slows down and you can easily slip into a state of meditation. Chanting AUM with attention on the third eye for 15 minutes will bring tremendous concentration on the third eye, which may result in the opening of the eyebrow center (ajna chakra), raising the kundalini upward and allowing you to slip into meditation. Inhale fully and chant AUM as long as your breath lasts. You may sit either in siddhasana, in a relaxed posture, or on a chair with your spine remaining straight. You should make yourself comfortable and well set, since you are now ready to go into meditation.

Prayer (shaktipat or -samadhi) is the final step of this two-hour practice. When you finish, you will be ready to go into a state of meditation and, one day, you will just slip into samadhi, your final goal. Sit in a relaxed posture on the ground or in a chair, with your spine straight, neither too relaxed nor too tense. Close your eyes and keep your attention on your third eye. You are already in a calm state of serenity and ready to slip into meditation. Visualize yourself sitting on top of the world, rising higher and higher toward the absolute. Feel liquid white light filling every part of your body. The same light is filling your body from the crown center to make your body immune to all decay, imperfections, diseases, and injury for the rest of life. Feel the light accumulate in your root center, pelvic center, navel center, heart center, throat center, and eyebrow center. All your chakras are open and providing their full power to you. Mother Kundalini has awakened from its seat at the base of your spine and is rising through your spine and reaching your crown center.

You are enjoying bliss and happiness. Nectar in the form of white light is filling your head, neck, left shoulder, and left hand, then your right shoulder and hand. Your hands feel longer and heavier than before because now they are filled with white light. The light now fills your spinal column, heart, lungs, kidneys, stomach, reproductive organs, left leg, and right leg. You are filled with light, surrounded by light; you have become ight itself.

Liquid white light is God consciousness itself. Feel the beautiful hand of God on top of your head; energy and vibrations from his hand are entering your body. You are now vibrating with the vibrations of God himself. You receive shaktipat from God and you realize you are God yourself, through his own blessing, because this is the only way. He is the ocean of love and mercy. He has understood your faults, mistakes, or sins as you have created them and has helped you release your karma through the awakening of Mother Kundalini. You can ask your mind to think what you want it to think; you can ask your body to do what you want it to do. You are neither the mind or the body; both respond to your beliefs; all are transitory. Feel that you are a pure being, an awareness other than the mind and body; feel that you are the dimensionless Atman, who is witness to everything.

Feel that you, as Atman, are rising up from the physical, to the astral, mental, intuitional, and soul planes. On the soul plane, you can see the guru, Sat Nam, Pythagoras, Master Jesus, Lord Krishna, Mother Goddess, or any enlightened being who has helped you. They have magnificent smiles and beautiful deep eyes. They are looking at you with love.

Rays of energy and divine vibration are coming from their bodies and entering yours. They are blessing you with their right hands, from which the rays come out and pour through your body. You are vibrating with the vibration of God. This is God's direct shaktipat.

You are the soul and become one with the supersoul. The drop merges with the ocean and the ocean merges with the drop. Atman and Paramatma become one; the two are made from the same material. Enjoy the bliss of union and be absorbed. You are in Samadhi.

To meet the requirements of the jnana yoga (path of wisdom), make it a habit to read scriptures and stories about realized people. This will quicken the process of awakening the kundalini through discernment and clarity. Layers of ignorance will dissolve one by one. I recommend two hours a day; it can be more or less, depending on your choice.

The requirements of bhakti yoga (path of devotion) can be met through the chanting of a mantra that serves the double purpose of attracting spiritual energy from the cosmos and developing love for God. The kundalini-awakening process becomes faster. Thousands of years of research by yogis and rishis shows that repeating the names of God, even mechanically, brings results. Mechanical nonfeeling is gradually converted into heartfelt reverence. The union of Atman and Paramatma becomes easy and smooth. In using a simple mantra, such as "Om Namaha Shivaya," the technique is to feel the beginning sound of AUM emanating from the seat of kundalini and gradually rising toward the eyebrow center with a pulling motion. The last two words, "Namaha Shivaya," should be spoken with a push into the position of third eye. The Sufis have a very good technique for repeating the name of God that is similar to the one suggested here. During a conference at a Florida retreat in December 1996, I learned one of the mantras Lord Jesus used to chant—*Yod Hey Wod Hey* repeated using a technique similar to the one above. In alchemy, you also chant a mantra to bring about the union of *chang* and *chi*, the male and female principles of the personality. As for the duration of chanting, I suggest 2 hours to gain results; it can be more or less, depending on how you feel.

Last, but not least, is the technique of regulated sex. Many, if not most, realized persons and yogis were married or in spiritual partnership.[2] They used sex as a tool for generating an experience and transcending it, opening thereby the doors of higher perception, rather than only for sensual pleasure or procreation. Just as only a thorn can remove a thorn from the body, transcendence from sexual desire can be achieved only through sex.

A single path can bring the desired results, although it can be difficult. For example, the path of selfless action (karma yoga) requires that a person live the life of a Mahatma Gandhi or Mother Teresa—not so easy for a normal person. Similarly, the path of devotion (bhakti yoga) requires that a person be devoted in the service of God day and night, like Mira, Surdas, or St. Teresa of Avila. The path of knowledge (jnana yoga) requires that a person study truth or thinking and concentrate day and night, like king Janaka, Ramana Maharishi, Socrates, or Richard Maurice Bucke. The path of sex (tantra yoga) requires that an individual be engrossed in tantric rituals day and night. There is a chance practitioners may become eccentric in this way, since a single path does not develop the personality in a balanced manner. Hence the researching yogis developed a path combining the elements from various disciplines so one could continue to live in the natural way and yet achieve liberation. This gave birth to kundalini yoga and the Integral Path. Gautam Buddha taught the middle way between asceticism and material living, and Sri Aurobindo advocated the Integral Path in his own style. The path presented here meets those requirements.

The sage Patanjali was a great exponent of yoga. The eightfold path he advocated has the following steps:

1. *Yama*, meaning moral conduct, such as nonviolence, nonstealing, truthfulness, continence, and noncovetousness.

2. *Niyama*, meaning religious observances, such as purity of mind and body, contentment, self-discipline, study of scripture and devotion to God.

3. *Asana*, meaning yogic postures.

4. *Pranayama*, deep breathing or breath control.

5. *Pratyahara*, meaning withdrawal of senses from external objects.

6. *Dharna*, meaning determination.

7. *Dhyana*, meaning meditation.

8. *Samadhi*, meaning final absorption leading to oneness with the supreme.

The Integral Path presented in this chapter meets all of Patanjali's requirements in a modernized fashion that suits the requirements of present day humanity. Moreover, factors like prayer and regulated sex have been added for power and increased effectiveness.

The complete Integrated Path is a way of life that is easy to adopt in a short time, although it may appear difficult. I found it very convenient while living the life of a university professor. And my feeling is that one can achieve results in a single lifetime, although the period may vary from a few weeks to a few years, depending on how much one puts into it. However, there are certain yogic postures practicants may not like to do, or certain disciplines one may not like to incorporate. Likewise, one may practice only two hours a day instead of six. When a person perseveres, however, progress is bound to take place. Over time, other elements may be added according to personal suitability.

The whole process may be understood, again, through the example of water. To boil water, the fire must be powerful enough to bring the water to the boiling point. But once the water reaches the boiling point, it will instantly convert into steam. Similarly in yoga, you may have to make several kinds of effort to bring yourself to your personal "boiling point"; once this is done, personality is converted into Godhood. And then you cease being simply human and begin to live as God. But remember, there is always one step more. Godhood is an everlasting journey, from perfection to perfection. The only difference is that you have the bliss of being on the path and have knowledge of the truth, while previously you lived and suffered in ignorance and material attachment. When your kundalini is awakened, you know you have broken the chain of further births.

The Awakening of Kundalini

There are characteristic symptoms of awakened kundalini.[3] A list of these symptoms, though not an exhaustive one, is presented here:

1. Throbbing of the root center (mooladhar), shaking of the whole body, and involuntary inhaling and exhaling of breath with loss of control of the body.

2. Trembling of the body, involuntary laughing or weeping, twisting of the tongue and deformed sounds coming from it, fear and frightening visions, hair standing on its roots, passing semen.

3. Fixed posture and concentration between the eyebrows, revolving of the eyeballs and automatic holding of breath in the lungs (*kumbhak*), cessation of breath, creation of a void in the mind.

4. Fixed posture and involuntary coming of the three locks—root, navel, and throat (moolbandha, uddayanbandha, and jalandhar bandha)—the

tongue pushing back and rising toward the palate (*khechri mudra*), forcibly stretching out the hands and legs.

5. Feeling of the spiritual energy (prana) being active in the body day and night, concentration of mind filling the mind with joy and bliss, the body beginning to shake or toss, a feeling that the spiritual energy is rising to the crown center every moment, whether attending to the call of nature, sleeping, or dreaming.

6. Feeling that mind and body are possessed by some heavenly agency or spirit and, under that influence, the body performs involuntary yogic postures without pain or fatigue and accompanied by strange breathing.

7. Hearing of different kinds of internal sounds (*naad* or *shabda*), feeling of absence of body and experience of vibrations in the spinal column, eyelids opening and closing without effort, a feeling of electrical currents passing through nerves, convulsions.

8. Automatic repetition of mantras all the time, accompanied with waves of blissful beatitude and passing of spiritual currents to the cerebrum.

9. Body possessed by some heavenly agency beginning to rotate like a grinding stone, loss of control of breathing, sitting in a cross-legged position, the body beginning to jump like a frog here and there, the body becoming motionless like a dead person and feeling as if you have passed away.

10. The moment you sit with eyes closed, the body begins to throw its limbs forcibly and to utter deformed sounds or sounds like those of various animals and birds.

11. Wherever attention is fixed in the body, the spiritual energy, prana, begins to flow there, with nerves undergoing jerks, as if electricity is passing through.

12. Feeling intoxicated without taking any drug, walking like a drunk and unable to do any work, steps falling majestically, lack of interest in talking to or hearing others, a feeling of having drunk divinity.

13. Shaking of the body and singing of hymns with joy and ecstasy whenever sitting for prayers, music and poetry coming out involuntarily, speaking languages not known.

14. Maintaining a balanced mind, undisturbed in all situations, having inexhaustible energy, not feeling tired even after many hours of work,

feeling the body light as air, filled with joy and buoyancy and happy even in dreams.

15. Falling into a dreamy state of mind in meditation, sensing divine visions, smells, sounds, tastes, figures, touches, and instructions.

16. While in meditation, the secrets of the future and the hidden meanings of scriptures beginning to unfold before you, removing all doubts. You begin to understand spiritual works at a glance and acquire self-confidence so that you do not feel the need to approach anyone for knowledge, including Brahma himself. You acquire strange powers of oratory and influencing an audience.

17. While in meditation, you achieve quick concentration between the eyebrows, breathing slows down, and you plunge into the ocean of bliss, khechari and shambhavi mudras come into operation and you experience the pleasure of savikalpa samadhi.

18. In mornings and evenings, you regularly become charged with divine influences and feel possessed by a heavenly agency.

It is important to point out here that, thankfully, everyone does not have all the symptoms mentioned here. Only some of them will appear in each person, depending on the temperament, karma, and preparation of the individual. For example, if a person has been doing the necessary yogic postures as a part of a regular practice, the involuntary postures will not manifest on awakening of the kundalini, since he or she has already met those requirements. In a person who has lived a natural sex life, excessive heating of the head or other parts of the body will never take place on awakening. Someone who has covered all the factors included in the Integral Path will have a very smooth awakening of kundalini, with no, or few, side effects. Only positive symptoms will manifest.

Chapter Twenty-Six

THE PHYSIOLOGY OF KUNDALINI

The physiology of kundalini can be understood through its supporting elements—the three *nadis* (subtle channels) and the seven chakras (energy centers) as shown in figure 1 on page 226. The connection of the chakras with the glands of the body is shown in figure 2 on page 228.

The three nadis—*ida*, *pingala*, and *sushumna* create chakras one through seven (see figure 1), whose function is to govern all aspects of our being and supply energy to meet basic needs. The seat of kundalini is at the base of the spine, between the first and second chakras, where it lies dormant in the symbolic form of a snake coiled three-and-a-half times around the *swayambhu linga*, and closing the opening of the *linga* with its mouth. The name kundalini is derived from *kunda,* meaning "cavity" (in which it resides) and, *kundala*, meaning "coils." The feminine form of the masculine kundala is kundalini, meaning that this energy is recognized in the female form of Mother. She is responsible for guiding our attention to the highest level of realization. She has a built-in archive recording all our previous existences, as well as an intelligence of her own. She gives her loving care to us as the Mother and guides us in the most nurturing way possible.

Since Mother Kundalini is herself pure, she rises in a person who has also achieved purity. On arousal, the expression on the face of the practicant becomes radiant; one begins to look younger, active, beautiful, and magnetic. Kundalini repairs damage, cures illness, and rejuvenates the body; the successful practitioner can pass on the same healing to others. The power received is in direct proportion to the openness for and trust in kundalini.

The Nadis

In the set of the three nadis, ida (moon channel) manifests at the left, pingala (sun channel) manifests at the right, and sushumna constitutes the central channel. Ida and sushumna begin at the mooladhara chakra; pingala begins at the swadhishthan. All of them cross at the ajna chakra, where ida moves to the right, pingala moves to the left, and the three nerves join again at the sahasrara.

Ida nadi represents *tamo-guna* (inertia), the past, and the subconscious. Its positive aspects are existence, emotion, joy, desire, and auspiciousness. Its negative aspects are conditioning, superstition, lethargy, guilt, self-pity, fear, addictions, sexual perversion, blind faith, and black magic. Since emotion is born out of desire, the left side of the body represents the emotional side. If the left side is weak, one becomes prone to emotional extremism, the negative aspects of the nadi are manifested, and the growing pressure on the brain can lead to a psychotic breakdown. A balance can be achieved through *rajo-guna*, or activity of the right channel. If the left side is strong, the positive aspects of the nadi are manifested, and joy, buoyancy, and happiness are expressed.

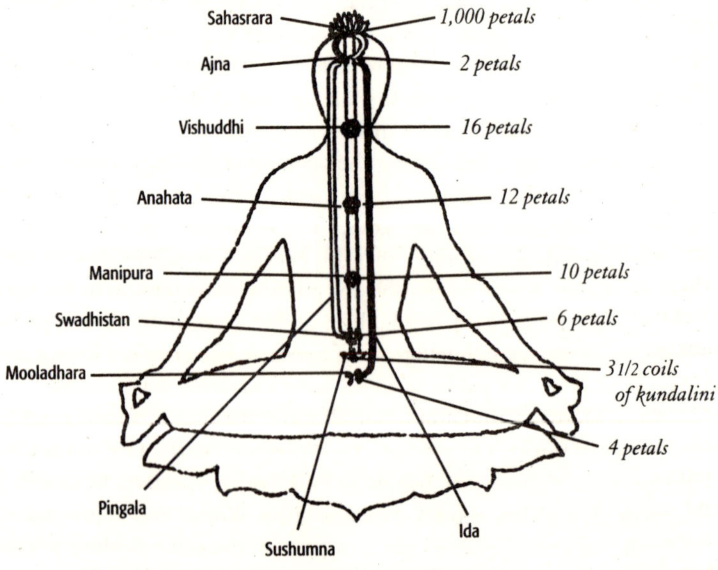

Figure 1. The three nadis and the chakras

Pingala nadi represents *rajo-guna* (activity, desire), the future, and supraconsciousness. Its positive aspects are physical and mental activity, creativity, and self-respect. Its negative aspects are egotism, temper, domination, cunning, exploitation, vanity, lack of shame, fanaticism, and asceticism. With a strong right side, the person is known to be egotistic, selfish, and aggressive, and the emotional side may become paralyzed. However, logic and wisdom are seen to depart and they become ignorant. A balance is achieved by moving to the central channel (sushumna nadi) and believing strongly that one is not the doer.

The sushumna nadi represents *sattva-guna* (purity), the present, and the unconscious. It has only the positive aspects of faith in spirituality, nurturing, and revelation. Our evolution takes place through this channel. When partly active, it provides awareness, virtue, and knowing. An awakening kundalini first ascends sushumna to ajna chakra, and then descends through ida and pingala in a melting form. The disparate factors of our being begin to integrate into a whole, connecting the mind to Atman. Passing through the gate of ajna chakra, one reaches *sahasrara*, which is the kingdom of God. Maintaining thoughtless awareness and meditation makes sushumna strong. One lives in the eternal now, transcending time and space.

The arousal of kundalini through the ida nadi manifests the negative aspects of ida; arousal through the pingala nadi manifests the negative aspects of pingala. Only arousal through the sushumna nadi leads to the kingdom of God.

The Chakras

Ripples are created by the respective powers of the ida and pingala nadis in the two channels, and then the seven chakras are created at the points where these ripples meet. The chakras are vortices of energy, moving in a clockwise direction. Each chakra corresponds to a plexus and a certain number of petals express its qualities. Each petal corresponds to a subplexus. Seen from above, the chakras appear as overlapping circles. They are energy storehouses for the corresponding plexus to use to meet the physical, mental, emotional, and spiritual demands of the sympathetic nervous system. Before the awakening of the kundalini, the chakras have a limited and exhaustible energy supply, like a battery. After awakening, they are connected to the unlimited divine powerplant through the kundalini and then their energy is inexhaustible. These chakras evolve and develop at various stages; they represent milestones on the evolutionary path.

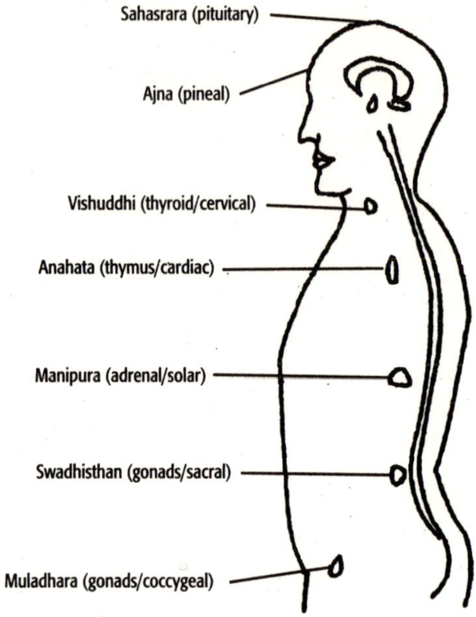

Figure 2. The chakras and the glands

The first is the *mooladhar* chakra (root center), situated below the seat of kundalini. It has four petals and earth is its element. Literally, *mool* means "root," and *adhara* means "support." This chakra represents innocence, eternal childhood, chastity, motherly love, and wisdom. It is responsible for sex and excretion. Its negative aspects are adultery, perverted sex, pornography, lustful attention, materialism, apathy to spirituality, and constipation. The elephant god, Lord Ganesh, is its presiding deity. Lord Ganesh is known as the remover of obstacles and the source of absolute wisdom. After awakening, one transcends sexual desire and learns to develop respect for one's own chastity and that of others. Childlike minds experience maturity. Freedom from sin is achieved. Sin in yogic terms is the intentional repetition of known mistakes. Realizing this, we take back our power to avoid sin. With the understanding of selfishness, one lives in the spirit of gratitude.

The second chakra is the *swadhishthan* chakra (navel center), suspended like a satellite on a cord from the *manipura* (third) chakra in the spinal region just above the genitals. It has six petals and fire is its element. The kundalini first awakens in the manipura chakra, passes enlightenment to the swadhishthan chakra through the cord, and then returns to the manipura chakra. This chakra represents intellectuality, creativity, inspiration, knowledge of the beyond, and aesthetics. It is responsible for the kidneys, liver, spleen, pancreas, and uterus. Its negative aspects are excessive thinking and excessive involvement in artistic things, ego-oriented life, domination or slavery, alcohol, drugs, self-destructive eating habits, and artificial and crude behavior. In a positive sense, it bestows intelligence and creativity in conjunction with the pingala nadi, since its presiding deities are Lord Brahma and his power, Sri Saraswati (Brahma is the creator and Saraswati is the goddess of music and arts). Since pingala draws its power from sushumna, an imbalance may be created that may result in diseases like diabetes or heart attack. A balance may be restored through nonmaterialism and nonegotism. Excessive thinking and negative attention can pressurize the liver. Interest in knowledge of the dead or black magic are pursuits that can damage this chakra. The aim of achieving a state of thoughtless awareness (*nirvichar samadhi*) and developing genuine humility is the goal. Increased awareness, well-reasoned discourse, or writing prose or verse are gifts of this chakra. Transcendence of greed, lust, anger, attachment, and ego is achieved and one's mind dwells in the beauty of the Most High. The poet may touch the level of a prophet.

The third, or *manipura,* chakra (navel center) is at the level of the solar plexus. It has ten petals and water is its element. It represents harmless action, *dharma* (sustenance), evolution, health, and material well-being. The stomach, intestines, spleen, and liver are governed by this chakra's life force. Its negative aspects are involvement in domestic problems, dominance over spouse, excessive fasting or excessive interest in food, asceticism, materialism, and dependence on alcohol. In a positive sense, it advocates the Ten Commandments as guidelines for Self-realization. Kundalini first awakens in manipura, piercing it from one extreme to the other. The presiding deities are Lord Vishnu and Sri Lakshmi. Dharma and the stomach seem to be related. Whenever revolting against dharma, the stomach becomes upset. However, after seeing the truth and beauty of the spirit on awakening, one no longer cares for worldly things and becomes a witness to the Self. One has faith in Providence, and gains strength in taking responsibility and enjoying duty. Addiction to alcohol and demand for special foods or fasting vanishes, and one's appetite is easily satisfied. One attains the power to create and destroy worlds through the power of speech. The presence of a saintly person brings a sense of quiet and stillness into a group of tumultuous people. Manipura is at the boundary between the physical and spiritual worlds; its awakening normally brings visits to higher realms through the astral body in dreams, trances, or visions.

The fourth chakra is the *anahat* chakra (heart center), located at the spinal center in the region of heart. It has twelve petals and air is its element. *Anahata* means "unstruck." The awakening of this chakra promises hearing with the inner ear of the cosmic sound—AUM or Word—created without the striking of two objects. It is heard when all the internal noises of the mind have stopped through sustained practices. This chakra represents existence, love, and truth. After its awakening, truth-attention-joy (*sat-chit-anand*) abide. Its negative aspects are extreme physical and mental activity, unbalanced relations (especially with the mother), drugs, and a lack of faith in God (universal consciousness) or anti-God activities. The presiding deities are Lord Shiva and Sri Parvati, the Atman or spirit. On awakening, one loses identification with body, mind, and feelings, and becomes spirit or Atman through an open heart. Forgiveness, all-pervading attention, and care of Sri Jagadamba (Mother of the Universe) are received. One develops reverence for one's physical mother, who has a place at the left of the heart, and one's father, who has a place at the right of the heart. One realizes we actually choose our parents. Pure love is detached and unconditional, flowing like a river. Transcendence of self-will removes self-protective screens, enabling one to put oneself in another's shoes (or heart) through understanding.

The fifth is the *vishuddhi* chakra (throat center), located at the juncture of the spine and medula oblongata. It has sixteen petals and ether is its element. It represents collective consciousness, divine attitude, androgynous personality, and playful witness. The presiding deity is Lord Krishna, with Sri Radha, his consort, representing the center. Lord Krishna is the eternal witness, watching the cosmic drama in complete detachment. The deity of the left side is Lord Krishna's sister, Sri Vishnumaya, representing the brother-sister relationship on the positive side, and immorality, guilt, sarcastic attitude, and foul tongue on the negative side. The deity of the right side is Bal Krishna (Lord Krishna as child), the positive side representing witnessing of the Self. Smoking, problems with colds or bronchial tubes sinus problems, and continual swearing represent the negative side. Awakening this chakra transcends the negative aspects of the left, right, and central chakra and realization of all positive aspects. Vishuddhi chakra takes care of the physical parts—

arms, face, throat, mouth, and teeth—and suggests a protection from colds, smoking (or other drugs), addiction, and negligent dental care. Awakening promises freedom from worldly desires, because they have served their purpose. The energy hitherto used for achieving worldly goals is now free and redirected upward, opening the gateway of liberation. Realization of eternity comes from mooladhara and all other knowledge, coming through manipura, is now combined by the union of the subjective and objective at the vishuddhi, giving the true meaning of yoga—union. Clarity comes from shifting from the intellectual to deeper levels, giving peace of mind, understanding of the past, and clear visions of the present and the future. Increased awareness and greater discernment clearly show what can be done and what should be avoided. One becomes merciful to all, knowing that, since one's experience is a product of one's own choices, one can only be a victim of one's own ignorance.

The sixth is the *ajna* chakra (eyebrow center), also known as the center of command or the third eye. It is located at the center of the brain and has two petals. The presiding deity of the central chakra is Lord Jesus Christ, representing forgiveness and resurrection; the deity of the left chakra is Lord Mahavira, representing the subconscious (superego); the deity of right chakra is Lord Buddha, representing *ahankar* (ego). The positive aspects of the center are sight, hearing, and thought, and the negative aspects are bad association and wandering eyes; the positive aspects of the left are memories and conditioning from the past, and the negative aspects are addictions and self-indulgence. The positive aspect of the right is I-ness and the negative aspects are worry, harmful attitudes toward others, and incorrect notions of God. Ajna is supposed to be the most important chakra, because this is where ida and pingala join. With the arrival of kundalini at this chakra, serene awareness brings the blissful silence that is the heart of creation; one is in direct communication with creation and commands are received here. Yogis undergo an experience of death, ego is fragmented into millions of pieces, and one enters the state of *shoonya* (void), or absolute nothingness. This is one's second birth from Mother Kundalini with the blessings of Paramashiva. According to the message of Lord Jesus, one is resurrected and born again into a new awareness of the Self. Karma is the result of past actions of the ego, but oneness with spirit takes one beyond ego and karma. Vestiges of imperfection are purified and karma is burned away. God's compassion is expressed through our forgiveness. This is the spiritual definition of forgiveness—that one no longer judges others as wrong and accepts them as they are, as other manifestations of God. One is now androgynous, *ardhanareeshwara*—half male, half female—and has a perfect balance of intellect and intuition. One recognizes more than three or four dimensions of reality that cannot be described, only experienced.

Compassion, expressed previously only to friends, relatives, and those deemed worthy, is, at this stage, extended to all beings, since one's compassion reaches the level of divinity. One begins feeling grateful even to those who have been one's personal enemies. However, temptations continue to come, even in the lives of saints and yogis, but now they are more subtle. The guru can also err, or at least commit what our limited understanding judges as error. Saints, gurus, or seekers who, in your opinion, are on the wrong path and must be put into the light are in reality mirrors showing you your own error in judging others. Ajna chakra gives the power of awareness and discernment, and it is crowned with compassion.

The three nadis—ida, pingala, and sushumna—are represented by three great rivers in mythology: Ganga, Jamuna, and Saraswati. The *sangam*, or the meeting place or the convergence, of the three rivers is called Triveni. This is near present-day Prayag, or Allahabad, in India. According to Hindu belief, every twelve years, when the sun is in Aquarius, a dip at the point of confluence purifies the person. Ajna chakra is very important and is symbolically represented by this point of confluence. Its awakening signifies expansion of awareness, transcendence of duality, and precipitation of stored karmas to the surface. This, when faced and squared with great effort, transforms the person from ego-human to God-realized. Women in India apply *sindur* (vermilion) at the exact point of ajna chakra, meaning to maintain a constant conscious and unconscious awareness of this chakra. This mark is not a religious mark or a beauty spot, as is incorrectly thought today. Men also apply *tilak* (sandalwood paste) on the third eye. The purpose of sindur or tilak is to exert constant pressure on the nerve running from *bhrumadhyaa* (the center of eyebrows) to the medulla oblongata. Many who practice this ritual have forgotten the intention behind its performance. The health of the pineal gland, responsible for the development of ajna chakra, can be regenerated and maintained through yogic techniques, such as *trataka* (concentration in front of third eye) and *shambhavi mudra*.

A sixth, or intuitive, sense works through an awakened ajna chakra, also giving rise to the faculty of astral projection and inner visions in the dream state. One is now standing under the *kalpataru* (wish-fulfillment tree) and mental resolves in accordance with dharma are immediately converted into fruit. Now one is a detached observer, a witness of all of life's events, and hence immune to disturbance. One participates in all the affairs of life and lives fully, but now as a detached observer. One surrenders and moves freely with the fast-moving current of a flowing life, awakened from the dream of life and conscious of higher realms through dreams and visions.

This chakra has two petals. The left signifies the ida nadi, the right signifies the pingala nadi. The two meet with the central nadi, sushumna, just below ajna chakra. The letters inscribed on the two petals are *Ham* and *Ksham*, the *bija* (seed) mantra for Shiva and Shakti. The importance of *shivalingam* can now be understood. It is not a phallic symbol, but a symbol of one's astral body. *Lingam* in mooladhara, called *dhumra lingam*, has a smoky color, representing the undeveloped state of consciousness with instincts. Lingam at ajna chakra, called *itarakhya lingam*, has a black color, representing I-awareness and various powers associated with it. Lingam in sahasrara, called *jyotir lingam*, is luminous, representing an illuminated state of consciousness. During meditation, consciousness passes from one stage to another—instinctive and restless, calm and quiet, illuminated. Practitioners witness the three lingam during the course of their inner journey. Successful arrival at ajna is indicated by the realization of its deity, Paramshiva, who, according to traditional terminology, shines like a chain of lightning flashes during meditation on ajna chakra.

On meditating at the awakened ajna chakra, one sees a flaming lamp shining like the morning sun. Results of meditation on various chakras are collectively realized by meditation on ajna chakra alone. One has realized one's unity with Brahman and, according to one's grooming and interest, acquires certain superpowers (*siddhis*). For example, for writers, their writings become very effective and powerful through divine influence.

The next and last station is *sahasrara* chakra, which is the culmination of the journey of kundalini. However, "it is not important for us to know how to reach sahasrara from ajna chakra, but it is essential for us to know how to awaken ajna."[1] If ajna chakra is awakened before the other chakras, the practitioner faces far fewer difficulties. Awakening other chakras one by one can bring several unprecedented difficulties. Hence it is highly advisable to concentrate on ajna chakra first and then on the others. Since mooladhara chakra is internally connected to ajna chakra, the awakening of ajna automatically triggers the awakening of mooladhara, and the opening of other chakras also becomes easier.

The seventh is the sahasrara chakra (crown center), located four finger-widths above the crown of the head. It has 1,000 petals. It represents integration, silence, and cosmic consciousness, and is manifested as vibrations and cool breezes. The positive aspects are going beyond duality and above the three states of being or gunas, called *tamas* (inertia), *rajas* (activity), and *sattva* (purity). Its negative aspect is disbelief in God consciousness. Since the location of sahasrara is beyond the physical body, it is not, in fact, a chakra. It is the culmination of the yogic process and the crown of expanded awareness, signified through the 1,000 petals. It is Brahman—represented by *shoonya* (void)—nothing and everything. Transcending all concepts, it is, nevertheless, the source of all concepts. The arrival of kundalini at sahasrara marks the union of Shiva and Shakti and the beginning of samadhi, that is, Self-realization. Between ajna and sahasrara is the experience of death, absolute nothingness or shoonyata (void), and the merging of the seer, seeing, and seen. This is Nirvana, enlightenment, *nirvikalpa samadhi*, Self-realization, or the kingdom of God. It is supramental awareness, awareness of one's own Self as God.

Awareness is of three kinds: sensual awareness (sight, touch, taste, smell, and sound), awareness of mind -(time, space, and object), and supramental awareness (process or range of experience, or samadhi). Samadhi is further classified into three categories by Patanjali: *savikalpa samadhi* (samadhi with fluctuations), *asampragyata* (samadhi without awareness), and *nirvikalpa samadhi* (samadhi without fluctuations). Just as one cannot know when childhood ends and youth begins, or when youth ends and old age begins, also one cannot know when meditation ends and samadhi begins. One cannot pinpoint it; it is an interaction between two states. The whole process occurs in continuity, each state fusing into the next and transforming gradually. When kundalini ascends through various chakras, experiences are indicative of the evolving nature of consciousness. They are within the realm of savikalpa samadhi, with illumination and darkness occurring now and then. At the point of the experience of death at the ajna chakra, savikalpa samadhi ends and nirvikalpa samadhi begins. According to Swami Satyananda Saraswati:

> From here, energies fuse and flow together to sahasrara, where enlightenment unfolds. Kundalini awakening and samadhi are the same thing. If you understand the teachings of Buddha and the other great saints and teachers, you will find that they have all spoken about the same thing but in different languages.[2]

Patanjali's raja yoga is an intellectual approach leading to the highest point of nirvikalpa samadhi, while tantra is an emotional approach leading to the highest point of sahasrara. Awareness in both cases is the same.

Many Methods, One Goal

Just as the food in a pot cannot be cooked over the flame of a candle, kundalini cannot be awakened through limited prayers or worship. If the pot is placed over a powerful heat, the food will be cooked in a very short time. If the spiritual pressure reaches the boiling point, kundalini can be awakened in a single lifetime. The concept of religion through duality (external and internal God) has become obsolete. That is why followers of different religions fight against each other. The power and understanding has not awakened in them, because they have not undergone inner transformation. If Krishna, Buddha, Jesus, Mohammed, Zoroaster, Confucius, Lao Tse, Gurdjief, Mahavir, Nanak, and Pythagoras were seated at a round table, they would have perfect understanding and love for each other. Each of them had their spiritual power awakened through an event or crisis, leading them all to one and the same God. It is a pity that their followers, in general, never know of and learn to bring spiritual pressure to bear on their own existence and thus remain ordinary. Of course, there have been and will always be a few in each faith who know the secret and reach the goal.

The Integral Path presented here, if followed in the correct manner, can awaken the kundalini in one lifetime and then all can join those who know themselves to be as and of God. The Integral approach covers most of the disciplines of development and there is very little chance, if any, of its failure or of its giving rise to abnormalities in a practitioner that sometimes result from one-sided methods. Bronwyn Fox, an Australian researcher and best-selling author of *Panic: Don't Panic*, agrees that the main cause of psychic disorders from which a large number of people in Australia are suffering today is an uneven way of living and spiritual development. Kundalini is energy of an infinite order and it is often overlooked in the quest for spiritual development.

The various methods discussed in chapter 25 are not mutually exclusive; perfection of any one path will invariably include elements from many other paths. For example, whatever method one follows, one's stages of development are always seen in dreams. Guides of different faiths have always advised practitioners to pay regular attention to dreams and receive benefit from them. Paths of knowledge, devotion, and karma are usually seen to run parallel in a yogi—more for some, less for others—and yogis remain aware of their dreams as well. Most practitioners are married and traditional religions tell them to avoid sex, which is a sinful act according to them. So practitioners are in a dilemma; they want to transcend sex but they cannot, so they live with guilt. So whatever path they may be following, they have to know a way to transcend sexual desire. Love, prayer, and solitude are each independent paths in themselves. But whatever path a practitioner may be following, one has to have intense love, since love is God. One needs to live in solitude for a sufficient period of time so the spirit can interact with the person. And prayer is a part of most disciplines, in a natural way.

So you see, more than one discipline is lived simultaneously, and it is for this purpose that ashrams were built with the assistance of experienced guides. However, if one has the ability to learn and practice, the external guru is unnecessary, although it may take a little longer to get to the goal. Once you reach the goal, the same experience is there for all.

The Point of No Return

God has no life; he is existence, and the experience of this existence is called samadhi. Normally, when the "inner atom bomb" explodes—that is, when kundalini reaches sahasrara—there is a brief experience of death and resurrection. One passes through samadhi and the experience of Self or God, and then comes back to normal life with a change. The change is received through a second birth; one is reborn, mere human-ness ends, and Godhood begins. But in later encounters with this reality, and sometimes even in the first encounter, the person may be absorbed and gone forever; one may not return from this sojourn to the normal existence one had before samadhi. One is dead on the physical level, and the translation into a higher realm has taken place. This is called "the point of no return." Meher Baba was lost in such a state for four to five days; he did not know what he was wearing or eating or doing. Ramakrishna would go into such a state just by hearing the name of Ram or Krishna, or by seeing a temple or any religious forms.

Great awareness is needed at such a juncture. Meher Baba returned because his disciples were ever-present; Ramakrishna stayed primarily because of one of his nephews. Whenever Ramakrishna went into such a state, his beloved nephew fed him or gave him massage to restore his breathing. The world knows the name of Vivekananda, who spread the teachings of Ramakrishna, but nobody knows the name of his nephew who saved him for this world. Ramakrishna also kept himself on earth to carry the message to the world by maintaining a taste for delicious and new varieties of food. Someone asked him the reason for the tasty food. He explained the interest in food was keeping him alive for the world, but then he lost that interest when it was pointed out to him. Three or four days later, he was dead. No attachment could hold him on earth any longer. Unless surrounded by a school, a group, or an ashram, one will either not be able to go into samadhi, or, once there, one will not be able to return to normal life unless one has sufficient development. Hence, some kind of organization is recommended for the person who is likely to go into samadhi. Naturally, karmic destiny may support some in not needing an outside agency to keep them on earth. Their presence meets a need the world has for them and they stay until their responsibility to that need is met.

The state of samadhi is extremely blissful and it becomes very difficult to cut the experience short. As I pointed out earlier, one touches this state and comes back. Perhaps this is a design of nature. But on repeated occurrences, one fine day, one may be plunged into it, never to return. I can say so from my own experience, and I remind myself of this fact before going into samadhi when I am alone. Of course one day it will happen, but those who can convey the truth to the world in one way or another, and those who do not want to leave even this attachment behind—because this can be the seed of another incarnation—would like to keep the allotted existence on earth in a natural way.

Let me say here that the rule of "fixed destiny" does not apply to yogis, who are the ones gone beyond the force of gravitation. A yogi makes his or her own destiny and is free to choose the time of death. There have been innumerable realized souls who are unknown to the world because they had no literary training or could not have a known impact on the world for one reason or the other. And it is only those who have gone beyond who can tell of their experiences and teach us about what is beyond, to whatever extent it may be possible within communication constraints. There is no other source. It is not unusual to find that special interests in the lives of saints and prophets or other realized souls kept them alive and on earth. Hence, such people should not be criticized on the basis of those special interests and must be preserved as the advocates of truth.

AFTERWORD

I FEEL PART OF THE INTENT AND VALUE of this book is in its pointing out the parallel foundations in all orthodox religions. There are always two main paths in a world based on a belief in polarity. These are value judgments such as right and wrong, good and evil, and in or out. We can search for mutual peace by exploring all the external dogmatic teachings of the various competing religions and, after a comprehensive explorative comparison of them all, come to the understanding that fundamentally they all demand the same thing. Religion demands adherence. Most of the world's people have been conditioned to believe that chasing after this goal of religious law, outside themselves, will lead to peace, happiness, and ultimately the experience of a particular definition of heaven. If only they can convince or coerce every other person on the planet that they are the possessors of the only regulations that are right or that God approves of. There would be peace if only someday everyone can be taught God's one and only true name, whatever that may be. What religious competitors commonly forget are the two most powerful tenants basic to all scripture—love and compassion—the complete spiritual opposites of religious competition and judgment.

There is a reason, despite all the energy expended over thousands of years, that this peace has not yet come about in a lasting way. Peace, happiness, love, and heaven are not found outside of our own hearts. Peace, happiness, love, and heaven are in our own being-ness. Love is what we are created of. The people of the world all want the same two things, happiness and an escape from suffering. And, as always, there is another method to discover this. The orthodox study and observation of what we are not can lead us to what we are. This will bring us to the other path.

Cosmic consciousness is a state already existing and waiting to be uncovered within everyone. Within the state of cosmic consciousness, the reality of who we truly are dawns like the sun dawns each morning. Sunshine comes because it has always been there, only during the night it was hidden in the shadow of the earth's body just as our fearful beliefs are a dark shadow separating us from our hearts, love, and the true nature of all that is. Something similar occurs when we identify ourselves as our bodies and fear their loss will also be the loss of who we feel we are. Our cosmic consciousness is overshadowed by our confusion that we are our bodies. Cosmic consciousness is the direct experience of not only the universe and God's true nature; it is also the experience of our own true being as well. In that first instant of dawning, the fearful shadow of misunderstanding begins to evaporate before the light of universal love. This is a purely natural phenomenon that cannot be forced or counterfeited and will manifest in all beings at some point in every being's infinite spiritual evolution. Perhaps we can delay its coming by sleepwalking through life, but our ultimate awakening is as inevitable as the birthright of our existence. There is also the strong possibility of encouraging and speeding its coming.

Arousal of kundalini energy is one way to begin the dawning of cosmic consciousness and to attain freedom from life after life of experience founded on fear and judgment. This book has the information to assist spiritual aspirants in finding their own path. Cosmic consciousness lies within us, just as the path to realize it also lies within.

Our own life experiences and those of the people around us give hints of the universe's nature, just as dreams and visions show us the possibility of other truths and realities. Near-death experiences, in which the events witnessed are later verified as accurate, and past-life memories that have been verified as true events are two examples of other realities. The slowing of perceived time during a dangerous crisis can generate an understanding of the illusion of time and the limited truth of the speed of light. Indeed, everything we perceive as reality is fundamentally a quantum event. These types of experiences will lead to a realization of four basic, unchanging cosmic truths:

1. We exist infinitely with no beginning and no end. We are not born and cannot die.

2. We are part of all that is and all that is, is within us.

3. The law of cause and effect; what we put out is what we get back, without exception and in the tiniest detail.

4. With the exception of these laws, everything in the universe is in a constant state of transformation.

A desire for understanding expands awareness, thus creating possibility for expanded experience. Defining and judging contract awareness and deny our natural openness for greater experience. Expansion of awareness can come through an educated desire or with natural spontaneity. A near-death experience is naturally spontaneous, and consciously directed out-of-body soul travel to other places on earth or to the astral realms can be the result of educated desire. The desire for awakening can come as part of the personality drive at birth or evolve slowly over a lifetime of acquiring enough knowledge to discover that awakening exists and is an achievable reality. On the arrival of awakening and Self-realization, much of the burden of judgmental, polarized knowledge is released back into the illusion it spawned from. This freedom, so sought after by humankind, is freedom from our own belief in fear and judgment. We are searching for salvation from our own beliefs. God-realization is that salvation; it comes from within. All humankind is ultimately a candidate for cosmic consciousness, whether it occurs as a spontaneous event arising out of crisis or is consciously pursued with an open heart. Learning of the commonality in the natural source of the awakening is a conformation for both the spiritually educated, trained students of liberation, and for those in whom the experience is sudden and unexpected.

This book offers a glimpse into the reality of cosmic consciousness and a variety of ways to discover that same reality within us. There are also more ways than those detailed here; as always it is up to us to choose our own path. We will always be offered polarity's two pathways—the inner or outer—taking responsibility or giving our responsibility away, going toward what excites us or running from our fears. There need not be confusion over which path is most suitable, as the intention for taking any given path will generate the results.

The mind and body are interconnected and supportive of one another. Kundalini is a physical energy requiring a physical mind and body to manifest through. A healthy body and clear mind give kundalini energy a place to work. One reason we may be embodied in an organic physical form is to have a vehicle through which to generate the transformation.

The path to consciousness can be traveled more easily with training, as we are less likely to believe the experiences are hallucinatory or that we are losing our minds. Our own karmic destiny is supplying us with all the tools we need. Each person's life is a constant stream of choice and opportunity. The simple trust that whatever your soul is providing you with or guiding you toward is the most perfect and most compassionate possible. It is all that your beliefs will allow. This trust in perfection and love will see you through all of life's transformations.

Throughout time, we have had a fascination with healing. Usually, that idea of healing has been limited to connections with the physical and emotional body and we have thought of healing as a singular event. We see something as wrong and we want to fix it, to change it from wrong to right. There is another way to view healing. We live in a time-stream of existence. In the same way that we view a river as a whole entity composed of several elements, the stream of existence is composed of elements such as love, compassion, peace, and healing. And it is eternally flowing. Every moment, we are in a constant state of healing. Perhaps what we are in physical bodies to heal may not actually be our bodies at all. Maybe we are experiencing ourselves as physical to give a reference point for our consciousness to realize that the only thing we can truly heal is our fearful beliefs. The rising of kundalini and subsequent expansion of awareness are powerful tools in our ability to heal and spiritually evolve. The healing of fear and separation and spiritual evolution are mutually dependent. Kundalini is energy of clarity. There may be much opportunity for confusion as it rises in partial stages, but when fully risen, the ability to clearly focus and to understand the underlying and unified compassionate nature of reality dawns with the clear light of the soul.

—JONATHAN BARBER

NOTES

Abbreviations: n.d. = no date given, n.p. = no place given, JRPR = Journal of Religion and Psychical Research

Front Matter

1 C. G. Jung, *Memories, Dreams, Reflections* (New York: Vintage Books, 1989), p. 314.

2 Robert Jay Lifton, MD, *The Broken Connection* (Washington, DC: American Psychiatric Press, 1979), p. 47.

Chapter 1

1 Dr. Don Morse, *Searching for Eternity* (Memphis, TN: EagleWing Books, Inc., 2000).

2 Among them Edgar Cayce, Dr. Ian Stevenson, Dr. Michael Newton.

3 Swami Prabhupad, *Bhagavad-Gita As It Is* (Los Angeles: The Bhaktivedanta Book Trust, 1968).

4 C. G. Jung, *Man and His Symbols* (New York: Double Day & Co., 1964).

Chapter 2

1 Swami Prabhupad, *Bhagavad-Gita As It Is* (Los Angeles: The Bhaktivedanta Book Trust, 1968).

2 Aldous Huxley, *The Perennial Philosophy* (New York: Harper & Row Publishers, 1944).

3 Echo Bodine, *Echoes of the Soul* (Novato, CA: New World Library, 1999).

4 Paul Twitchell, *Stranger by the River* (Minneapolis, MN: Eckankar, 1987).

5 Gary Zukav, *The Seat of the Soul* (New York: A Fireside Book, 1989).

6 Terrill Wilson, *How I Learnt Soul Travel* (Minneapolis, MN: Eckankar, 1987).

7 Michael Newton, *Journeys of the Soul* (St. Paul, MN: Llewellyn Publishers, 1994).

8 Rosemary Ellen Guiley, *Harper's Encyclopedia of Mystical and Paranormal Experiences* (San Francisco: HarperSan Francisco, 1991).

9 Ravindra Kumar, *Kundalini for Beginners* (St. Paul, MN: Llewellyn Publishers, 2000).

10 Bodine, *Echoes of the Soul.*

Chapter 3

1 Michael Newton, *Destiny of Souls* (St. Paul, MN: Llewellyn Publications, 2000).

2 To read the experiences of individual souls on the astral plane or other realms, refer to the works of Swain (1974), O'Brien (1989, 1991), Haslop (n.d.), Borgia (n.d.), Sted (1897), Yogananda (1986), Sherwood (n.d.), Rocher (n.d.), Pike (n.d.), Myers (1954), and many others. See also Dr. Stevenson's landmark book, *20 Cases suggestive of Reincarnation* (1974).

3 Rosemary Ellen Guiley, *Harper's Encyclopedia of Mystical and Paranormal Experiences* (San Francisco: Harper, San Francisco, 1991), p. 399. Barbara Harris Whitfield (1995) and Diane Globe (1993) are two writers personally known to me who had similar experiences. They have given a wonderful account of life beyond. Other notable writers in this direction are Atwater (1988), Moody (1975), Ring (1984, 1993), Ring and Rosing (1990), Grosso (1992), Doyle (29), and Zaleski (1987).

4 Jasper Swain, *On the Death of My Son* (London, UK: Turnstone Books, 1974).
5 Herald Klemp, *The Eck Dream 2 Discourses, No. 11* (Minneapolis, MN: Eckankar, 1990).
6 There is a series of books by Stephen O'Brien of Swansea, UK, about life in the worlds beyond. He holds sessions with several hundred people in a hall and makes them exchange information with their dead relatives and friends using him as a medium. O'Brien has visited the lower subdivisions of the astral plane several times and met with people who had created their own hell. Sri Yukteshwar Giri, guru of Swami Yogananda, stated in a posthumous appearance that he (Giri) is constantly busy helping people on the higher realm. Paul Twitchell and Harold Klemp have been regular visitors to different subdivisions of the astral plane and their experiences confirm the text of this paragraph.
7 Martinus, *The Fate of Mankind* (Copenhagen: Martinus Institute, 1933). Translated into English in 1986.
8 Paramahansa Yogananda, *Autobiography of a Yogi* (New Delhi, India: Jaico Publishing House, 1986). Swami Muktananda, *Chitshakti Vilas (The Play of Consciousness)* (Maharashtra, India: Gurudev Siddhapeeth, 1972). Swami Sivananda, *Kundalini Yoga* (Sivananda Nagar, Tehri Garhval, India: The Divine Life Society, 1991).
9 Harold Klemp, *Letters of Light and Sound 1* (Minneapolis, MN: Eckankar, 1992) p. 46.
10 M. Rajeshwar Rao, *The Legend of Sri Shirdi Sai Baba and His Teachings* (Secunderabad, India: Sri Sai Baba Mandir, n.d.).
11 C. W. Leadbeater, *The Astral Plane* (Madras, India: The Theosophical Publishing House, 1933).
12 Martinus, *The Fate of Mankind*, pp. 22–23.

Chapter 4

1 C. W. Leadbeater, *The Astral Plane* (Madras, India: The Theosophical Publishing House, 1933), p. 5.
2 C. W. Leadbeater and Madam Annie Besant had knowledge of the astral plane gained through the third eye or through astral projections. *The Other Side of Death* and *The Astral Plane* were written by Leadbeater (1933), and *Death And After* by Annie Besant (1923). These contain wonderful details of the astral plane. James A. Pike gave a scientific description of the world beyond in the book *The Other Side* (n.d.). British medium Ivor James also talks about the seven subdivisions of the astral plane in *The Astral World* (AudioTape, London, UK: 1996).
3 See, for example, the books by Yogananda, Muktananda, Sri Aurobindo, and Gopi Krishna.
4 Alexandra David-Neel, *Magic and Mystery in Tibet* (New York: Dover Publications, 1971).

Chapter 5

1 Yukteswar Giri, *The Holy Science* (Los Angeles: Self Realization Fellowship, 1984).
2 One of the well-known books in this direction is *Raymond* written by Raymond Lodge after he contacted his famous scientist father, Sir Oliver Lodge, sometime after the latter passed away. Another book, *Post-mortem Journal*, was written when Lawrence of Arabia encountered his writer friend Jane Sherwood soon after her death. *Beyond the Horizon* was written when Mr. Gordon contacted his writer friend Grace Rocher after his death. *After Death* has been translated into many languages and has appeared in several editions. It was written when W. T. Sted contacted his friend Julia after her death. *Life in the World Unseen* and *More About Life in the World Unseen* are two books written when Monsigner Robert Hufbenson contacted Anthony Borgia after Borgia's death.
3 C. W. Leadbeater, *The Astral Plane* (Madras, India: The Theosophical Publishing House, 1933), p. 6.
4 Pundrik C. Mehta, *The Fundamentals of Indian Philosophy* (A correspondence Course, Hindu University, Florida: 1994). D. R. Vaze, *Upanishads Chetna Sanstha and Kundalini* (Pune, India: Research Thesis, n.d.).
5 J. D. Goyal, *Mrityu ke Bad (Occult Science)* (New Delhi: Hind Pocket Books, 1996).

Chapter 6

1 Mohini M. Chatterji, *Viveka-cudamani* (Adyar, India: The Theosophical Publishing House, 1932), p. 165.
2 Jasper Swain, *On the Death of My Son* (London: Turnstone Books, 1974).
3 John White, "The Awakening of Kundalini," *Ascent Magazine*, 07 fall 2000, Montreal, Canada, pp. 11–12.
4 Gene Kieffer, "Mr. Krishna, the Biggest Story of the Century," *Ascent Magazine*, 07 fall 2000, Montreal, Canada, p. 40.
5 Rober Scheer, "Kundalini in Peru," *Ascent Magazine*, 07, Fall 2000, Montreal, Canada, pp. 46–47.

Chapter 7

1 Erik Gerner Larsson, *Martinus* (Copenhagen: Martinus Institute, 1963).
2 Ronald S. Lello, *Revelations-Glimpses of Reality* (London: Shephard-Walwyn Ltd., 1985).
3 Larsson, *Martinus,* p. 31.
4 Larsson, *Martinus,* p. 34.
5 Larsson, *Martinus,* p. xiv.
6 The twentieth century has produced many spiritual giants in recent years who have given a lucid and exhaustive explanation of soul and God in their writings. Notable among them are Ramakrishna Paramahansa, Vivekananda, Yukteswar (1984), Yogananda (1986), Meher Baba (1967), Muktananda (1972), Sivananda (1991), Gopi Krishna (1975), Vishnu Tirtha (1993), Asaramji (1994), Satyananda Saraswati (1984), and Vimalananda (1994). Anne Bancroft (1976) has given a brief survey of the saints of the present century in *Twentieth Century Mystics and Sages*.
7 Nick Herbert, *Quantum Reality* (New York: Double Day, Anchor Books, 1987), p 15.
8 R. L. Morris and M. L. Edge, *Foundations of Parapsychology* (Boston: Routledge and Kegan Paul, 1986).
9 Quantum properties enumerated by the physicist Amit Goswami (1993) are presented later.
10 Helena P. Blavatsky, *Collected Writings* 16 Vols. (Wheaton, IL: Theosophical Publishing House, 1980–1988).
11 Satprem, *Evolution II* (New York: Institute for Evolutionary Research, 1992), pp. 4–5.
12 Joel Beversluis, *A Source Book for Earth's Community of Religions* (Grand Rapids, MI: CoNexus Press & NY: Global Ed. Associates, 1995), p. 285.
13 Claire G Walker, *The Psychic Revolution of the 20th Century and Our Psychic Sense* (Seal Beach, CA: Psychic Sense Publishers, 1997), p. 135.

Chapter 8

1 C. G. Jung, *Memories, Dreams, Reflections*, recorded and edited by Aniela Jaffe. (New York: Random House, 1961), pp. 274–275.
2 Satya Prakash Singh, *Sri Aurobindo and Jung* (Aligarh, India: Madhuchhandas, 1986), p. 73.
3 Sri Aurobindo, *The Life Divine* (Pondicherry, India: SABDA, Sri Aurobindo Ashram, 1970), p 357.
4 Sri Aurobindo, *The Life Divine*, pp. 268–269.
5 Ibid., p. 644.
6 Singh, *Sri Aurobindo and Jung*, p. 42.
7 Ravindra Kumar, "Journey Back Home-IV, Personality Transformation with Chakras," *JRPR*, Oct. 94.
8 Jung, *Memories, Dreams, Reflections*, p. 5.
9 Rashid Field, *The Last Barrier* (New York: Harper & Row Publishers, 1976), p. 82.
10 Sri Aurobindo, *The Synthesis of Yoga* (Pondicherry, India: SABDA, Sri Aurobindo Ashram, n.d.), p. 779.
11 Sri Aurobindo, *Savitri* (Pondicherry, India: SABDA, Sri Aurobindo Ashram, n.d.), pp. 311–312.

12 Sri Aurobindo, *Letters on Yoga,* Part III (Pondicherry, India: SABDA, Sri Aurobindo Ashram, 1958), p. 1070.
13 R. M. Bucke, *Cosmic Consciousness* (Secaucus, NJ: The Citadel Press, 1961).
14 Aurobindo, *Letters on Yoga*, p. 316.
15 Aurobindo, *The Life Divine*, p. 660.
16 Ibid., p. 108.
17 Jung, *Memories, Dreams, Reflections*, p. 69.
18 Jung, *Memories, Dreams, Reflections*, Vol XIV, p. 122.
19 Jung, *Memories, Dreams, Reflections*, Vol. IX, Part I, p. 171.
20 Jung, *Memories, Dreams, Reflections*, Vol. V, pp. 391–393.
21 Mohini M. Chatterji, *Vivek Chudamani or The Crest Jewel of Wisdom of Sri Samkaracharya* (Adyar, Madras, India: TPS, 1932), p. 94.
22 Aldous Huxley, *The Perennial Philosophy* (New York: Harper & Row Publishers, 1944).
23 Meher Baba, *Discourses by Meher Baba Vol. I, II, III.* (San Francisco: Sufism Reoriented Inc., 1967), p. 39.
24 Aurobindo, *The Life Divine,* p. 1019.

Chapter 9

1 Satprem, *On the Way to Supermanhood* (New York: Institute for Evolutionary Research, 1985), pp. 157–159.
2 Satprem, *On the Way to Supermanhood*, pp. 268–269.
3 Satprem, *On the Way to Supermanhood*, p. 331.
4 For details, see Satya Prakash Singh, *Sri Aurobindo and Jung* (Aligarh, India: Madhuchhandas, 1986), p. 72, and Satprem, *On the Way to Supermanhood*, p. 275.
5 Satprem, *On the Way to Supermanhood*, p. 299.
6 Joel Beversluis, *A Source Book for Earth's Community of Religions* (Grand Rapids, MI: CoNexus Press & NY: Global Ed. Associates, 1995), pp. 84–85, 285.
7 Sri Aurobindo, *Savitri* (Pondicherry, India: SABDA, Sri Aurobindo Ashram, n.d.), pp. 594–595.
8 Leroy E. Zemke, *Thoughts for Transformation* (Florida: Emberlight Publishers, 1996), p. 156.
9 Saint Asaramji, *Suchha Sukh* (Sabarmati, Ahmadabad, India: Saint Asaramji Ashram, 1994).
10 Helena Blavatsky, *Collected Writings* 16 Vols. (Wheaton, IL: Theosophical Publishing House, 1980–1988), p. 75.
11 Gary Zukav, *The Seat of the Soul* (New York: Fireside Book, Simon & Schuster, 1989).
12 Annie Besant, *Initiation: The Perfecting of Man* (Chicago, IL: Theosophical Press, 1923), p. 213.
13 Claire G. Walker, *The Psychic Revolution of the 20th Century and Our Psychic Sense* (Seal Beach, CA: Psychic Sense Publishers, 1997), p. 77.
14 C. G. Jung, *The Collected Works* Vol. XII (New York: Bollingen-Pantheon, nd.), pp. 43–45.
15 Jung, *The Collected Works* Vol XII, p. 200.
16 Jung, *The Collected Works* Vol. VIII, pp. 151–152.
17 Jung, *The Collected Works* Vol. VIII, pp. 414, 318.
18 Jung, *The Collected Works* Vol. VIII, pp. 282–283.
19 Jung, *The Collected Works* Vol. IX, Part II, p. 261.
20 Singh, *Sri Aurobindo and Jung*, p. 118.
21 Jung, *The Collected Works* Vol. V, pp. 136–137.
22 Jung, *The Collected Works* Vol. VIII, p. 181.
23 Jung, *The Collected Works* Vol. VI, (New York: Bollingen-Pantheon, n.d.), p. 593.
24 Jung, *The Collected Works* Vol. VI, p. 588.
25 Jung, *The Collected Works* Vol. VIII, p. 414.
26 Sri Aurobindo, *The Synthesis of Yoga* (Pondicherry, India: SABDA, Sri Aurobindo Ashram, n.d.), pp. 206–207.

27 Ibid., pp. 206–207.

28 Ibid., p. 843.

29 Ibid., p. 170.

30 Sri Aurobindo, *Letters on Yoga* Part III (Pondicherry, India: SABDA, Sri Aurobindo Ashram, 1958), p. 1070.

31 Aurobindo, *Letters on Yoga* Part III, p. 279.

32 Singh, *Sri Aurobindo and Jung,* pp. 133–134.

33 Brad Steiger, *In My Soul I Am Free* (Minneapolis, MN: Eckankar Books, 1988).

34 Amit Goswami, Richard E Reed, and Maggie Goswami, *The Self-Aware Universe* New York: Jeremy P. Tarcher / Putnam Book, G.P.Putnam's Sons, 1993), p. 9.

Chapter 10

1 Chakrapani, "Chamatkar hi tha Vah" *Manohar Kahania*, 281 Muthi Ganj, Allahabad, India, March '97.

2 A Hamid, A. "Ma Ka Dil," *Manohar Kahania*, 281 Muthi Ganj, Allahabad, India, March '97.

3 Chakrapani, "Trikal Siddhi," *Manohar Kahania*, 281 Muthi Ganj, Allahabad, India, May '97.

Chapter 11

1 Claire G. Walker, *The Psychic Revolution of the 20th Century and Our Psychic Sense* (Seal Beach, CA: Psychic Sense Publishers, 1997), p. 20.

2 Amit Goswami Richard E. Reed, and Maggie Goswami, *The Self-Aware Universe* (New York: Jeremy P. Tarcher / Putnam Book, G. P. Putnam's Sons, 1993), p. 9.

3 Nick Herbert, *Quantum Reality* (New York: Double Day, Anchor Books, 1987), pp. 16–27.

4 Herbert, *Quantum Reality*, pp. 27–29.

5 Walker, *The Psychic Revolution*, p. 134.

6 Herbert, *Quantum Reality*, p. 15.

7 For more details on the attributes of Atman, refer to *Perennial Philosophy* by Aldous Huxley (New York: Harper & Row Publishers, 1944).

8 Manly P. Hall, *An Encyclopedic Outline of Masonic, Hermetic, Qabbalistic and Rosicrucian Symbolical Philosophy* (San Francisco: H. S. Crocker & Co., 1928). Max Long, *The Huna Code in Religions* (California: Huna Research Publications, 1965).

9 Mohini M. Chatterji, *Vivek Chudamani or The Crest Jewel of Wisdom of Sri Samkaracharya* (Madras, India: TPS, Adyar, 1932), p. 94.

10 Meher Baba, *Discourses by Meher Baba* Vol. I, II, III (San Francisco: Sufisism Reoriented Inc., 1967).

11 Anne Bancroft, *Twentieth-Century Mystics and Sages* (London: Penguin Group, 1976).

12 Ravindra Kumar, "Journey Back Home-IV, Personality Transformation with Chakras," JRPR, Oct. '94.

13 Nisargatta Maharaj, *I Am That* (n.p.: Advaita Press, n.d.).

14 A well-known physics equation in which "E" stands for energy released on the disintegration of an atom, "m" stand for mass, and "c" stands for the velocity of light.

Chapter 12

1 Sri Aurobindo, *The Life Divine* (Pondicherry, India: SABDA, Sri Aurobindo Ashram, 1970), p. 357.

2 Ibid., pp. 1124–1125.

3 Ibid., p. 1118.

4 Ibid., pp. 603–604.

5 *The Collected Works*, Vol. VI, pp. 695–696.

6 Satya Prakash Singh, *Sri Aurobindo and Jung* (Aligarh, India: Madhuchhandas, 1986), p. 39.
7 C. G. Jung, *The Collected Works* Vol. IX, Part II (New York: Bollingen-Pantheon, n.d.), p. 275.
8 Chaturbhuj Sahai, *Sadhana ke Anubhav* (Mathura, India: Ramashraya Satsanga, 1987).
9 Jung, *The Collected Works*, Vol. IX, Part II, p. 180.
10 Jung, *The Collected Works*, Vol. VIII, p. 25.
11 Jung, *The Collected Works*, Vol. VI (New York: Bollingen-Pantheon, n.d.), p. 225.
12 Ravindra Kumar, "Psychic Individuation and Self-Realization-I," JRPR, July '97.
13 Singh, *Sri Aurobindo and Jung*, p. 156.
14 Ibid., p. 157.

Chapter 13

1 Satya Prakash Singh, *Sri Aurobindo and Jung* (Aligarh, India: Madhuchhandas, 1986), pp. 161–162.
2 Ibid., p. 163.
3 Sri Aurobindo, *The Life Divine* (Pondicherry, India: SABDA, Sri Aurobindo Ashram, 1970), p. 266.
4 Sri Aurobindo, *Letters on Yoga,* Part III (Pondicherry, India: SABDA, Sri Aurobindo Ashram, 1958), p. 89.
5 Aurobindo, *The Life Divine*, pp. 262–264.
6 Aurobindo, *Letters on Yoga*, p. 725.
7 Singh, *Sri Aurobindo and Jung*, p. 170.
8 Aurobindo, *The Life Divine*, pp. 1970–1972.
9 Singh, *Sri Aurobindo and Jung*, p. 175.
10 Ibid., p. 177.

Chapter 14

1 Erik Gerner Larsson, *Martinus* (Copenhagen: Martinus Institute, 1963), pp. 10–11.
2 Ibid., p. 27.
3 Ibid., pp. 30-33.
4 Ibid., p. 36.

Chapter 15

1 Sri Aurobindo, *The Yoga of Divine Works-Karmayoga* (Pondicherry, India: Sri Aurobindo Ashram, 1986).
2 Ibid., p. 327.
3 Ibid., p. 21.

Chapter 16

1 Sri Aurobindo, *Thoughts and Aphorisms* (Pondicherry, India: Sri Aurobindo Ashram, 1982), pp. 1–35.
2 Ibid., p. 25.
3 Ibid., p.19.
4 Ibid., p.15.
5 Ibid., p. 16.
6 Ibid., p. 27.
7 Ibid., p. 28.
8 Ibid., p. 17.
9 Sri Aurobindo, *The Eternal Wisdom* (Pondicherry, India: Sri Aurobindo Ashram, 1993), p. 239.
10 Ibid., p. 239.

11 Ibid., pp. 239–240.
12 Ibid., p. 246.
13 Ibid., p. 246.
14 Ibid., p. 244.
15 Ibid., p. 244.

Chapter 17

1 Swami Prabhupad, *Bhagavad-Gita As It Is* (New York: Bhaktivedanta Book Trust, 1969).
2 Hanumanprasad Poddar, *The Philosophy of Love* (Rajgangpur, India: Orissa, 1978).
3 Chaturbhuj Sahai, *Saint Sri Mirabai* (Mathura, India: Ramashraya Satsanga, 1990).
4 Prabhupad, Bhagavad Gita *As It Is*, pp. 6, 47.
5 Bhakti Sutra, line 25.
6 Poddar, *The Philosophy of Love* p.185.
7 Ibid., pp. 197–199.
8 Ibid., pp. 208–209.
9 Prabhupad, *Bhagavad-Gita As It Is*, pp. 611–635.
10 Ibid., p. 268.
11 Ibid., p. 629.
12 Ibid., p. 630.
13 Ibid., p. 631.
14 Ibid., p. 632.
15 Ibid., p. 634.
16 Poddar*The Philosophy of Love*, p. 247.
17 Ibid., p. 248.
18 Sri Aurobindo, *Thoughts and Aphorisms* (Pondicherry, India: Sri Aurobindo Ashram, 1982).
19 Chaturbhuj Sahai, *Saint Sri Mirabai* (Mathura, India: Ramashraya Satsanga, 1990).

Chapter 18

1 Swami Prabhupad, Bhagavad Gita *As It Is* (New York: Bhaktivedanta Book Trust, 1972), pp. 621–626.
2 Hanumanprasad Poddar, *The Philosophy of Love* (Rajgangpur, India: Orissa, 1978), pp. 241–254.

Chapter 19

1 With its headquarters in Minneapolis, MN.
2 Martinus, *The Fate of Mankind* (Copenhagen: Martinus Institute, 1933). Translated into English in 1986.
3 Ibid., p. 20.
4 Swami Sivananda Radha, *Kundalini Yoga* (Delhi, India: Motilal Banarsidass Publishers, 1992).
5 Henry Reed, "Recovering Spirituality From Dreaming," *Venture Inward,* A.R.E./Edgar Cayce Foundation, Atlantic University, Sept./Oct. 1995.
6 Reed, "Recovering Spirituality From Dreaming," p. 39.
7 Herman Riffel, *Your Dreams: God's Neglected Gift* (New York: Ballantine Books, 1981).
8 Ibid., p. 12.
9 Ibid., p. 13.
10 Ibid., pp. 20–21.
11 Ibid., p. 60.
12 C. G. Jung, *Man and His Symbols* (New York: Double Day & Co., 1964).
13 Ibid., pp. 177–195.
14 Ravindra Kumar, *Kundalini for Beginners* (Minneapolis, MN: Llewellyn Publishers, 2000), pp. 202–204.

Chapter 20

1 P. M. H. Atwater, *Coming Back to Life* (New York: Dodd, Mead, 1988).
2 Rosemary Ellen Guiley, *Harper's Encyclopedia of Mystical and Paranormal Experiences* (San Francisco: Harper, 1991).
3 Carol Zaleski, *Other World Journeys: Accounts of Near-Death-Experience in Medieval and Modern Times* (New York: Oxford University Press, 1987).
4 Barbara Harris Whitfield, *Spiritual Awakening* (Deerfield Beech, FL: Health Communications, 1995), pp. 25–28.
5 Ibid., p. xi.
6 Martinus, *The Fate of Mankind* (Copenhagen: Martinus Institute, 1933), p. 6. Translated in English in 1986.
7 Whitfield, *Spiritual Awakening*, pp. 15–16.
8 Diane Globe, *Through the Tunnel* (Palm Harbor, FL: S.O.U.L. Foundation, 1993).
9 Ibid., p. 36.
10 Ibid., p. 33.
11 Nils Bjorn Kvastad, *Problems of Mysticism* (Oslo: Scintilla Press, 1980).
12 Ibid., p. 352.
13 Ravindra Kumar, *Kundalini—An Autobiographical Guide to Self/God Realization* (New Delhi, India: Sterling Publishers, 1999).

Chapter 21

1 Barbara Harris Whitfield, *Spiritual Awakening* (Deerfield Beech, FL: Health Communications, 1995), p. 9.
2 Paul Twitchell, *Stranger by the River* (Minneapolis, MN: Eckankar, 1987).
3 Ronald S. Lello, *Revelations-Glimpses of Reality* (London: Shephard-Walwyn Ltd., 1985).
4 Ibid., pp. 18–19.
5 Ibid., pp. 32–33.
6 Ibid., Preface.
7 Ibid., p. 75.
8 Ibid., p. 94.
9 Ibid., p. 118.
10 Ibid., p. 128.

Chapter 22

1 Osho Rajneesh, *From Sex to Superconsciousness* (Cologne, West Germany: The Rebel Publishing House GmbH, n.d.).
2 Anne Bankroft, *Twentieth-Century Mystics and Sages* (London: Penguin Group, 1976).
3 Swami Satyananda Saraswati, *Kundalini Tantra* (Bihar, India: Bihar School of Yoga, Munger, 1984).
4 Gopi Krishna, *The Awakening of Kundalini* (New York: Kundalini Research Foundation, 1975).
5 Elisabeth Haich, *Sexual Energy and Yoga* (New York, NY: Aurora Press, 1982).
6 Ibid., p. 49.
7 Ibid., pp. 54–55.
8 Barbara Harris Whitfield, *Spiritual Awakening* (Deerfield Beech, FL: Health Communications, 1995), p. 135.
9 Ravindra Kumar, *Kundalini for Beginners* (Minneapolis, MN: Llewellyn Publishers, 2000).
10 Rajneesh, *From Sex to Superconsciousness*, p. 112.
11 A. K. Dey, *KHAJURAHO—The Immortal Ancient Sculpture* (Delhi, India: Jayana Publishing Co., n.d.).
12 Sir John Woodroffe, *The Serpent Power* (Madras, India: Ganesh & Co., 1981).
13 Ravindra Kumar, *Kundalini for Beginners* (St. Paul, MN: Llewellyn Publications, 2000).

Chapter 23

1 Baba Haridass, *From Sweeper to Saint* (Santa Cruz, CA: Sri Ram Publishing, 1980).
2 Amit Jayaram, "Meditations: Freedom From Choice," *The Hindustan Times*, New Delhi, September 22, '97, p. 12.
3 P. K. Jain, "God-less Karma for Salvation," *The Hindusatn Times*, New Delhi, September 15, '97, p. 12.
4 Sonam Wangchuk, "The Beauty of Bhavana," *The Hindustan Times*, New Delhi, May 11, '98, p. 12.
5 Nergis Dalal, "Towards a Higher Awareness," *The Hindustan Times*, New Delhi, March 23, '98, p. 12.
6 Barbara Harris Whitfield, *Spiritual Awakening* (Deerfield Beech, FL: Health Communications, 1995), p. 4.
7 Aiyoshi Kawahata, *Universal Meditation* (CA: Heian International Inc., 1984).
8 Rahul Agarwal, "Martial Arts Are a Way of Life," *The Hindustan Times*, New Delhi, October 22, '97.
9 Maulana Wahiduddin Khan, "Pilgrimage-Highest form of Worship," *The Hindustan Times*, New Delhi, March 30, '98, p. 12.
10 Anthony Storr, *Solitude: A Return to the Self* (New York: Ballantine Books, 1988).
11 Ibid., p. ix.
12 Ibid., p. ix.
13 Ibid., p. 60.

Chapter 24

1 Ravindra Kumar, *Kundalini for Beginners* (Minneapolis, MN: Llewellyn Publishers, 2000).
2 Osho Rajneesh, *From Sex to Superconsciousness* (Cologne, West Germany: The Rebel Publishing House GmbH, n.d.).
3 Rajneesh, *From Sex to Superconsciousness*, p. 138.
4 Kumar, *Kundalini for Beginners*.
5 Rajneesh, *From Sex to Superconsciousness*, p. 210.
6 Leroy E. Zemke, *Thoughts for Transformation* (Florida: Emberlight Publishers, 1996), p. 40.
7 Osho, *Kundalini Yoga* (Delhi: Sterling Publishers, 1997).

Chapter 25

1 Swami Vishnu Tirtha, *Devatma Shakti-Kundalini* (Muni-Ki-Reti, Rishikesh, India: Yogshri Peeth Trust, 1993).
2 Ravindra Kumar, *Kundalini for Beginners* (Minneapolis, MN: Llewellyn Publishers, 2000).
3 See for example, *Kundalini: The Secret of Life* by Swami Muktananda (1979), *Mahayoga Vijnana* by Yogendra Vigyani (1938), *The Serpent Power* by Sir John Woodroffe (1981), and *Devatma Shakti-Kundalini* by Swami Vishnu Tirtha (1993).

Chapter 26

1 Swami Satyananda Saraswati, *Kundalini Tantra* (Bihar, India: Bihar School of Yoga, Munger, 1984).
2 Ibid., pp. 204–205.

GLOSSARY

Achara dharma: ethical discipline
Adattadana viramana: to accept not when not rightly bestowed
Adi: the beginning
Adi lok: plane in the beginning
Agun: absolute, without attributes
Ahankar: ego
Ahimsa: noninjury to others
Ajna chakra: eyebrow center
Akashik elements: etheric substance
Anahata chakra: heart center
Ananda: bliss
Anandamaya kosh: unconscious, transcendental dimension
Annamaya kosh: physical body
Anupama: having no parallel
Ardhanareeshwara: half male, half female, Shiva and Shakti in one, representing balance of masculinity and femenity
Asampragyata: samadhi without awareness
Asanas: yogic postures
Ashram: place of yogic practices
Atman: soul or spirit, the pure Self, beyond body and mind
Atmic: pertaining to Atman or soul or spirit
Bal Krishna: Lord Krishna as a child
Bhairvi: female tantric deity
Bhakti: devotion
Bhakti sutras: elements of bhakti (devotion)
Bhakti yoga: path of devotion
Bhajana: religious song
Bhoga: worldly pleasures
Bhoolok: physical plane
Bhrumadhya: eyebrow center
Bhuvarlok: astral plane, next to the physical plane
Brahmachari: celibate
Buddhic: intellectual
Chakras: seven centers or vortices of energy on the spine

Chaitya purusa: psychic being
Chhaya sharira: etheric double
Comatose torpor: dull trance, defined by Sri Aurobindo
Darshan: seeing in person
Devachan: heaven
Devarsi: superior among all devas (gods)
Dharma: social or religious discipline
Dharmshala: resting place, hotel or motel
Drsti: direct sight
Dukha: misery, pain or suffering
Durga: benevolent female deity, sitting on a tiger, representing wisdom and power; symbol of the awakened and controlled kundalini
Eckankar: religion of light and sound, based in Minneapolis, MN
Girdharilalji: a name of Lord Krishna
Golok: plane of God
Grahastha: householder
Gunas: virtues
Hatha yoga: path of physical yogic practices, which includes asanas (postures), pranayama (breath control), kriyas (cleansing practices), bandhas (locks) and mudras (seals)
Hiranyalok: particular division of the astral plane representing the womb of consciousness
Ida: moon channel running to the left of sushumna
Jalandhar bandh: throat lock
Japa: chanting of names
Jivatma: Atman, soul
Jnana lok: plane of wisdom
Jnana yoga: path of knowledge
Kali: ferocious goddess, killer of demons, representing freshly awakened and untamed kundalini
Kalpataru: wish-fulfillment tree
Kama lok: plane of desires
Kamakhya Devi: goddess of sexual power/energy
Kanhaiya: another name for Lord Krishna
Karana sharira: causal body
Karma yoga: path of selfless action, acting without attachment to the fruits or results of one's actions
Khechri mudra: reverting back of the tongue and its rising toward the palate
Kirtan: singing the glories of God
Krodha: anger

Kshem: safety of one's possessions
Kundalini: also known as the serpent power or Shakti, the creative cosmic energy, the female counterpart of God unmanifest, belongs to the causal plane, hence is invisible on the physical plane, lies dormant at the base of the spine
Kundalini yoga: yoga system specially designed for the awakening of kundalini
Lakshmi: consort of Lord Vishnu, and goddess of wealth
Lobha: greed
Maana: pride
Mahapurusha: great soul who has realized God
Maharlok: upper division of the mental plane
Maharsi: greatest among the rishis
Maithuna viramana: to desist from sex
Manasik lok: mental plane
Mandala: psychic pictures
Manipura chakra: navel center
Maya: illusion, deceit
Mirsavada viramana: to desist from telling a lie
Moksha: liberation, Nirvana
Monad: spark of God
Monadic: pertaining to the monad, the first manifestation of the Unmanifest
Mooladhara chakra: root center
Mool-bandh: root lock
Mudras: yogic postures
Naad: internal cosmic sound
Nadis: channels of energy running throughout the body for its nourishment and maintainance
Namaz: holy scripture of Muslims
Narad Muni: devotee saint of Lord Narayana, who used to travel to different planes by appearing and disappearing at will
Narayana: God, Lord Krishna
Nirguna Brahman: Brahman without attributes
Nirodha: renunciation
Nirvana: liberation from the cycle of death and rebirth
Nirvichar samadhi: thought-less awareness
Nirvikalpa samadhi: samadhi without fluctuations
Padmasana: lotus posture
Paramatma: supersoul, God
Paramashiva: Lord Shiva

Parigraha parimana: to fix the size of acquisition
Parvati: consort of Lord Shiva
Pingla: sun channel running to the right of sushumna
Prana: cosmic life energy
Pranamaya kosh: etheric double, conscious dimension
Pranayama: deep breathing and breath control
Pranatipata viramana: to desist from killing
Pret lok: plane of ghosts and spirits
Purusa: psychic being
Radha: consort of Lord Krishna
Raja: king
Raja yoga: kingly path, superior to all other kinds of yoga, postulated by Patanjali; beginning with the stability of mind, it takes the practitioner to the highest state of samadhi
Rajayogi: one devoted to the path of raja yoga
Rajasic: belonging to activity
Rajogun: properties of action/activities
Rasalila: group dance
Rigveda: Veda devoted to the path of jnana yoga
Rishis: yogic masters of ancient times
Rooh-va-tavajjah: Ray of God, creative energy, kundalini
Ruha: soul, spirit, Atman
Saccidananda: sat-chit-ananda, existence-knowledge-bliss
Sadachara: right conduct
Sadhana: yogic practice
Sadhu: monk
Sadhvi: nun
Saguna: divine manifestation of God with attributes
Sahasrara: crown center
Salokya: residence in the abode of God
Samadhi: deep absorption
Samaveda: Veda devoted to the path of bhakti yoga
Samipya: living in close proximity to the Lord
Samyaka-charitra: right conduct
Samyaka-darshan: right belief
Samyaka-jnana: right knowledge
Sangam: meeting point of three rivers—Ganga, Jamuna, and Saraswati
Sankalpa: will
Sankatamochan Mahavirji: monkey god Hanuman
Sankhya: classification of all that is known, without reference to God, ancient scientific philosophy of India

Sanyasa: renunciation
Saripya: having form similar to Lord
Saraswati: goddess of wisdom
Sarsti: enjoying the same powers as the Lord
Satguru: inner guru, spiritual teacher or guru
Satogun: proprties of purity
Satsanga: company of religious or God-intoxicated people
Sattvic: belonging to purity
Satya lok: plane of truth
Savikalpa samadhi: samadhi with fluctuatioins
Sayujya: absolute identity with Lord
Shabda: internal cosmic sound
Shakti: female counterpart of God, creative energy
Shaktipat: direct transmission of spiritual power by a guru
Shambhavi mudra: gazing at the eyebrow center
Shunyata: void
Siddha: adept
Siddhi: paranormal or super powers
Sindur: vermilion
Smriti: inspired memory of truth
Sravaka: layman
Sravika: laywoman
Sruti: direct hearing
Sthool lok: physical plane
Sthool sharira: physical body
Sukha: comfort, happiness
Sukshma sharira: astral body
Surati: creative energy kundalini
Sushumna: central channel, pathway of the awakened kundalini
Swadhishthan chakra: Pelvic center
Swargalok: heaven, lower division of mental plane
Swayambhu linga: pillar (linga) around which kundalini remains coiled, closing the opening of the linga with its mouth
Tamasic: belonging to inertia
Tamogun: properties of inertia
Tantra yoga: path leading to the union of Shiva and Shakti, or the masculine and feminine forces, resulting in liberation; using different kinds of yoga, rituals, worship, discipline, meditation and attainment of powers
Tap lok: plane of austerities
Tapas: will of the transcendent spirit, defined by Sri Aurobindo

Tat-tvam-asi: that-thou-art
Tilak: sandalwood paste applied at eyebrow center by men
Trataka: concentration in front of third eye
Trikal siddhi: power to control the past, present, and future
Triveni: place of convergence of three rivers—Ganga, Jamuna, and Saraswati—situated in Allahabad, India
Tulpa: monkey, created through the power of mind, by Alexandra David-Neel
Twice-born: one who is spiritually awakened and liberated
Uddiyan bandh: navel lock
Upasana: absorption in one's own consciousness
Vaikunth lok: plane of God
Vanaprasthi: belonging to the part of life, after married life is completed
Varna: caste or division of society one belongs to
Vasana sharira: astral body
Vasudeva: Lord Krishna
Vigyanmaya kosh: subconscious or unconscious dimension, intuitive aspects
Vipassana: particular kind of meditation
Vishnumaya: sister of Lord Krishna
Vishuddhi chakra: throat center
Yajna: sacrifice on the sacred fire
Yajurveda: Vedas devoted to the path of karma yoga
Yog: providing the needs
Yoga: divine unity of soul and supersoul
Yogi: one who takes to the discipline of yoga

BIBLIOGRAPHY

Abbreviations: n.d. = no date given
JRPR = Journal of Religion and Psychical Research

Agarwal, Rahul. "Martial Arts Are a Way of Life," *The Hindustan Times,* New Delhi, October 22, 1997.

Asaramji, Saint. *Sachcha Sukh.* Sabarmati, Ahamadabad, India: Saint Asaramji Ashram, 1994.

Atwater, P. M. H. *Coming Back to Life.* New York: Dodd, Mead, 1988.

Aurobindo, Sri. *The Life Divine.* Pondicherry, India: SABDA, Sri Aurobindo Ashram, 1970.

———. *The Synthesis of Yoga.* Pondicherry, India: SABDA, Sri Aurobindo Ashram, n.d.

———. *Savitri.* Pondicherry, India: SABDA, Sri Aurobindo Ashram, n.d.

———. *Letters on Yoga.* Pondicherry, India: SABDA, Sri Aurobindo Ashram, 1958

———. *Thoughts and Aphorisms.* Pondicherry, India: Sri Aurobindo Ashram, 1982.

———. *The Yoga of Divine Works: Karmayoga.* Sri Aurobindo Ashram, Pondicherry, India: Sri Aurobindo Ashram, 1986

Aurobindo, Sri, and The Mother. *The Psychic Being.* Pondicherry, India: Sri Aurobindo Ashram, 1989.

Baba, Meher. *Discourses by Meher Baba Vol. I, II, III.* San Francisco: Sufism Reoriented Inc., 1967

Bancroft, Anne. *Twentieth-Century Mystics and Sages.* London: Penguin Group, 1976.

Besant, Annie. *Initiation: The Perfecting of Man.* Chicago: Theosophical Press, 1923.

———. *Death—And After.* Madras, India: The Theosophical Publishing House, 1966.

Beversluis, Joel. *A Source Book for Earth's Community of Religions.* Grand Rapids, MI: CoNexus Press & NY: Global Ed. Associates, 1995.

Blavatsky, Helena P. *Collected Writings.* 16 Vols. Wheaton, IL: Theosophical Publishing House, 1980–1988.

Borgia, Anthony. *More About Life in the World Unseen.* London: Uddam Press Ltd., n.d.

Bucke, R. M.. *Cosmic Consciousness.* Secaucus, NJ: The Citadel Press, 1961.

Chakrapani. "Chamatkar hi tha Vah." *Manohar Kahanian* (March 1997).

———. "Trikal Siddhi." *Manohar Kahanian* (May 1997).

Chatterji, Mohini M. *Vivek-Chudamani or the Crest Jewel of Wisdom of Sri Samkaracharya.* Madras, India: TPS, Adyar, 1932.

Dalal, Nergis. "Towards a Higher Awareness," *The Hindustan Times* (March 23, 1998).

David-Neel, Alexandra. *Magic and Mystery in Tibet.* New York: Dover Publications, 1971.

Devi, Shri Nirmala. *Sahaja Yoga.* New Delhi, India: Printographics, n.d.

Dey, A. K. *Khajuraho: The Immortal Ancient Sculpture.* Delhi, India: Jayna Publishing Co., n.d.

Doyle, Arthur Conan. *The Coming of the Fairies.* London: Hodder & Stroughton, 1922.

Field, Rashid. *The Last Barrier.* New York: Harper & Row Publishers, 1976.

Globe, Diane. *Through the Tunnel.* Palm Harbor, FL: S.O.U.L. Foundation, 1993.

Goswami, Amit, with Richard E. Reed and Maggie Goswami. *The Self-Aware Universe.* New York: Jeremy P. Tarcher / Putnam Book, G.P. Putnam's Sons, 1993.

Goyal, J. D. *Mrityu ke Bad (Occult Science).* New Delhi, India: Hind Pocket Books, 1996.

Grosso, Michael. *Frontiers of the Soul.* Wheaton IL: Quest Books, 1992.

Guiley, Rosemary Ellen. *Harper's Encylopedia of Mystical and Paranormal Experiences.* San Francisco: HarperSan Francisco, 1991.

Haich, Elisabeth. *Sexual Energy and Yoga.* New York: Aurora Press, 1982.

Hall, Manly P. *An Encyclopaedic Outline of Masonic, Hermetic, Qabbalistic and Rosicrucian Symbolical Philosophy.* San Francisco: H. S. Crocker Co., 1928.

Hamid, A. "Ma Ka Dil." *Manohar Kahanian* (March 1997).

Haridass, Baba. *From Sweeper to Saint.* Santa Cruz, CA: Sri Ram Publishing, 1980.

Haslop, F. *Life Worth Living.* London: Brook House, n.d.

Herbert, Nick. *Quantum Reality.* New York: Double Day, Anchor Books, 1987.

Huxley, Aldous. *The Perennial Philosophy.* New York: Harper & Row Publishers, 1944.

Jain, P. K. "God-less Karma for Salvation," *The Hindustan Times,* New Delhi, September 15, 1997.

James, Ivor. *The Astral World.* London: Audio Tape, 1996.

Jayaram, Amit. "Meditations: Freedom from Choice," *The Hindustan Times*, New Delhi, September 22, 1997.

Jung, C. G. *The Collected Works.* 18 vols. New York: Bollingen-Pantheon, n.d.

———. *Memories, Dreams, Reflections.* Recorded and edited by Aniela Jaffe. New York: Vintage Books, 1989.

———. *Man and His Symbols.* New York: Double Day & Co., 1964.

Khan, Maulana Wahiduddin. "Pilgrimage: Highest Form of Worship," *The Hindustan Times*, New Delhi, March 30, 1998.

Klemp, Herald. *Soul Travellers of the Far Country.* Minneapolis, MN: Eckankar, 1987.

———. *The Eck Dream 2 Discourses, No. 11.* Minneapolis, MN: Eckankar, 1990.

———. *Letters of Light and Sound 1, No. 8.* Minneapolis, MN: Echkankar, 1992.

Krishna, Gopi. *The Awakening of Kundalini.* New York: Kundalini Research Foundation, 1975.

Kumar, Ravindra. *Secrets of Numerology.* New Delhi, India: Sterling Publishers Pvt. Ltd., 1992.

———. "Journey Back Home-IV: Personality Transformation with Chakras." *JRPR* Oct. 1994.

———. *Destiny, Science and Spiritual Awakening.* New Delhi, India: Sterling Publishers Pvt. Ltd., 1997.

———. "Psychic Individuation and Self-Realization-I." *JRPR,* July 1997.

———. *Journey Back to Our True Home: Through Spiritual Energy Kundalini.* New Delhi, India: Sterling Publishers Pvt. Ltd., 1999.

———. *Kundalini for Beginners.* Minneapolis, MN: Llewellyn Publications, 2000.

Kvastad, Nils Bjorn. *Problems of Mysticism.* Oslo, Norway: Scintilla Press, 1980.

Larsson, Erik Gerner. *Martinus.* Copenhagen: Martinus Institute, 1963.

Leadbeater, C. W. *The Astral Plane.* Madras, India: The Theosophical Publishing House, 1933.

Lello, Ronald S. *Revelations: Glimpses of Reality.* London: Shephard-Walwyn Ltd., 1985.

Long, Max Freedom. *The Huna Code in Religions.* California: DeVorss & Company, 1965.

Martin, Joel, and Patricia, Romanowski. *We Are Not Forgotten.* New York: Berkley Books, 1991.

Martinus. *The Fate of Mankind.* Copenhagen: Denmark: Martinus Institute, 1933. (Translated in English in 1986).

Moody, Raymond A. Jr. *Life After Life.* New York: Bantam Books, 1975.

Morris, R. L. & M. L. Edge. *Foundations of Parapsychology.* Boston: Routledge and Kegan Paul, plc, 1986.

Muktananda, Swami. *Chitshakti Vilas (The Play of Consciousness).* Maharashtra, India: Gurudev Siddhapeeth, 1972.

———. *Kundalini: The Secret of Life.* Ganeshpuri, India: Gurudev Siddha Peeth, 1979.

Myers, W. W. Frederic. *Human Personality and Its Survival After Death.* Vols. 1 and 2. New York: Longmans, Green & Co., 1954.

Newton, Michael. *Journey of Souls.* Minneapolis, MN: Llewellyn Publications, 2000.

O'Brien, Stephen. *Voices from Heaven.* London: The Acquarian Press, 1991

———. *Visions of Another World.* London: The Acquarian Press, 1989.

Osho. *Kundalini: In Search of the Miraculous.* New Delhi, India: Sterling Publishers (P) Ltd., 1997.

Pike, James. *The Other Side.* London: W. H. Alan, n.d.

Poddar, Hanumanprasad. *The Philosophy of Love.* Rajgangpur, India: Orissa, 1978.

Prabhupad, Swami. *Bhagavad-Gita As It Is.* Los Angeles, CA: Bhaktivedanta Book Trust, 1968.

Radha, Swami Sivananda. *Kundalini Yoga.* Delhi, India: Motilal Banarsidass Publishers, 1992.

Rai, Dina Nath. *Kundalini Awakening: A Practical Guide.* Lucknow, India: Kundalini Yoga Research Institute, 1997.

Rajneesh, Osho. *From Sex to Superconsciousness.* Cologne, West Germany: The Rebel Publishing House GmbH, n.d.

Rao, M. Rajeshwar. *The Legend of Shri Shirdi Sai Baba and His Teachings.* Secundarabad, India: Sri Sai Baba Mandir, n.d.

Reed, Henry. "Recovering Spirituality from Dreaming," *Venture Inward,* A.R.E./Edgar Cayce Foundation, Atlantic University (Sept./Oct. 1995).

Riffel, Herman. *Your Dreams: God's Neglected Gift.* New York: Ballantine Books, 1981.

Ring, K. *Heading Towards Omega.* New York: Morrow, 1984.

Ring, K., and C. Rosing. "The Omega Project." *The Journal of Near Death Studies,* 8, no. 4: 211–239.

Rocher, Grace. *Beyond the Horizon.* London: Messrs James Clark & Co., n.d.

Sahai, Chaturbhuj. *Sadhana ke Anubhava.* Mathura, India: Ramashraya Satsang, 1987.

———. *Saint Sri Mira Bai*. Mathura, India: Ramashraya Satsanga, 1990

Satprem. *On the Way to Supermanhood.* New York: Institute for Evolutionary Research, 1985.

———. *Sri Aurobindo or the Adventure of Consciousness*. New York: Institute for Evolutionary Research, 1991.

Sherwood, Jane. *Post Mortem Journal.* London: Messrs Naville Spairman Ltd., n.d.

Singh, Satya Prakash. *Sri Aurobindo and Jung*. Aligarh, India: Madhucchandas, 1986.

Sted, W. T. *After Death*. 10th ed. London, 1921.

Steiger, Brad. *In My Soul I am Free*. Minneapolis, MN: Eckankar Books, 1988.

Storr, Anthony. *Solitude: A Return to the Self.* New York: Ballantine Books, 1988.

Svoboda, Robert E. *Kundalini*. New Delhi, India: Rupa & Co., 1994.

Swain, Jasper. *On the Death of My Son*. London: Turnstone Books, 1974.

Tirtha, Vishnu. *Devatma Shakti (Kundalini): Divine Power.* Muni-Ki-Reti (Rishikesh), India: Yogshree Peeth Trust, 1993.

Twitchell, Paul. *Eckankar: The Key to Secret Worlds*. San Diego, CA: Illumined Way Press, 1969.

Vaze, D. R. *Upanishads Chetna Sanstha and Kundalini.* Pune, India: Research Thesis, n.d.

Walker, Claire G. *The Psychic Revolution of the 20th Century and Our Psychic Sense*. Seal Beach, CA: Psychic Sense Publishers, 1997.

Wangchuk, Sonam. "The Beauty of Bhavana," *The Hindustan Times,* New Delhi, May 11, 1998.

Woodroffe, Sir John. *The Serpent Power.* Madras, India: Ganesh & Co., 1981.

Yogananda, Paramahansa. *Autobiography of a Yogi*. New Delhi, India: Jaico Publishing House, 1986.

Zaleski, Carol. *Other World Journeys: Accounts of Near-Death Experience in Medieval and Modern Times*. New York: Oxford University Press, 1987.

Zemke, Leroy E. *Thoughts for Transformation*. Florida: Emberlight Publishers, 1996.

Zukav, Gary. *The Seat of the Soul*. New York: Fireside Books, Simon & Schuster, 1989.

INDEX

TESTIMONIAL FOR RAVINDRA KUMAR

I HAVE KNOWN DR. RAVINDRA KUMAR closely since 1995 when he worked with me as a professor of comparative religion at the Belk Research Foundation in Charlotte, North Carolina. Before this, at several international conferences, I had listened to him speak with great authority on the subject of life after death. He spoke with eloquence and confidence, his ideas clearly based on his personal investigation of other realms of existence. His revelations—coming as they did from a Self-realized soul with a scientific background—were all the more convincing.

Dr. Kumar obtained his Ph.D. in mathematics from the Indian Institute of Technology, New Delhi, in 1968. After that he did postdoctoral research at the Lancaster University, UK, and the Imperial College, London. He was also affiliated for seventeen years as a professor of mathematics with the Indian Institute of Technology, Delhi, and later with universities at Iraq, Nigeria, Zimbabwe, Ethiopia, Fiji Islands, Tanzania, and USA in the same capacity (as a visiting professor). During this period he wrote more than thirty research papers and four books in the field of applied mathematics.

In 1987 Dr. Kumar experienced the awakening of the kundalini, a unique event that transformed his whole life. As he lost interest in the material world, his focus of attention turned to spirituality. Within a decade he was able to author eight practical handbooks on hatha yoga, kundalini yoga, kriya yoga, chakras and nadis, mantra, auras, dreams, and psychic development. He also wrote *Secrets of Numerology* (1992) and *Destiny, Science and Spiritual Awakening* (1997). Dr. Kumar is further concentrating on writing books that combine classical wisdom with modern scientific findings. After *Kundalini for Beginners* (2000), *The Kundalini Book of Living and Dying* is the fourth in his widely acclaimed series that illustrates the common link in all religions of a spiritual energy, referred to here as kundalini.

Dr. Ravindra Kumar has evolved a method called the "Integral Path," which includes yogic exercises, pranayama (breath control), meditation, prayer, study of scriptures, and regulated sex. This Integral Path is a scientific combination of various yogic disciplines and is possibly the shortest path to awaken kundalini energy and to experience Self-/God-realization within a single lifetime.

Dr. Kumar's approach is in consonance with ancient Vedic teachings as well as the findings of several Masters. His absorbing and enlightening workshops (which comfortably stretch up to two hours) on the awakening of the kundalini—a vast potential of energy lying dormant within each of us—command an ever-growing international response.

Dr. Kumar has already established Kundalini Yoga and Quantum Soul centers at New Delhi, Bradenton (Florida), Copenhagen, and London. He is looking forward to establishing additional centers around the world, but he is now concentrating on writing books in which he intends to show how all religions have a common link in the spiritual energy known as kundalini.

Dr. Kumar was recently trained in the art of Shaktipat (direct transmission of energy from guru to disciple) by his guru. Through Shaktipat, the kundalini can be awakened in a very short time. Dr. Kumar is now accepting disciples for Shaktipat training.

—WILLIAM HENRY BELK II
Founder Director, Belk Research Foundation
Charlotte, NC, USA